PENGUIN  CLASSICS

THE CISTERCIAN WORLD

Pauline Matarasso read modern languages at Lady Margaret Hall, Oxford, and was awarded a Doctorat de l'Université de Paris in 1958. Her thesis, *Recherches historiques et littéraires sur 'Raoul de Cambrai'*, was published in 1962. She has also translated *The Quest of the Holy Grail* and *Aucassin and Nicolette and Other Tales* for Penguin Classics, and has written an in-depth study of the former, *The Redemption of Chivalry*, published in 1979. *Queen's Maid*, her combined biography of Anne of France, Anne of Brittany and Louise of Savoy, will be published by Ashgate in 2001.

The Cistercian World

MONASTIC WRITINGS OF THE TWELFTH CENTURY

Translated and Edited with an Introduction by
PAULINE MATARASSO

PENGUIN BOOKS

PENGUIN BOOKS

Published by the Penguin Group
Penguin Books Ltd, 80 Strand, London WC2R 0RL, England
Penguin Putnam Inc., 375 Hudson Street, New York, New York 10014, USA
Penguin Books Australia Ltd, 250 Camberwell Road, Camberwell, Victoria 3124, Australia
Penguin Books Canada Ltd, 10 Alcorn Avenue, Toronto, Ontario, Canada M4V 3B2
Penguin Books India (P) Ltd, 11 Community Centre, Panchsheel Park, New Delhi – 110 017, India
Penguin Books (NZ) Ltd, Cnr Rosedale and Airborne Roads, Albany, Auckland, New Zealand
Penguin Books (South Africa) (Pty) Ltd, 24 Sturdee Avenue, Rosebank 2196, South Africa

Penguin Books Ltd, Registered Offices: 80 Strand, London WC2R 0RL, England

www.penguin.com

First published 1993

022

Typeset by Datix International Limited, Bungay, Suffolk
Set in 9.5/12 pt Monophoto Bembo
Printed in England by Clays Ltd, St Ives plc

ISBN 978-0-14-043356-2

www.greenpenguin.co.uk

To the community of Mount Saint Bernard, who have made me welcome over the years and provided a living witness to the continuing vitality of their tradition.

Contents

Acknowledgements

My particular thanks to Hilary Costello O.C.S.O. for acting as a sounding-board, wrestling with linguistic teasers, fielding queries and undertaking extra manual labour in ferrying books between library and guest house, all with unfailing cheerfulness; to Professor Brian Patrick McGuire, head of the Medieval Centre at Copenhagen University, for much friendly encouragement and wise advice; to Jeannine Alton for the unfailing support of her friendship, and for leading me to both title and cover illustration; and to my son François for gifts of mind and heart placed at my disposal during the preparation of this book.

Introduction

The ruins of the great Cistercian houses that sprang up all over
Europe in the twelfth and thirteenth centuries stand today as silent
witnesses to an Order for which silence was an integral part of the
spiritual life. It is not too hard, when wandering among the blanched
and fretted remains, to rebuild and even to repeople in the mind's
eye the abbeys in their later splendour. It is harder to understand
what took men to the first foundations, what induced them to settle
in small groups in outlandish and infertile spots, to opt for a way of
life so austere in the early years that their own contemporaries
viewed it with a mixture of horror and admiration. Happily, they
left another witness, less monumental but less subject to decay: the
written word. They were not only great exponents of monastic
spirituality; they chronicled their beginnings and, as one generation
of monks followed another, committed to parchment all the memora-
bilia of the heroic years in an attempt to fan their own zeal to a
comparable flame.

The Cistercian Order came into being in Burgundy at the turn of
the twelfth century as part of a movement of radical renewal then
gathering momentum. It was an offshoot of the Benedictine tree, and
it was not the first time that a fresh wind had shaken those spreading
branches. For over a hundred years the great Burgundian abbey of
Cluny, itself the product of an earlier reform, had exerted a revitalizing
influence, both directly and through its many dependent and affiliated
houses. Its power was now at its height, its fervour perhaps on the
wane. The Cluniacs observed the spirit, as they saw it, of St Benedict's
Rule, adapting the letter to the conditions of their time. A greatly
lengthened liturgy, in particular, left the monks no time for manual
labour. The life was exacting but not harsh, and the Order, though
subject only to Rome, remained tightly enmeshed in feudal society.

Rapid economic and social changes in the late eleventh century ushered in a period of self-questioning and a search for identity among different classes and groups, not least or last the professed religious. Neither the traditional Benedictine abbeys nor Cluny with its liturgical splendours satisfied a growing hunger for the Gospel values of poverty and simplicity. Those years saw the founding of half a dozen new orders dedicated to prayer and ascesis; of these the Cistercians, or white monks, were to become by far the largest and indeed in time absorbed some of the others. But nothing in their beginnings gave any hint of the phenomenally rapid growth to follow. The initial impetus was given in 1098 by Robert, Abbot of Molesmes. Feeling that this community, which he had himself established twenty years before, was falling short of his vision, he went in search of greater isolation and austerity, taking a score of brothers with him. They settled in a marshy clearing in the woodland south of Dijon bearing the name of Cîteaux. Here they found that 'howling waste of the wilderness' through which God led his people after their escape from slavery in Egypt. The community's experience of living out the exodus in all its rigour proved no less searching than the Israelites', and manna was not at once forthcoming. The first setback was the loss of their leader. Abbot Robert's abandoned flock at Molesmes sued to the Pope for his return, and the following year he obeyed an injunction to rejoin them. At least half the brothers chose to accompany him back, and Cistercian chroniclers never quite forgave what they saw, perhaps unjustly, as his return to the fleshpots of Egypt. The remaining monks, first under Abbot Alberic, then under the authority of the Englishman Stephen Harding whose Charter of Charity was to guarantee unity and uniformity throughout the Order, eked out in the early years an existence of great hardship.

Their professed aim was a literal enactment of St Benedict's Rule. The overgrown office was pruned back to restore the right balance of prayer, *lectio divina* (the meditative reading of Scripture and the Fathers) and manual labour. The monks' day varied with the seasons: more time for reading in the winter, longer hours in the fields during the summer months. The biggest break with the recent monastic past was the Order's rejection of any interdependence with feudal society. Gifts of land were accepted, but the Order had neither tithes, tenants nor serfs. The world was kept at bay: no schools, no parishes, no funeral ceremonies for lay patrons, no relics for public veneration, hence no pilgrims and no crowds. Breaking with custom was not easy; it was only under Stephen Harding that the community succeeded in preventing Hugh II, Duke of Burgundy and a good friend of the abbey, from holding his court on major feasts in the church his father had built for them.

The centralized yet flexible structure that was to preserve the Order from anarchy and fragmentation during its period of meteoric growth was the fruit of the organizational genius of Stephen Harding. Under his rule the New Monastery, as it was called, began to prosper. Gifts of land increased and granges were established to exploit those farthest from the monastery. This was to lead in time to a major new initiative, a break with custom and, indeed, the Rule. Finding it impossible to cover fully both their choir duties and their field work, and determined not to fall back into the trap of the manorial system, the white monks introduced a lay brotherhood of men under vows but living apart under a simplified regime. Within a generation these had become the chief labour force.

From around 1110 converts began to arrive in sufficient numbers to allow the founding of a daughter house, La Ferté, in 1113. Some time before this emigration an extraordinary young man presented himself at the gate, along with most of the male members of his family and a group of friends. Tradition has it that they numbered thirty. This youth was to become known throughout Christendom as Bernard of Clairvaux, after the third daughter house of Cîteaux, of which he was appointed abbot at the age of twenty-five. Bernard had come to Cîteaux because of its reputation for exceptional austerity, the very characteristic which many had found daunting. Such was his magnetism that within a few years men were thronging not in their tens but in their hundreds to Cîteaux, to Clairvaux above all, and to the abbeys springing up throughout France, Italy, Germany, England, Spain, Portugal, and eventually as far afield as Scandinavia and Poland. The narratives recounting the Order's early years were written after the Bernardine experience and sought to incorporate it. The result was a distorted picture of an heroic remnant miraculously saved from extinction. In fact the expansion of Cîteaux had begun in a small way before Bernard's arrival.[1] Furthermore, since relatively few of that army of recruits can have met him in person, and since the influx continued unabated for many years after his death, his call to the contemplative life founded on the practice of ascesis clearly met a great, if unformulated, need. It was one of the historic junctions of man and moment.

The Order in its early years attracted some of the most gifted men of their generation. There was no lack of fine minds or literary talent. Indeed it has been said of the' first Cistercians that they renounced everything except the art of writing well. Bernard himself, William of St Thierry, Aelred of Rievaulx, to name but the greatest, left works that were to become classics of the spiritual life, deserving of a place beside *The Imitation of Christ* and *The Cloud of Unknowing*. They were at once reformers and traditionalists. The Church habitually renews itself by returning to its apostolic origins, by seeking to tap afresh the source of evangelical simplicity and fervour that imbued its first beginnings, and the Cistercians took this path. They turned to St Benedict in an attempt to reach beyond him to the Desert Fathers and the Church of the apostles. Scripture was their nourishment. They partook of it direct, but also as it came to them presented by Ambrose, Augustine and Gregory the Great. They were not concerned with breaking new intellectual ground, but with gleaning after those who had already tilled and harvested. Theological speculation was merely a vaulting form of the idle curiosity condemned by St Benedict; and so in the works of these radical reformers we have, paradoxically, a last and vigorous flowering of the patristic tradition.

They wrote not about belief, but about faith, and love, and contemplation. Whereas St Benedict makes little mention of contemplation, seeing it rather as the reward of the blessed in heaven, St Bernard's propensities and graces tilted the balance of the monastic life markedly, as far as the Cistercians were concerned, in the contemplative direction. In fact, for a hundred years or so the Cistercians were seen as embodying the mystical tradition in the Church, though not in any exclusive sense, for Bernard's works and those of William of St Thierry, often covered with the cloak of Bernard's name, circulated far beyond the cloister, while Bernard shared with Gregory the Great the honour of being the first doctor of the Church to be translated into the language of the people – in this instance French.

Neither Bernard nor William were strangers to controversy, but the Cistercians were above all versed in the tradition of meditative theology, which they had inherited from the Fathers, a theology which has been defined as 'a prayerful reflection upon God's revealed word and all the depths of meaning which it contains'.[2] Central to this tradition was the allegorical reading of the Scriptures, dating back to Origen and beyond, and springing from a desire to make sense of the Old Testament. The New Testament pointed the way by representing the Old as foreshadowing and prophesying the coming of Christ. The Fathers extended the principle from key passages and themes to the entire text of Scripture. Where they found the Old Testament abstruse, they approached it obliquely by means of allegory and surprised it into rendering a meaning. Their conceptual tools were not definitions, but types and symbols and analogies. To define is also to limit. The Fathers, and the monastic writers after them, in inviting us to meditate on symbols, lead us into a mystery that has no limits.

St Bernard mirrors the soul of Clairvaux, but it is not to his writings that one turns to find out how the body functioned, nor indeed to study the psychological make-up. It is the lesser men – the secretaries, the intimates and the successors – who throw light on the minutiae of daily living and hold up a glass to their own and their contemporaries' strengths and weaknesses, aspirations and beliefs. It is, to an indefinable degree, a distorting glass. These men were not historians dedicated to the recording of uninterpreted facts. They wished above all to edify: themselves, succeeding generations of religious, and no doubt the world beyond the cloister, which would furnish them with new recruits. Theirs was not, however, a propaganda exercise in any crude sense. The desire to edify certainly influenced the choice of anecdote, hence the preponderance of visions and 'miraculous interventions of providence'. But in a community whose eyes were fixed on the afterlife and on the 'Jerusalem of the saints', for which the present was merely a penitential preparation, these would be the experiences remembered, recounted and handed down. The spiritual favours accorded to one brother increased the wealth of all. No doubt a certain amount of embellishment slipped in with the retellings, but not from a conscious wish to falsify; rather was it culturally determined. Visions and spiritual experiences of all kinds were a mark of grace accorded to men of known virtue, but they tended, not unnaturally, to conform to a pattern established by Scripture and tradition, and as they passed from mouth to mouth the pattern would be reinforced, while the men who wrote them down, working within a given hagiographical tradition, would add such details as brought them more closely within the norm.

But whether they were recounting anecdotes, revising sermons or composing treatises, the motivation was the same: the desire to make God known to men and to bring men closer to God. If Bernard of Clairvaux was, by the quality, the quantity and the variety of his writings, pre-eminent among them, he was by no means alone. His role on the European stage and his many and complex gifts have tended, even in his own day and certainly since, to throw into shadow the lives and charisms of his contemporaries. It is only in this century that William of St Thierry has been fully drawn out from under Bernard's wing and that some of Aelred of Rievaulx's works have become available in translation. The writings of such men as Isaac of Stella, Guerric of Igny, Gilbert of Swineshead and John of Ford have been until recently (although the Cistercians themselves are now working hard at tearing down the fences) the preserve of scholars, with language difficulties rising like a Keep Out sign in the way of many would-be explorers. The purpose of this anthology is to give back resonance to these voices, some strikingly individual, which have come to us out of the great silence compounded of time and neglect and a language comprehensible to fewer and fewer people, and to prove that they can, with a minimum of decoding, speak to us today. At times we may find them alien, even forbidding; at others surprisingly and comfortingly familiar; while on occasion we may be moved to wonder at a way of life that could produce what William called 'tales homines' – such men as these.

Translator's Note

As compiler as well as translator it has been my privilege to determine the shape of this book, and I have been very aware of thus mediating in a dual capacity between the twelfth-century authors of these writings and those who might wish to read them today. Because the past may be approached from many angles, I have given importance to variety. There are monks talking about God, monks talking about monks and, on occasion, about cabbages and kings. The human element also figures large, for it affords the easiest access to the past, and the twelfth century, with its growth in self-awareness, offers rich pickings. I have tried, in the space allotted, to make a representative selection – representative, that is, of the gold and not the dross, and rejecting material which has only historical significance. Which brings me to that final and inevitable arbiter: personal preference. I have included nothing that does not move, interest or appeal to me in the hope of proving, in turn, representative of the readership.

The arrangement is, in the main, chronological, once pride of place has been allocated to St Bernard himself. In the sections given to Bernard and to Aelred of Rievaulx I have placed the Life – written of course by someone else – before the writings, thinking that readers might wish to read the latter in the light of the former.

A translator has other problems, not unknown to the twelfth century. 'You must know, my daughter, that any written work, when translated from one language into another, will lose in the foreign idiom something of its flavour and coherence, just as a liquid, decanted, suffers some change either of colour or of taste and smell.' So wrote Adam of Perseigne to Blanche, Countess of Champagne, when sending her the copy of his sermons – in Latin – which she had requested. Happily, modern English is a more diversified and subtle medium than the French of Adam's day, which was still short of the vocabulary of argument and dialectic. Yet what he said remains largely true. Often, when translating the Cistercians, I have found that 'flavour' and 'coherence' are bad bedfellows, inclined to elbow one another out. The translator has to choose between rendering as far as possible the style, which is the man set in the context of his time, and providing the best vehicle for the message; rarely can one fully combine the two. Where there has been conflict I have opted for the second, believing that the spirit is more important than the body it inhabits, yet always aware that the spirit is only perceptible when embodied, and that, reincarnated, it may be subtly or even grossly changed.

The scriptural content of the writings presents another stumbling-block. There is scarcely a sentence that does not contain a reference to Scripture or an expression drawn from Scripture. Quotations serve to buttress argument. Sometimes a chain of aptly selected verses will constitute the argument. Monastic writers can slip into and out of Scripture without any change of style. In English today there is no one universally known and accepted translation of the Bible. I have used sometimes the R.S.V., sometimes the Jerusalem Bible, sometimes a hybrid version – whatever best fitted the context. Often the Vulgate differs substantially, particularly the text of the Psalms, from any of the modern translations. I have had, on such occasions, to fall back on my own rendering, the Douai Bible being too archaic. Nor, as Stephen Harding's *Monitum* makes plain, did the Vulgate itself exist in the twelfth century as a standard text. Quotations can therefore vary according to the version familiar to the writer, the accuracy of his memory and the freedom with which he adapts the words of Scripture to suit his purpose – i.e., a reference may be literal, glancing, slightly altered or substantially padded. Some quotations and allusions have been omitted for simplicity's sake. Others have suffered a sea change in the attempt to integrate them better into the English sentence, but where a reference is given the reader can be sure that the connection in the Latin is plain.

References are given to the Vulgate, the chief difference being in the numbering of the Psalms. The abbreviations are those in current usage. Sir. for Sirach denotes Ecclesiasticus; Ecc. denotes Ecclesiastes.

Integral translations of many of the texts included in this selection can be found in the continuing Cistercian Fathers series brought out by Cistercian Publications. If I have not referenced them individually, except where I have made use of their critical apparatus, it is because of their relative unavailability in libraries outside the USA.

Abbreviations

PL	*Patrologia Latina*, ed. J. P. Migne (Paris, 1844–)
CC, Cont. Med.	*Corpus Christianorum, Continuatio Mediaevalis* (Turnhout, 1971–)
SBO	*Sancti Bernardi Opera*, eds. Jean Leclercq, Henri Rochais and C. H. Talbot (Editiones Cistercienses, Rome, 1957–77)
AC	*Analecta Sacri Ordini Cisterciensis* (Rome, 1945–64). Since 1964, *Analecta Cisterciensia*
Cist. Pub.	Cistercian Publications, originally Spenser, Mass., now Kalamazoo, Mass. Available in England from Mowbray
CFS	Cistercian Fathers Series, Cist. Pub.

The Monastic Horarium

The monks' day was built around the singing of the office: the *opus Dei*, or work of God. Times varied as between winter and summer, and any given are at best approximate.

Vigils or *matins*, followed at once by *lauds*, were sung at some time between midnight and 4 a.m. The morning hours were *prime*, *terce* and *sext*. Mass was celebrated after *terce* in winter, before in summer. The afternoon hours were *none* (2 p.m.) and *vespers*, with *compline* closing the day around 6–6.30 p.m. There were normally two periods of work, morning and afternoon. Dinner followed *sext* in winter, *none* in summer, except during Advent and Lent and on other fast days, when no food was taken until the evening.

CÎTEAUX: THE EARLY YEARS

The remnant of fewer than a dozen monks who stuck it out at Cîteaux after the fainter hearts had followed Abbot Robert back to Molesmes were deeply marked by that traumatic scission. The pain of what was felt as a betrayal welded them together in a unity of mind and will that was to shape the future and become as it were the hallmark of the Order. They left little tangible witness to their lives; their legacy was their lived experience, drawn from their understanding of St Benedict's Rule and covering the whole spectrum of monastic life, so that every aspect of their existence welled from the same spring.

The earliest texts emanating from Cîteaux – the Exordium Parvum and the Carta Caritatis, the latter guaranteeing at once the autonomy of each monastery and the unity of the Order and its customs – are riddled with as many problems as a colander has holes. Circumstance, dating, authorship: nothing is incontrovertibly established. The Exordium Parvum, or Little Exord (to distinguish it from the Great Exord written a century later) chronicles the beginnings of the Order. Its initial ring of authenticity – 'We monks of Cîteaux, the first founders of this church' – is reinforced by the incorporation in the narrative of all the letters and documents authorizing the establishment of the New Monastery and its subsequent separation from Molesmes. It is clear, however, that, in the latter part, hindsight has been at work, and that we have here an updated version of an original possibly written around 1120 by Stephen Harding or someone close to him. It may be no less true for that, but it is certainly less genuine. Yet if the Exordium Parvum is not quite what it purports to be, it still gives a vivid picture of the search for authenticity, the stripping away of accretions, the return to first principles that inspired those who broke with Molesmes.

Having arrived at what they believed to be the essence of the Rule, they were then free to reinvent it. As so often, the return to the well-springs was a liberation, and a great surge of creativity in every sphere – spiritual, organizational, architectural and agricultural – was to distinguish the Order during its first hundred years.

The Little Exord

1   We monks of Cîteaux, the first founders of this church, inform our successors by this present text through whose agency and in what circumstances the monastery and our way of life came into being, and on what canonical authority they rest; so that, when the whole truth is laid before them, they may have a stronger love for the place and for the observance of the holy Rule, which we, in one way or another, implanted here with the help of God's grace; that they may pray for us who have, unflagging, borne the burden of the day and the scorching heat; and that they too, on the strait and   Mt. 20:7 narrow path traced by the Rule, may sweat it out until they breathe their last and, having laid down their mortal load, repose happily in everlasting rest.

*   *   *

The text goes on to relate how Robert of Molesmes and six brothers, among them Stephen Harding, approached Hugh, Archbishop of Lyons and apostolic legate, to seek his support in leaving Molesmes and founding a community dedicated to a stricter observance of St Benedict's Rule. Hugh provides them with a letter of authority.

*   *   *

3   Thereafter the abbot and his disciples, strong in the authority of so great a prelate, went back to Molesmes and chose from that community companions wholly devoted to the Rule, numbering, with the monks who had spoken with the legate at Lyons, twenty-one in all. Such was the serried company that set out eagerly for a wilderness known as Cîteaux, a locality in the diocese of Chalon where men rarely penetrated and none but wild things lived, so densely covered was it then with woodland and thorn bush. When the men of God

arrived there and realized that the less attractive and accessible the site was to laymen, the better it would suit themselves, they began, after felling and clearing the close-growing thickets and bushes, to build a monastery; and this at the wish of the Bishop of Chalon and with the agreement of the lord Odo, Duke of Burgundy, to whom the place belonged. The duke, delighted with their holy fervour and encouraged thereto by a letter from the legate, later completed at his own expense the wooden monastery they had begun, and for a long time after saw to all their needs and made them generous gifts of lands and livestock.

* * *

A brief account of the circumstances surrounding Abbot Robert's return to Molesmes and the election of Alberic as his successor is supported by an array of letters and documents culminating in the Roman Privilege, which confirmed the independent existence of the New Monastery under the protection of the Pope.

* * *

15 Thereafter Abbot Alberic and his brethren, mindful of their solemn promise, took the unanimous decision to institute and keep in that locality the Rule of blessed Benedict, rejecting whatever contravened it: namely, long-sleeved tunics and furs, fine linen shirts, caps and breeches, combs, quilts and coverlets,[1] and a variety of courses in the refectory, as well as lard[2] and everything else that militates against the purity of the Rule. And thus, drawing the integrity of the Rule over the whole tenor of their life – liturgical observance as well as daily living – they followed faithfully in its track, and, having stripped off the old self, they rejoiced to have put on the new.

Finding no evidence in the Rule or in the life of St Benedict that he, their teacher, had possessed churches or altars, offerings or burial dues, other men's tithes, ovens or mills, villages or peasants, and no sign either that women had entered his monastery or that the dead were buried there, save only his sister, they renounced all these privileges, saying: 'When blessed Father Benedict teaches that a monk should set himself apart from secular conduct, he gives a clear witness that such matters should find no place in the conduct or hearts of monks, who should strive to live out the meaning of their name by shunning such things as these.' They also said that the holy Fathers, who were the mouthpiece of the Holy Spirit and whose statutes it is sacrilege to transgress, had distributed tithes four ways: one part, that is, to the bishop, another to the parish priest, a third for the needs of travellers, of widows and orphans, or of the poor without other means of sustenance, and a fourth for the repair of the church. Finding no mention in that reckoning of the monk, who lives by working his own lands with the help of his cattle, they declined to arrogate wrongly to themselves another's right. The world's wealth thus held at naught, and poor as Christ was poor, his new recruits debated among themselves by what exercise of brains or brawn they might provide for themselves and for the guests, rich and poor, whom the Rule bids us receive as Christ.[3] It was then that they decided, with the bishop's permission, to take in bearded lay-brothers, whom they would treat as themselves in life and in death – the status of monk apart – and also hired men, because without such backing they did not see how they could fully observe, day and night, the precepts of the Rule. They would accept lands as well, in isolated places far from human habitation, and vineyards, meadows and woods, and streams for driving mills, but for their own use only and for fishing, and horses too, and the different sorts of livestock useful for men's needs. And since they had set up farmsteads here and there for cultivating their lands, they resolved that the aforesaid lay-brothers, rather than the monks, should manage these steadings, because monks, according to the Rule, should live in their own cloister. And knowing that blessed Benedict had built his monasteries not in cities, towns or villages, but in places unfrequented and remote, they vowed to imitate him. And just as he had set up the monasteries he built with twelve monks and an abbot, they affirmed themselves ready to do the same.

16   A certain sadness weighed on God's servant, Abbot Alberic, and his monks, because it was rare in those days that anyone came to emulate them. The holy men had a passionate desire to commit to successors their heaven-sent treasure of virtues for the salvation of many yet to come, but almost everyone seeing and hearing of the exceptional and almost unheard-of harshness of their life, instead of drawing near, made haste to put heart and body at a distance, and could not understand their perseverance. But, as what follows will make plain, the mercy of God, which had inspired them to enter

this spiritual militia, proceeded in notable fashion to enlarge and perfect it to the advancement of many.

17   Alberic, man of God, after nine and a half fruitful years spent training himself in Christ's school in the discipline of the Rule, passed over to the Lord, resplendent in faith and virtues and therefore well deserving that God should bless him in eternity. He was succeeded by a certain Stephen, a brother of English birth who had himself come with the others from Molesmes to Cîteaux and loved both the Rule and the place. It was in his time that the brothers, in conjunction with their abbot, prohibited the Duke of Burgundy or any other lord from ever holding court in the church, as had formerly been their custom on great festivals. From then on, to ensure that God's house, in which they desired to serve him devoutly day and night, was empty of anything redolent of pomp or superfluity, or tending to corrupt the poverty – guardian of the virtues – which they had unconstrainedly embraced, they settled that they would keep neither gold nor silver crosses, but only ones of painted wood, nor more than one branched candlestick, and that of iron, nor censers, save of copper or iron, nor any but fustian or linen chasubles without silk or gold or silver, nor albs or amices except of linen, and likewise without silk, gold or silver. As regards all mantles, copes, dalmatics and tunics, these they eschewed entirely. They did, however, keep chalices, not gold but silver ones, or preferably silver gilt, and a silver communion tube, again, if possible, gilded; stoles too and maniples of plain silk without gold or silver. And they laid down, too, that the altar cloths should be made of linen and have no ornamentation, and that the wine cruets should be without gold or silver.

In those days the church at Cîteaux grew in lands and vineyards, meadows and farmsteads, without any decrease in fervour, and God in consequence visited that place and poured out his mercies on those who called on him, entreating him with tears, and with sighs dragged day and night from their inmost core, as they neared the threshold of despair over their almost total lack of followers. For God's grace at one stroke sent that church as many as thirty recruits – lettered clerks of gentle birth and laymen just as noble and wielding dominion in the world – who enthusiastically entered the novices' cell together and, fighting successfully against their own vices and the incitements of evil spirits, completed their probation.

Meanwhile, young men and old, of divers conditions and places, inspired by their example and seeing that what they had previously dreaded as impossible in the keeping of the Rule was in fact being achieved by these, started hastening to Cîteaux to submit their proud necks to Christ's gentle yoke, and, embracing with ardour the hard and gruelling precepts of the Rule, they brought to that church a wonderful renewal of joy and vigour.

18   Abbeys thereafter were established in different dioceses, which in time, through God's ample and active blessing, grew until, eight years later, counting those which had sprung from Cîteaux itself and others to which these daughter houses had given birth, a total of twelve monasteries were found to have been built.

The Admonition of Stephen Harding

Stephen Harding was one of a number of outstanding Englishmen who graced the Cistercian Order in the twelfth century. William of Malmsbury was proud to claim him both as a compatriot and a brother monk. 'One of ours,' he wrote, recalling that he had once worn the black habit of the older order.[1] Born around 1060 of noble Saxon parentage, he entered the monastery of Sherborne as an oblate but left a few years later in circumstances that remain obscure. He studied in France, travelled to Rome, and on the return journey sought entry to Molesmes. We may assume that he was a leading spirit in the subsequent migration to Cîteaux. Appointed prior under Alberic, he succeeded him in 1108 and gave to the Order during the next ten or fifteen vital years its characteristic structure. Even if he did not pen the text of the Charter of Charity that has come down to us, there is no doubt that it represents Stephen's vision of the Order, which began under his rule its period of swift expansion. He had seen at Molesmes a similarly idealistic project lose its way through outside intervention and the lack of firm direction. In this new venture he was determined to avoid both dangers, and triumphantly succeeded.

Under his abbacy the scriptorium at Cîteaux produced some illuminated manuscripts of exceptional beauty. No such figurative illustrations would be seen again, for the chiller wind of Bernard's rigour blowing through Cistercian cloisters left behind it only an infinitely elegant script and discreetly ornamented capitals. All that Stephen Harding touched bears witness to his pursuit of authenticity, of the spirit that only the authentic letter can set free. He tried to ensure that both text and melody of the hymns sung at Cîteaux were genuinely those of St Ambrose. Wishing his monks to have access to a Bible that was not only beautiful but accurate, he set about producing one that still bears his own account of how he established the text, together with a stern warning to any who might be tempted to tamper with it.[2] Besides this Monitum, *the encyclical letter on the Ambrosian hymns and one written late in life to the abbey of Sherborne, we have nothing that is certainly from his pen. Correspondence there must have been, but probably little else. Stephen Harding was essentially a builder and left it to his successors to provide the decoration and the furnishings. When he died in 1133, his spiritual building was already well advanced, and he had also seen, with what feelings we cannot say, Bernard's earliest compositions displayed with all their jewel-like coruscations to a mainly admiring world.*

*   *   *

The writing of this book was completed in the year of our Lord 1109, while Stephen, the second abbot, was governing the monastery of Cîteaux.

Brother Stephen, abbot of the New Monastery, to the servants of God, present and to come, greetings. When we were preparing to write this history, having collected together a number of books, including some from different churches, in order to follow the most accurate, we came up against one that was often at variance with almost all the others. Putting our trust in that particular one because we found it fuller than the rest, we based this present text upon it. But the discrepancies in the narratives left us, on later reflection, much disturbed; for reason teaches that what one interpreter (in this case blessed Jerome, whom our countrymen even today accept to the exclusion of all others) has translated from a single source of Hebrew truth should speak with a single voice. There are certain books of the Old Testament which were translated by Jerome not, in fact, from Hebrew but from Aramaic, since this, as he writes in the prologue to Daniel, was the language in which he found them in the Jewish Scriptures; and these, like the rest, we accept in his rendering. Astonished therefore at the discrepancies in our books, which all come from one translator, we approached certain Jews who were learned in their Scriptures, and inquired most carefully of them in French about all those places that contained the particular passages and lines we found in the book we transcribed, and had since inserted in our own volume, but did not find in the many other Latin copies. The Jews, unrolling a number of their scrolls in front of us, and explaining to us in French what was written in

Hebrew and Aramaic in the places we questioned them about, found no trace of the passages and lines that were causing us so much trouble. Placing our trust therefore in the veracity of the Hebrew and Aramaic versions and in the many Latin books which, omitting these passages, are in full agreement with the former, we completely erased all these unnecessary additions, as is indeed apparent in many places, especially in the books of Kings, where most of the errors were found. To all future readers of this book we make the strongest appeal not to put back these passages and superfluous lines. Where they were is made plain enough by the erasures on the parchment. On the authority of God and of our congregation we forbid anyone from presuming to mishandle this book, whether by defacing the text with his nail or by jotting anything in the margin of a volume that has cost much toil and care.

BERNARD OF CLAIRVAUX

Bernard of Fontaines was born near Dijon, probably in 1090, one of six sons of Tescelin le Sor, or Rufus, a trusted vassal of the Duke of Burgundy. His mother, Aleth, was the daughter of Bernard, Count of Montbard. All the boys, unusually for the time, seem to have received some education. Bernard certainly was given a thorough grounding in grammar and rhetoric by the canons of St Vorles at Châtillon-sur-Seine, where the family had a house. In his early twenties, without having gone on to study dialectic and theology, he made a dramatic entry into the little-regarded monastery of Cîteaux, sweeping along with him all his brothers save the youngest and a number of his kinsmen and friends. Within three years the postulant had risen to be abbot of a new foundation, Clairvaux, destined to become within his lifetime the brightest star in the monastic galaxy.

The next fifteen years saw, first, a breakdown in his health from which he never fully recovered, a long process of spiritual growth, the first tractates to come from his pen (the controversial *Apologia*, *On the Steps of Humility and Pride* and the celebrated work *On Loving God*), as well as the beginnings of a voluminous correspondence. He made few forays into the outer world, but the world increasingly sought him out.

The death of Honorius II in 1130 and the ensuing schism in the Church marked the end of this relative reclusion. Invited to the council of Étampes, Bernard came out strongly in favour of Innocent II and against Anacletus. The French king and bishops having followed his lead, the Abbot of Clairvaux travelled the roads of Europe to win the support of rulers and prelates to Innocent's cause. It was not until 1137, when the pope finally re-entered Rome, that his champion was able to make good his escape and return to the monks he had seen little of for seven years.

Any respite was short-lived. The next decade saw Bernard constantly embroiled in the affairs of Church and State, and as constantly protesting that his wish was for solitude and quiet. We may, without impugning his sincerity, wonder whether so natural a leader of men did not find satisfaction in exercising his talents in this sphere. He was a man of many paradoxes and it is doubtful whether he fully understood himself. A letter written during this period to Peter the Venerable, Abbot of Cluny, has him stating: 'I have decided to stay in my monastery and not go out except once a year to the general chapter of abbots at Cîteaux.'[1] In fact, the reverse obtained. Appealed to by William of St Thierry, he entered the lists against Peter Abelard, obtaining the condemnation of his books, acted as intermediary in a protracted and bloody dispute between Louis VII and Thibault, Count of Champagne and patron of Clairvaux, and put his eloquence at the service of the Cistercian pope, Eugenius III, who required him, in 1147, to preach the Second Crusade. Another mission, undertaken in failing health and with great reluctance, took him through Languedoc preaching against the Cathars. His authority was constantly invoked in the settling of disputes, the reform of abuses within the Church and, of course, the administration of his dramatically proliferating Order: by the time of his death Clairvaux alone had a network of over 160 affiliated houses.

If Bernard can seem to have channelled the energies of his maturity into activities that he himself felt to sit uneasily with his monastic state, it is important to remember that, from 1135, when the Church was in schism, until death interrupted him eighteen years later, he was working on the series of sermons on the Song of Songs which are the finest flowering of his spirituality. A certain diminishment of his authority, which followed the calamitous outcome of the Crusade, together with chronic illness, put an end to his journeyings and ensured a measure of tranquillity to his final years, reflected in the last sermons on the Canticle, which have been compared to Beethoven's late quartets, and in one of his best-known works, *On Consideration*, written for Eugenius III. He died at Clairvaux in 1153.

The 'events' in Bernard's life were the least important part of it. Indeed it could be said that in them we often see the shadow side of this gifted and complex man. Certainly, in accepting a role in the full glare of history, he exposed himself to its judgements as stay-at-home abbots did not. He both reflected his age and affected it on many levels, but, if his life as a whole must be seen in the perspective of his century, it is with the inner man that we are more immediately concerned. His was an essentially passionate nature, a combination of deep emotions and a strong will. It was his natural emotivity that made Bernard a fond brother, an affectionate friend, an always vulnerable individual. As for the love of God, or *caritas*, William of St Thierry defines this as 'nothing else than a vehement will for good'. It would be hard to imagine a more vehement will for good than Bernard's, and that will translated itself into the solicitude with which he loved his monks and the often combative passion with which he defended the Church.

Although seemingly destined from childhood for ecclesiastical office, and thereby spared the tough apprenticeship that made a knight and could turn the same knight into a competent peasant in the abbey fields, there was a certain part of Bernard that remained intensely the knight he had never been. It was not merely his predilection for military metaphor, nor his tractate extolling the ideal of the Templars; his very entry to Cîteaux at the head of a band of men who had surrendered to his superior power has been likened to the arrival of a paladin bringing his prisoners back to Arthur's court.[2] The battles he fought were not his own but those of the Church, the Bride of Christ, forever in peril, forever forsaken. Bernard was her knight errant and saw himself as such. Referring to the controversy with Abelard, he speaks in one letter of the Bride of Christ crying out that she is being strangled in the forest of heresy and among the undergrowth of errors, and in another of himself, 'the least of all', called out to single combat with the new Goliath.[3]

Partisan by temperament, and in that too a man of his combative age, he was quick to give credence to his own, not only espousing their causes on insufficient grounds but also tending to blacken the opposition. He was a man of peace who wielded the sword of rhetoric with ease and vigour, and, one suspects, a certain pleasure; a man whose enemies never questioned his humility, yet who can appear in his letters hectoring and overbearing. He was a reformer, but no innovator; indeed, in theology he was deeply conservative, eschewing speculation. He was naturally eloquent, a master of the spoken and the written word, a poet in prose. The combination of his eloquence, his personality and, quite early, his reputation for holiness rendered him as a preacher almost irresistible. William of St Thierry, a fine scholar himself, marvelled at the ease, elegance and skill with which Bernard deployed his scriptural knowledge both when speaking and writing. Part was learning, part natural gift and part application. No doubt he could and did preach powerfully off the cuff, but, when time afforded, and even by his own admission when it didn't, he was a highly conscious craftsman, polishing his texts until they scintillated.

St Bernard dominated his time by force of personality allied to singleness of purpose. His zeal for the Church was simply an extension of the love of God which directed and informed his whole life and being. If he counted some enemies, he had a host of friends and disciples and was venerated, to his embarrassment, as a saint in his lifetime. It is impossible to do justice to such a man in a brief selection from writings which fill, in the Leclercq–Rochais edition, nine volumes. Because he was many-faceted, I have drawn from a wide spectrum in the hope of affording different glimpses both of the man and of his message.

From the *Vita Prima* by William of St Thierry, Arnald of Bonneval and Geoffrey of Auxerre

The Vita Prima, *the most authoritative of the four twelfth-century lives of St Bernard, consists of six sections or books, and was composed by three men writing successively: William of St Thierry, Arnald of Bonneval and Geoffrey of Auxerre. All the Lives were written as supporting evidence for Bernard's eventual canonization, and, while such a premise does not necessarily make a work inaccurate, it certainly means it is selective.*

The author of Book I was William of St Thierry, whom we shall meet again under his own imprint. Around 1145 he was discreetly approached by certain monks of Clairvaux as the best person to write the abbot's Life before death took too great a toll of his family and intimates. Geoffrey of Auxerre, who was at that time Bernard's secretary and in a position to learn at first hand as well as glean from the older men, handed over to William his notes and jottings, now known as the Fragmenta. *These William worked on, incorporating his own experiences and memories of a friendship stretching back to 1118. Unfortunately, William died in 1148, before his task was finished and five years before his friend. His account, which has been chiefly drawn on here, after an outline sketch of Bernard's childhood and schooldays, covers the early years at Cîteaux and at Clairvaux. Given the purpose of the Life, William is remarkably frank on the first years of Bernard's abbacy, which saw him walking a knife-edge between psychological maturity and breakdown. The portrait of the young man who descended from his spiritual Sinaï incapable of communicating with his monks on a level they could understand, and then despaired of his own inadequacy, provides a striking contrast with descriptions of the older Bernard left by Geoffrey of Auxerre, let alone with the almost legendary figure of later anecdotes.*

William of St Thierry's death brought the work to a premature halt, but, as soon as Bernard had followed his biographer, Arnald, abbot of the Benedictine house of Bonneval, was asked to take over the abandoned task.

Arnald's section, Book II, covers Bernard's activities during the eight-year schism, a role better presented and assessed by the historian with a wider and longer view. Arnald too died before completing his work. The Fragmenta were returned to Geoffrey, who set about composing his own memoir and chronicling the remaining years. Geoffrey had been a student of Abelard and left Paris dramatically in the Abbot of Clairvaux's wake, after hearing him preach in the Schools the famous sermon on conversion. During his years as secretary he gathered together and edited Bernard's letters, continuing as travelling companion until he was elected abbot of Igny. It was probably between 1162 and 1165, when he was briefly abbot of Clairvaux, that he revised the Vita Prima. Geoffrey's narrative comprises Books III, IV and V, and his Fragmenta have been published separately as the Vita Tertia.

A large part of Geoffrey's story is devoted to the healing miracles that seem to have occurred at every stage of the saint's many journeys, when people flocked to him with their infirmities and disabilities. There are many angles of approach to medieval miracle stories. One needs to take into account not only what was seen but how it was understood and what meaning the writer intended to convey. In different cases one may postulate hysterical symptoms, ignorance of physical laws, inaccurate reporting and wishful thinking. It would be a narrow view, however, that dismissed them all. There are not only the number and quality of the witnesses, the hard-headed as well as the soft-hearted: there are the initial reactions of Bernard's family (distrust, embarrassment and dismay finding vent in anger) and his own self-searchings on the subject, reported by Geoffrey.

The Vita Prima, for all its inevitable bias, is precious in supplying certain contexts unavailable elsewhere. Bernard is presented at the centre of a family group, close-knit even by the standards of the time. His brother Andrew's cry, after agreeing to follow his elder to Cîteaux, is revealing of the strength of feeling among them: 'Make sure that none of us brothers is left in the world, for I couldn't bear to be parted either from you or from them.' The dominant influence of their mother, Aleth of Montbard, is made clear, and her death when Bernard was still at school must have left him vulnerable. Both William and Geoffrey speak of his shyness (it slips in among the virtues under the guise of modesty), and one senses a highly strung boy, quick at his studies, passionately fond of literature. Many paths were open to the gifted youth, says William, who portrays him as looking apprehensively at the world around and seeing no safe haven − vanity of vanities, and all was vanity. Cîteaux was the farthest extreme, a challenge to tempt one of Tescelin's sons, of whom their father said that nothing would curb their zeal. Initially it did not tempt the others; the idea that Bernard was even thinking of it filled them with horror. Cîteaux was not the sort of Order one joined: there were no prospects, and one had to work with one's hands like a serf. Anything would be better than that. William describes their resistance and how it was overcome.

* * *

I, III, 9   When Bernard's brothers, whose affection for him was all too human, realized that he was seriously considering entering the religious life, they tried their utmost to deflect his mind to literary studies and enmesh him more tightly in secular life through a love for secular learning. And, as he himself would readily admit, their delaying tactics might well have succeeded, had it not been for the persistent memory of his holy mother. Again and again he fancied he saw her hurrying towards him, complaining reproachfully that he had not been softly nurtured for this sort of trifling, nor was it with this end in view that she had educated him.

There came a day, as he was riding to join his brothers engaged with the Duke of Burgundy in besieging Grancey Castle, when this anxiety preyed on him more intensely. Passing a church midway on his route, he turned aside and entered, and there he prayed with a flood of tears and hands upstretched, pouring out his heart like water before the face of his Lord and God. That was the day that saw his purpose firmly fixed in his heart.   Ps. 21:15, 141:3

10   Nor did he turn a deaf ear to the voice that says: 'Let him who hears say, Come.' From that hour on, as fire consumes the forest or   Rev. 22:17 the flame sets the mountains ablaze, running hither and thither and   Ps. 82:15 pouncing first on what lies to hand before ranging farther afield, so too the fire which the Lord had purposely kindled in his servant's heart first attacked his brothers, leaving only the last, too young as yet for the religious life, to be a comfort to their ageing father, before moving on to kinsmen, comrades, friends – wherever there was the slightest hope of conversion. His uncle Gaudry, the Castellan of Touillon, a man of rank and reputation and renown, was the first to vote with his feet, as the saying goes, and opt with his nephew for the monastic state. Swift on his heels came Bartholomew, youngest but one of the brothers and not yet knighted, and gave his ready assent to Bernard's words of wisdom. But Andrew, the next

in age to Bernard and himself a new-made knight, found it hard to accept his brother's counsel, until suddenly he exclaimed: 'I see my mother!' And indeed she appeared to him quite distinctly, smiling serenely and approving her sons' intention, whereupon, surrendering on the spot, another recruit left the ranks of the world for the army of Christ. Andrew was not alone in seeing his mother rejoicing over her sons: Bernard too confessed to a similar vision.

Guy, the oldest of the brothers, was a man of substance, already married and more firmly established in the world than the rest. Doubtful at first, he reflected long and deeply and then agreed to enter the religious life provided his wife gave her consent, a most unlikely step for a young noblewoman with infant daughters to bring up. Bernard, however, inspired with an unshakeable hope in God's mercy, promptly assured Guy that his wife would either come to share his feelings or die quite soon. After a while, as there was no moving her, her magnanimous husband, helped even then by that strength of faith of which he was later to offer so shining an example, conceived at God's prompting the bold plan of abandoning all outward trappings and living a peasant's life, working with his hands to keep himself and the wife whom he could not put away against her will. Bernard, meanwhile, who was chasing about, rounding up this man and that, arrived on the scene, and almost at once Guy's wife fell gravely ill. Realizing how it would hurt her to Acts 26:14 kick against the goad, she begged forgiveness of Bernard, who had been sent for, and sought assent for her own entry into religion. When she and her husband had finally been parted according to ecclesiastical practice, each taking a vow of chastity, she joined a congregation of women religious, where she serves God devoutly to this day.

11   The next in age after Guy was Gerard, a knight active in combat, prudent in counsel and loved by all for his remarkable courtesy and kindness. Worldly wisdom had him dismissing his brothers' quick compliance as mere frivolity, and he was resolute in rejecting Bernard's sound advice and admonishments. Finally Bernard, afire with faith and zeal for his brother's welfare, exclaimed in a fit of exasperation: 'I know, I know, it takes affliction to make a man receptive.' Then, putting a finger to Gerard's side, he added: 'The day will come, and soon, when a lance stuck here in your side will open a way to your heart for the words of salvation you treat with

such contempt; and you will fear for your life, but not lose it.' And as he foretold, so it turned out.

A day or two later, outnumbered by enemies and wounded as his brother had predicted, Gerard was taken prisoner in a skirmish and hauled off with a lance-head fixed in the very spot to which Bernard had pressed his finger. Fearing a death that seemed imminent, he kept shouting: 'I am a monk, I am a monk of Cîteaux!' This did not, however, prevent his being taken prisoner and shut up. A messenger was sent hotfoot to Bernard, but he did not come. 'I knew,' he said, 'and I foretold that it would be hard for him to kick against the goad. His wound is not mortal, though, but life-giving.' And so it proved. For Gerard, although he recovered from his wound faster than could have been hoped, did not change his resolve, or rather the vow he had made. Now that the love of the world no longer fettered him and only the chains of his enemies prevented him from entering the religious life, God's mercy came swiftly to his aid. His brother arrived and tried to get him freed, but without success. Forbidden even to speak with him, he stood close by the prison wall and shouted: 'Brother Gerard! We shall be leaving soon to enter the monastery. As for you, be a monk here since they will not let you out, and rest assured that what you want to do but cannot, will be deemed done.'

Acts 26:14
Rom. 7:10

12   A few days later, while Gerard was fretting more and more, he heard in his sleep a voice say to him: 'Today you will be freed.' It was the holy season of Lent. Early that evening, as he was pondering what he had heard, he bent to touch his shackles and one of the leg-irons fell off with a clatter in his hand, so that he was less restricted and could hobble along. But what was he to do? The door was bolted and there was a crowd of poor people at the gates. He stood up, however, and, less out hope of escape than from the tedium of lying there, and excited too by the idea of trying, he moved across to the door of the undercroft in which he was held in fetters. No sooner had he touched the bolt than the bar came away in his hand and the door opened. With the shuffling gait of a man in irons he made his way towards the church, where they were singing vespers. When the beggars waiting outside saw what was happening, providentially frightened out of their wits, they ran off without raising the alarm. As he was hobbling churchward, a member of the household, cousin to the man whose prisoner he was, chanced to

come out, and seeing him make what haste he could towards the church, called out: 'You are late, Gerard!' And as the other turned pale, 'Hurry up,' he added, 'there's still some left for you to hear.' His gaze was held fixed and he was quite unaware of what was happening. Not until he had given the still shackled Gerard a helping hand up to the steps of the church and the latter was passing inside did he realize what was going on and make an unsuccessful effort to detain him.

So it was that Gerard, freed in spirit and body alike from the world's grip, faithfully fulfilled the vow he had taken. At the same time the Lord made most powerfully plain the grace that his servant Bernard derived through the holy life he led so perfectly; for in the spirit of him who made what is to be, Bernard was enabled to see what was to come as though it had already taken place. When he placed his finger on the spot on his brother's side where the wound was soon to gape, the lance appeared to him in its very actuality, as he himself later confessed when questioned by those from whom he could not keep it secret.

Fragmenta, 11 While they were still at Châtillon (where they remained for some six months in the lay state in order to swell their numbers and to allow some of them to put their affairs in order), Bernard said one day to his brothers: 'I have a friend at Mâcon, Hugh of Vitry. He too must be brought here to become one of us.' Hugh was a clerk of noble birth, a few years older than Bernard, already richly beneficed and with family wealth besides. Those who knew him accused Bernard of aiming too high, but he sped off on his mission full of confidence. It was rumoured at the time that Bernard was planning to go to Jerusalem (in fact the Jerusalem he had in mind was not the city where the Lord once lived but the monastery where he now dwelled). In consequence, as soon as Hugh set eyes on him, he threw himself into his arms with tears and lamentation, but these were ignored by Bernard, who waited for Hugh to get his breath back and then disclosed his purpose to him. At this Hugh's grief burst out afresh and the fountain of tears flowed yet more freely; in fact there was not a moment when he was dry-eyed all that day. They slept together that night in a bed so narrow there was barely room for the two. Even then Hugh's tears continued to flow to the point where God's servant complained that they were keeping him awake. When Bernard did finally fall asleep, after invoking the Holy Spirit as was his habit, it seemed to him that he spoke to Hugh of conversion and the power of the Lord was in his voice.   Ps. 67:34

Morning dawned and to Bernard's annoyance Hugh was still in tears. He remonstrated strongly, but Hugh protested: 'I am not crying for the same reason today as yesterday; yesterday I was weeping over you, today it is over myself. I know your way of life, and I'm well aware that my need of conversion is much greater than yours.' 'Weep your fill!' cried Bernard, delighted. 'These are the right kind of tears; don't stop them!'

When Hugh's friends among clerks and clergy saw them joyfully walking and talking together and refusing to be parted for a moment, they tried to prize Hugh away from Bernard, fearing – indeed they already knew – that the two were one in spirit. They kept a tight hold on Hugh and would not allow God's servant to speak with him on any pretext. So Bernard went home sad, but still in his heart he trusted in the Lord.

Some days later he heard that the bishops were to meet in synod and hurried along in the expectation of meeting Hugh. When the latter's friends spied Bernard they glared at him as sourly as usual and hedged Hugh closely about wherever he went to prevent him being approached. They were all sitting in the open while the bishops consulted together. Bernard was sitting among the clerks and next to Hugh, but unable to speak to him because of his protectors; his tears, however, were flowing fast down his friend's neck. At that moment a sudden heavy shower soaked them all and sent them scurrying to the nearest village. But Bernard, holding Hugh by the hand, said: 'Stay here with me in the rain.' The swift return of fair weather found them alone in the field, and Hugh confessed to Bernard that he had sworn not to take monastic vows for a twelvemonth. He had done this to outmanoeuvre his companions by counting in the probationary year. Hand in hand the two walked back, their spiritual fellowship unassailably strengthened. From then on all despaired of Hugh, and nobody even attempted to detain him.

*   *   *

The Vita Prima *gives the date of Bernard's entry to Cîteaux as 1112. Whether it occurred then or a year later (see note 1, p. 305), the community, under Abbot Stephen Harding, must have found the influx overwhelming as well as inspiriting. New foundations were soon to follow and, three years after entering, a young, untried but clearly exceptional monk found himself leading a freshly severed nucleus, consisting in part of his own kinsmen, northward on the road to Troyes.*

* * *

I, V, 25 The same God who had set Bernard apart and called him out of the world in order – adding grace to grace – to reveal his glory in the man, and through him gather into one great flock his scattered sons; this same God in his own good time inspired Abbot Stephen to send out a group of monks to found the house of Clairvaux. As abbot to the departing group Stephen appointed Bernard, to the great amazement of these mature and active men with their dual experience of world and cloister, who feared for him on account of his tender years, his frailty and his comparative ignorance of practical matters. Clairvaux lay in the district of Langres, not far from the river Aube. It had once been a hide-out of robbers and was formerly known as the Valley of Wormwood, either because the plant grew there in abundance or because of the bitter ordeal of those who fell into the robbers' clutches. It was in
Dt. 32:10 that place of horror and desolation that these righteous men established themselves and turned a den of iniquity into God's temple and a house of prayer. There for some time they served God in simplicity, in poverty of spirit, in hunger and thirst, in cold and nakedness, and
2 Cor. 11:27 in long night watches. Many a time they prepared their broth with beech leaves. Their bread, like that of the Prophet, was made with
Ez. 4:9 barley, millet and vetch, and was such that a certain devout man, moved to tears, once smuggled out the portion served to him in the guest house, as it might be a miracle for general exhibition that any men should live on it, let alone such men as these.

26 But Bernard was little affected by such matters. The chief of his cares was the saving of many souls, a care known to have possessed his heart so intensely from the moment of his conversion to the present day that he seems to feel a maternal love for all mankind. This gave rise to an acute inner conflict where desire and humility were at odds. Now abasing himself, he would confess to being unworthy of producing any fruit; now forgetful of self, he would burn with so intense a fire that it seemed that nothing could satisfy his longing but the salvation of vast numbers. For love gave birth to

confidence, while humility came to check it. It happened once
during this time of struggle that he rose earlier than usual for the
night office, which left him with a somewhat longer stretch of the
night before lauds; so he went outside and walked around, praying
to God that he would accept his obedience and that of his brethren.
As he stood in prayer, being in that state of spiritual desire we have
just described, he suddenly saw, through half-closed eyes, such a
multitude of men of all sorts and conditions come thronging down
from the surrounding hills into the valley bottom that the valley
itself could not hold them. Today the meaning is plain for all to see.
Wonderfully comforted by this vision, Bernard exhorted his brethren, urging them never to despair of the mercy of God.

VI, 27   Before the onset of winter his brother Gerard, the bursar of
the community, complained to him bitterly that the household and
brothers were short of many necessities that he had not the means to
buy, but, although the need was pressing, he received no comfort
from Bernard, there being no funds to hand. He was, however,
asked what sum was needed to tide them over their present difficulties. Eleven *livres*, replied Gerard, whereupon the abbot sent him
away and had recourse to prayer. A short while later Gerard
returned to say that there was a woman from Châtillon outside who
wished to speak with him. When Bernard went out to her, this
woman fell at his feet and presented him with an offering of twelve
livres, imploring the help of his prayers for her husband who was
gravely ill. He spoke to her briefly and sent her away, saying: 'Go,
you will find your husband well.' And so she did when she got
home, while the abbot, putting new heart into his bursar, strengthened him for other trials the Lord might send.

This was no isolated instance. Often, when a similar crisis threatened, God would send Bernard help forthwith, and from some
unexpected quarter. In consequence men of discernment, realizing
that the hand of the Lord was upon him and that often his fine-
drawn spirit had but recently left the bliss of paradise, took pains not
to burden him with practical cares, consulting him only on spiritual
matters and the welfare of their souls.

28   But even in this respect they nearly suffered the fate of the
Israelites. When Moses, as we read, had spoken long with the Lord
on Mount Sinaï and came out of the cloud to go down to the
people, his face was so bright from his converse with the Lord that

Ex. 34:29–31 they fled in terror from his presence. So too when Bernard had been
standing a while before the face of God, as happened when he
attained in that monastic solitude and silence to the pinnacles of
contemplation, he seemed to return from heaven to earth bringing
with him an aura of purity whose source was in God rather than
man, and he frightened away almost all those men among whom he
was coming to live as abbot. When he spoke to them on the
spiritual life and the making of souls, he addressed men in the
language of angels and was scarcely understood. But above all
in matters of human behaviour his own generosity of spirit led him
to set them standards so sublime and to demand such perfection of
them that his words seemed hard, so little did they understand what
was being said to them. Again, when he heard them singly in
confession, accusing themselves of the various fantasies to which
human thought is prone and which none in this life can wholly
avoid, it was here above all that no common ground could be found
between his light and their darkness, for he discovered that those he
had taken for angels were in this respect mere men. Possessed
himself of an almost angelic purity and conscious that God had
given him in the past this singular grace, he jumped naïvely to the
conclusion that monks were proof against the temptations to which
the frailty of human nature exposes all mankind, and could not fall
into the mire of such imaginings. Or if they did so fall, they were
not true monks.

29   But those who were truly devout and combined piety with
prudence revered in his teaching even what they did not grasp. If
they were at times dumbfounded by the novelty of what they heard
when confessing their faults (since he seemed to be sowing the seeds
of despair in men already weak), they still felt that, by admitting
their wickedness to him instead of seeking excuses, at least, as Job
Job 6:10   said, they were not perversely denying the words of the Holy One,
Ps. 142:2   inasmuch as no man living is justified in the sight of God. So it came
about that holy humility became the mistress both of teacher and of
taught; for when the accused humbled themselves before their
accuser, he in turn began to question the righteousness of his
indignation in the face of their self-abasement. It reached the point
where he felt that his own ignorance was most to blame and
regretted having to speak at all since he did not know what to say.
He feared lest by speaking to men, not so much of things beyond as

28

of those beneath them, he might wound the conscience of his hearers. And again, he realized that he was demanding of simple monks a nicety of perfection which he had not yet attained himself. It occurred to him that they might well, in the silence of their souls, think upon better things and more germane to their salvation than they would hear from him; that they might work out their salvation more devoutly and efficiently on their own than through any example of his; that indeed his preaching might prove more of a stumbling-block to them than an aid to holiness. In this state of mental and emotional turmoil he decided to withdraw from all activities into himself and wait on the Lord in solitude and silence until he should, according to his mercy, show him his will in this matter.

God's mercy was not slow in coming to his aid. It was only a few days later that Bernard saw in a dream a boy standing by him and looking at him with love, who bade him with great authority speak confidently whatever words should be put in his mouth, for it would not be he who spoke, but the Spirit in him. From that time Mt. 10:20 on the Spirit did indeed speak more openly in and through him, giving greater power to his words and depth to his understanding of the Scriptures; increasing, too, the appreciation and respect of his hearers and endowing Bernard with a new sympathy with the poor and needy, the repentant sinner and the seeker after grace.

* * *

Bernard's year in the noviciate at Cîteaux had set a pattern that was to hold good for many years. The life was hard; he made it harder. The food was naturally poor and scant, the work heavy, the nights short. Bernard fasted more and slept less. He could not work harder than the others, being neither apt nor built for manual labour, but he did what he could and more than he should. During that first year his health broke down and he was never to recover it. Chronic gastric trouble would dog him for the rest of his life. He had not been long at Clairvaux before he fell seriously ill. The Bishop of Châlons-sur-Marne, William of Champeaux, who had lately ordained him, the see of Langres being vacant, went to the lengths of prostrating himself before the Cistercian abbots at the General Chapter to win for him a year's dispensation from the Rule, and permission (enforced by the bishop) to live on his own in a hut outside the monastery confines. It was there that William first met him.

* * *

I, VII, 26   Around that time I myself began to frequent the monastery and the man. I found him, when I first went to visit him with another abbot, in that little bothy of his, of the type normally built for lepers at public crossroads. And there I found him enjoying the freedom from all domestic cares, both indoor and outdoor, won for him by the order just described, with time for God and himself, and exulting as it were in the delights of paradise. As I stood in that royal chamber considering the dwelling and its inmate, as God is my witness, the place fired me with as much reverence as if I had gone

Ps. 42:4   in to the altar of God. So deeply affected was I by the aura of sweetness surrounding the man, so intense was my desire to live with him in that poverty and simplicity that, had the choice been given me that day, I should have wished for nothing more than to stay with him there for ever and wait upon him.

When he in his turn had welcomed us with joy, we asked what he did and what was his way of life there. 'The best possible,' he answered, with that generous smile of his. 'I, who till now had men – rational beings – obeying me, have by a just judgement of God been made subject to an irrational brute.' He was referring to a certain empty-headed bumpkin, under whose rule the bishop and abbots and his brethren had placed him, and who declared, from the vast depths of his ignorance, that he would cure Bernard of his illness. Eating with him there, we saw this man – whom we believed so ill that he was accorded whatever special dispensations were needed for his care – we saw him offered food by this physician of his that a healthy man, and famished at that, would have forborne to touch. Such was our horror that only the rule of silence kept us from letting fly at this murderer, this desecrator almost, with the rough edge of our tongues. Yet the object of these 'attentions' ate everything regardless and with apparent approval, as though, his sense of taste being impaired and virtually deadened, he hardly discriminated between one thing and the next. Indeed he is known to have eaten on several occasions raw lard, served to him in mistake for butter, and drunk oil instead of water: he was a prey to such mishaps. He used to say that the only thing he could taste was water because it refreshed his throat as it went down.

34   Unworthy though I was, I spent a few days with him, and

wherever I turned my eyes I was amazed to see as it were a new
heaven and a new earth, and the well-worn path trodden by the   Rev. 21:1
monks of old, our fathers out of Egypt, bearing the footprints left by
men of our own time.

35   That was the golden age of Clairvaux when men of virtue, once
rich in goods and honour and glorying now in the poverty of
Christ, established the Church of God in their own blood, in toil
and hardship, in hunger and thirst, in cold and exposure, in persecu-   2 Cor. 11:27
tion and insults, in difficulties and in death, preparing the Clairvaux   2 Cor. 12:10
of today, which enjoys sufficiency and peace. Nor did they care a   2 Cor. 9:8
whit for what they lacked, believing as they did that they lived not
for themselves but to serve Christ and their brothers, and in them,
God. They asked only to leave to their successors enough to keep
them from want and to give them at the same time some understanding of a poverty willingly embraced for Christ.

The first impression of those approaching Clairvaux down the
steep scarp was of God's presence in the little huddle of houses, for
the dumb valley itself proclaimed, through the poverty and humility
of the buildings, that of Christ's poor whose dwelling-place they
were. As further proof, in that very hive of activity, where none
might be idle but each was busy at his appointed task, a midnight
hush would greet the noontide visitor, broken only by work noises
or the chanting of the office, as might be. This much-talked-of
silence inspired such awe in laymen coming to the monastery that
they were afraid to pass any remark that was not essential to their
business, let alone a frivolous or improper one. There was a sense in
which the solitude of that valley, strangled and overshadowed by its
thickly wooded hills, in which God's servants lived their hidden
lives, stood for the cave in which our father St Benedict was once
discovered by shepherds – the sense in which those who were
patterning their lives on his could be said to be living in a kind of
solitude. They were indeed a crowd of solitaries. Under the rule of
love ordered by reason, the valley became a desert for each of the
many men who dwelt there: for just as one undisciplined man is his
own crowd even when he is alone, so here, thanks to unity of spirit
and the rule of silence, in an ordered crowd of men the order
safeguards the solitude of each man's heart.

VIII, 38   Such was the school of spiritual studies that flourished in
those days under Abbot Bernard in that far-famed and most beloved

valley. With such fervour was the rule observed when he, the moving spirit of the house, was building the tabernacle of God on earth, after the pattern shown to him on his spiritual Sinaï when he dwelt alone in the cloud with God. If only after that first essay in the monastic life, after he had gone some way towards learning to live as a man among men, and had come to understand the poor and needy and feel for the weak – if only he had treated himself with the same discreet and loving care he had for others. But as soon as he was loosed from his year's obedience and became his own master again, like a bow bent to its original tautness or a torrent dammed and then unleashed, he returned to his former ways as though he sought to penalize himself for that period of rest, or exact compensation for work left undone.

* * *

In fact, however harsh the regime he followed – and William details his austerities with loving attention – Bernard was never again to fall into the excesses of the first years. Geoffrey shows us the mature man shrinking from any form of singularity that might set him apart. And if he still would not pander in the slightest to his own ill-health, it was a different matter where others were concerned, as William discovered.

* * *

I, XII, 59   On another occasion, when Bernard learned that I too was laid up at our house, already much weakened and wasted by a protracted illness, he sent his brother to me (Gerard it was, of blessed memory), bidding me come to Clairvaux, with the promise of either a swift recovery or as swift a death.[1] Seizing this seemingly heaven-sent opportunity either to die with him or live with him a while (which I would then have preferred I do not know), I made my way to Clairvaux despite the pain and hardship of the journey. And there the promise made to me was kept and, I confess, just as I wished it. For health was restored to me after a severe and dangerous illness, yet physical strength returned by slow degrees. Ah! God of all goodness, what special good did that illness, that festival, that very holiday confer on me? In part what I myself desired. Bernard too was laid up at the time, and his illness served and coincided with my need. Both sick, we spent the the livelong day discussing the spiritual medicine of the soul and the remedies afforded by the virtues against the vices' various distempers. And all the while my illness lasted, he expounded the Song of Songs for me, but treating of the moral sense only and leaving aside the mysteries of that book – which was what I wanted and had asked of him. Each day, in so far as God and my memory enabled me, I fixed in writing all that I had heard on this subject lest it escape me; for with ungrudging kindness he would set forth for me and share with me the fruits of his understanding, both conceptual and intuitive, striving to teach my inexperience much that only experience can apprehend. And even though what he set before me lay then beyond my grasp, at least he gave me a clearer perception of the lack in me which prevented my understanding what he taught me. But enough said about that for now.

60   Septuagesima Sunday[2] was upon us, and on Saturday evening, having regained strength enough to get out of bed unaided and come and go on my own, I began to make plans for returning to my brothers. Bernard met this news with an unequivocal veto and forbade me all exertion and any hope of return until Quinquagesima Sunday. I gave way readily enough, seeing that his orders met my wishes no less than the requirements of my health. But from that Septuagesima Sunday on I wanted to abstain from meat, which I had been eating up to then, compelled by Bernard's orders and my need; this too he forbade me to do. And since I would not heed his warnings on the subject, nor listen to his pleas, nor obey his orders, that Saturday evening saw a mutual parting – he in silence to compline, I to my bed. Whereupon my illness revived in all its fury and as it were the first flush of its strength, and tore into me with such a paroxysm of ferocity, racking me past all bearing, that I despaired of life itself and thought I should not last out even till daybreak or what time I might exchange one last brief word with Bernard.

When I had dragged the night out in this torment, he came to me, summoned at first light, but not with his usual expression of sympathy, more one of disapproval. 'And what,' he said (but with a smile), 'will you eat today?' As for me, sure as I was, despite his silence, that yesterday's disobedience was the cause of my present suffering, I replied: 'Whatever you bid me.' 'Rest easy,' he said, 'you are not going to die now.' And off he went. What shall I say? My pain vanished instantly and completely, save that I could scarcely heave myself out of bed that day, so exhausted was I by the night-long agony. What was this pain and of what nature? I do not remember ever having been afflicted by a similar. By the following morning I had recovered health and strength, and a few days later, with the blessing and good grace of my kind host, I returned to my own community.

IX, 43   After Bernard had been some years at Clairvaux, it happened that a man of rank, who was also related to him, one Josbert of La Ferté-sur-Aube, the village nearest to the abbey, fell victim to a seizure, which deprived him of speech and understanding. It was a cause of much distress to his son, young Josbert, and to all his kinsmen that a great and greatly honoured man should die unshriven and without the sacrament. A messenger ran for the abbot, who happened to be away from the monastery, so that, when he finally got there, he found that the man had been lying insensible for three days. Taking pity on him and moved by the tears of his son and household, Bernard put his trust in God's mercy and spoke out boldly, saying: 'You are all aware that this man has been a flagrant robber of churches and oppressor of the poor, and has gravely offended God. But you may take my word for it that, if restitution is made to the churches and he restores to the poor the customary rights which he wrongfully usurped, he will recover his speech, confess his sins and receive the sacrament with devotion.'

The astonishment was universal: the son was overwhelmed, the household jubilant and Bernard's every direction was faithfully promised and carried out. But his brother Gerard and uncle Gaudry, consternated and shaken, took him aside, remonstrated with him and berated him bitterly for giving such an undertaking. His words in reply were few and simple: 'It is easy for God to do,' he said, 'what you find hard to believe.' And so, after praying in private, he went to offer mass, and as he was officiating a messenger came to say that Josbert, now speaking freely, was asking urgently for the abbot. When Bernard went to him after, he confessed his sins with tears and sighs, and received the sacrament. During the two or three further days that life and speech remained to him, he arranged for Bernard's instructions to be carried out to the letter, set his own household affairs in order and distributed alms. So it was that he finally breathed his last in a Christian manner and in good hope of God's mercy.

XI, 55   On one occasion a group of knights turned aside to Clairvaux to take a look at the place and its holy abbot. Lent was approaching and almost all these young men, given over to worldly chivalry, were going about in search of those detestable gatherings popularly known as tournaments. So Bernard set about asking them not to resort to arms during the few days left before the beginning of Lent. Faced with their obstinate refusal to agree, he said to them: 'I trust to God to give me the truce you have denied me,' and sent for a brother to fetch them some ale, which he blessed, telling them to drink to their souls' health. They did so, albeit reluctantly, for they were in love with the world and nervous of Bernard and God's power working through him, which they were soon to experience; for hardly had they passed the monastery gates when the fullness of their hearts burst out in talk and each was fired by the others' enthusiasm. Thus, inspired by God whose word runs swiftly, they   Ps. 147:15
turned back there and then and dedicated their sword arms to the pursuit of spiritual warfare. Some of these men are doing battle for God still and some are already reigning with him, freed from the   2 Tim. 2:4
body's bonds.

IX, 45   The abbot's brothers and sons after the spirit marvelled at what they heard and saw of him. They did not, however, allow it to turn their heads as is the way of the world; their care and anxiety – wholly spiritual – were for Bernard's youth and his lack of experience at that time in the religious life. His uncle Gaudry and his brother Guy led the field in this respect, as it were twin thorns in his flesh, divinely appointed lest the magnitude of his graces should exalt him. They certainly did not spare him, finding fault with his   2 Cor. 12:7
shyness, carping also at things well done, dismissive of seeming miracles and reducing that most gentle of men (who never said a word in contradiction) to tears with their taunts and reproaches.

Godfrey, Bishop of Langres, a holy man and a cousin of his who entered the religious life with him and was his inseparable companion through thick and thin thereafter, used to relate how Guy was present at the first miracle he saw worked by Bernard. They were passing through Château-Landon in the region of Sens, and a certain youth who had an ulcerated foot pleaded with the Father to lay his hands on him and bless him. Improvement was instant, and on their way back a few days later they found him completely healed. Yet not even that miracle could restrain Guy from upbraiding his brother and taxing him with presumption for agreeing to lay hands on the man: such were the depths of the elder's loving care.

*   *   *

Bernard's brothers were forced as time went on to let go the reins. The abbot's political role took him away for long periods, and they learned not only to do without him but to let him do without them. Arnald of Bonneval portrays him at Milan at the height of his authority.

*   *   *

II, III, 13   Among those who were troubled with evil spirits was an old woman of Milan, who was dragged by many hands as far as the church of St Ambrose in Bernard's wake. Over the years that he had been ensconced within her, the devil had virtually choked this once honoured matron, till she could neither see, hear nor speak. What with grinding her teeth and protruding her tongue like an elephant's trunk, she seemed more like a monster than a woman. Her filthy face, fetid breath and hideous expression were plainly enough the off-scourings of the evil lurking within.

The man of God knew at first sight of her that the devil would not be easily ousted from the dwelling he had occupied so long. Turning to face the huge congregation, he bade them pray with their whole attention, and told clerics and monks who were with him at the altar to bring the woman forward and keep her there. Some got hurt in the process, for she struggled with the devil's own strength and even succeeded in kicking the abbot, who treated this impertinence on the devil's part with quiet contempt. Tranquilly, humbly and with no trace of anger, he asked God's help in the riddance and proceeded with the mass. But as often as he blessed the host he turned towards the woman, and, with a sweeping sign of the cross, God's champion dealt his adversary a mighty blow. And each time a fierce outburst made it clear that the thrust had gone home as, all unwilling and lashing out against the unbearable goad, the evil one made his exit.

14   When the consecration prayer had been said, Bernard took stronger measures against the foe. Placing the sacred Body of the Lord on the paten, and holding it above the woman's head, he addressed him in these terms: 'Here present is your judge, foul spirit, here is the highest power that is. Resist if you can! Here is he who, before suffering for our salvation, said: "Now shall the ruler of this world be cast out." This is the body formed from the Virgin's flesh, Jn. 12:31 stretched on the tree of the Cross, laid low in the grave, the body that rose from the dead and ascended into heaven before the disciples' eyes. In the terrible power of this majesty I command you, evil spirit, to leave this servant of his, and I forbid you to come near her ever again.' Mk. 9:24

As the spirit was forced from the woman willy-nilly, it tormented her violently, its fury as fierce as its time was short. The abbot returned to the altar and, after the fraction of the blessed host, gave the kiss of peace to a priest that its blessing might be poured out on the people, and peace and wholeness returned on the instant to the woman. When she had come to her senses and recovered her reason, her tongue returned to its place and she gave thanks to God, throwing herself at the feet of the man who had saved her. A great shout went up in the church as young and old rejoiced in the Lord amid the sounding of gongs; and the whole city held God's servant in veneration and, if I may be permitted the expression, yearned after him with love.

III, VII, 20 God's servant turned these matters over and over in the privacy of his own mind, and it was only the fullness of his heart that led him to speak of them to certain members of his community. 'I am deeply puzzled,' he said, 'as to the meaning of these miracles, and to why God chooses to do such things through such a man as I am. I do not remember having read anything in Scripture about miracles of this kind. Wonders indeed are worked by holy men advanced in virtue and also by impostors. But as for me, I am neither the one nor the other. I know that I have no claim to the merits of the saints renowned for their miracles, and I trust I am not of the company of those who work wonders in the Lord's name and whom he does not know.' Mt. 7:22-3

These and similar matters he would discuss in private with men of spiritual understanding. Towards the end of his life he thought he had found a good way out of the impasse. 'Signs such as these,' he said, 'are not related to the holiness of one but to the salvation of many. And as for the man whom God uses, this much I know: it is not his holiness he takes into account but the opinion that men have of him. He uses him therefore to commend to men the virtue they believe him to possess. Nor are the miracles meant to benefit in any way those who are instrumental in their working, but those who see and hear about them. The Lord does not work miracles through men like me as a sign of their greater holiness, but to inspire greater love and holiness in others. There is nothing in these miracles that I can claim as mine, since I know they are procured by my reputation rather than my life, and are not for my commending but for a warning to others.'

THE LATER YEARS: A PORTRAIT

III, I, I His appearance was not without grace, but this was spiritual rather than physical. His face was lit with a radiance that had more of heaven than earth in it, and the eyes shone with an almost angelic purity and a dove-like simplicity. Such was the beauty of the inner man that his features bore the imprint and his outward aspect was infused with the fullness of his inward godliness and grace. He was slight and spare of figure, his fine skin lightly flushed over the cheekbones. Assiduous meditation and the workings of conscience had intensified a naturally ardent temperament. His fair hair was mixed with white, and towards the end of his life the reddish beard began to grizzle. He was of medium height but appeared taller. In other respects this treasure was housed in an earthen vessel, sadly battered and worn. Many infirmities plagued his flesh that the spirit might thereby be brought to its full perfection. The most serious was a constriction of the throat, which allowed nothing dry and only the smallest quantities of solid food to pass; more irksome was a stomach ailment and a weakness of the bowel. From these troubles he suffered constantly, besides others of frequent occurrence.

His chief concern was to avoid adulation and do as the others did. But renown dogged his every step, so that he was always having to change course to escape his would-be admirers. This proverb, often on his lips, was ever in his heart: Do as none does and the world marvels. With this in mind he conformed the more punctually to the common life and rule, so that nothing he did might smack of singularity. Witness the hair shirt he had worn in secret for many years: he chose to leave it off sooner than let the fact be known. To the practices common to all, however, he gave himself single-mindedly and with a quite uncommon devotion, neglecting nothing

Mt. 10:16
Eph. 3:16

2 Cor. 4:7

and fulfilling the least requirements with scrupulous care. The wise man, he would say, speaking from his own experience, is one who finds all things to his taste by reason of their existence.

2   Almost from his earliest years he avoided all foods that tempt the palate, seeking to eradicate as far as possible the very faculty to distinguish tastes. How often, deceived by some pious ruse of those who waited on him, did he not swallow one liquid, taking it for another? Once he even drank olive oil, presented to him in error, and was totally unaware of it. It was only when someone walking in was amazed to see it glistening on his lips that the mistake was noticed. His food was a mouthful of bread, well softened in warm water, and a very little broth. A moderate man, therefore; yet it was no moderate part that his stomach rejected undigested, that he might take no pleasure in food, he for whom eating spelled danger, digestion pain and rejection misery. Providence had so ordered it that this faithful servant should not lose the fruits of his remarkable abstinence, while yet by force of circumstance avoiding the admiration he always found so hateful. Regarding wine, he always said that, when a monk had to drink it, it was seemly that he should be seen not to have drained his cup. As for his own practice, whenever he let wine be served to him, the little vessel in which it was brought to him was scarcely ever seen to leave the table, even after a whole meal, less full than when he first put it to his lips.

Unable to stand for long, he was almost continually seated, moving very rarely. As often as he could get away from business, he would be either praying, reading or writing, or else busied with teaching and forming the brothers, or again, steadfast in meditation. His perseverance in these spiritual exercises had won him such exceptional grace that he experienced no tedium or difficulty of any sort. He was at freedom with himself, at large in his spirit's wide demesne, where he had prepared for Christ (as he used himself to counsel others) a spacious room.[3] No moment was too short, no place unsuitable for him to meditate. Yet often, when thus inclined, he would heed the Spirit's urging and leave his studies for more fruitful work, for he was schooled in seeking not his own but the general good. But whatever the press or tumult, unless there were some matter needing his attention, he would withdraw with effortless concentration into the enjoyment of that inner solitude which he carried with him wherever he went, deaf and blind to all besides.

VII, 22 I often heard him confess to feeling, in the midst of the honours and marks of favour heaped on him by commoners and princes, that he had become someone else, or better, that he was absent and the whole thing as illusory as a dream. But when the simpler brothers confided in him trustingly, as was their way, and he had leisure to enjoy it with the unassuming friendliness he always showed, then he rejoiced to find himself again and recover his true identity.

The shyness that had characterized him from boyhood remained with him to the end. Thus, for all his great and glorious gifts as a preacher, he never spoke (as he insisted repeatedly), however humble the gathering, without fear and awe. He would always have chosen silence had he not been spurred on by conscience, fear of God, or love of neighbour.

26 He was bold of spirit to a rare degree, yet combined it with such humility and gentleness that he seemed to fear none while reverencing one and all. He rarely had recourse to reprimands, preferring to warn or plead. If he spoke a harsh word, it was always reluctantly, never the lashing out of a sore heart. In fact, he controlled such impulses with particular ease and was always amazed at the bad faith of those who, once upset, would make difficulties about accepting an excuse however reasonable, or an apology however humble. Such men find their inner turmoil so exhilarating that they shun any remedy, blocking their ears, shutting their eyes, fending off with their hands and doing all they can to ensure that the passions aroused shall be neither calmed nor healed. With Bernard, on the contrary, a sharp, blustering response would often dry up his rebuke as swiftly as a submissive one. This led some to say that he pressed the compliant and yielded to the defiant.

28 What affected him most deeply was the spiritual good or ill of all men. His keenest desire, his greatest joy was the harvest of souls and the conversion of sinners. Yet he had sympathy and a kind understanding for the body's needs as well, and such was his tenderness of heart that he felt not only for men but for dumb beasts and birds and wild things. Nor was it empty sympathy without effect. Many a time on his journeys he saved with the sign of the cross a hare fleeing from the hounds or a bird marked by falcons; on such occasions he would tell the hunters that they were wasting their efforts and had no chance that day of satisfying their lust for plunder.

Fragmenta, 9   There was a time when God's servant had business to attend to in the region of Paris and broke his return journey to preach, as was customary, to the students there – a sermon on conversion. Evening found him downhearted and low. 'I fear you have utterly forgotten me,' he said to God in prayer. 'For the first time my journey has proved quite fruitless. I have gained nothing from these clerks on whose behalf I came, your word has opened no door to me among them.' Within the hour God consoled him, according to his promise that he should not go away empty-handed.   Dt. 15:13

Blessed be the day of the Lord! I was sitting in darkness and in the shadow of death and the light dawned on me. Blessed that day   Lk. 1:79
when the sun of justice, or rather mercy, visited from on high in his   Mal. 4:2
rising my most wretched soul, utterly recreating in a single word, in   Lk. 1:78
a moment, in the twinkling of an eye, by an inestimable change of   I Cor. 15:52
the right hand of the Most High, a man exceedingly contrary and   Ps. 76:11
perverse, and making another man of me, the embryonic beginnings of his creature. I shall never forget through all eternity the compassion which so bounteously forestalled me and changed me so suddenly as to leave men agape with stupefaction. There were many   Lk. 5:6
fish caught in the Lord's net in that haul, and more joined up with   Jn. 21:11
us on the road, so that after the probationary year there were twenty-one of our company professed. We were still raw recruits, and our Father was away, when I became ill in body and depressed in spirit. I know that Satan desired to have me that he might sift me like wheat. But what was being concocted around me was not   Lk. 22:31
hidden from the Father; and having a perfect knowledge through the Spirit – as I found out after his return – of all the thoughts that were occupying my mind and heart, he prayed that my faith might not fail. And then, O Lord my God, upon the person that I was you   Lk. 22:32
stamped in a most marvellous way the imprint of his heart. Thanks be to you, Lord, thanks be to you! But what a lodging for such a soul as that in such a breast as mine!

From *An Apologia for Abbot William*

The treatise known as the Apologia ad Guillelmum abbatem *is a witty and hard-hitting satire that can be enjoyed on its own merits without reference to its context. Yet this gem has an elaborate setting, worth looking at because it concentrates the sparkle. The crucible was the growing tension between black monks and white. Bernard had been ten years at Clairvaux when he was approached by William of St Thierry about writing a tract that would both refute current accusations that the Cistercians were running down the black monks' way of life and denounce the laxity of contemporary Cluniac practice. Bernard, after a moderate show of reluctance, prepared a first draft, which he sent to his friend Oger, a Canon Regular of Mont-Saint-Éloi, for perusal and comment. Oger in turn sent the draft text to William.[1] Presumably the criticisms and suggestions of both were carried back to Bernard, who in the summer of 1125 wrote a first edition, which was itself polished and expanded to form the definitive text.*

In his reply to William's initial request Bernard points out the difficulty of looking convincing in the dual role of prosecutor and counsel for the defence. 'Perhaps I could say first that the Order itself is quite praiseworthy and that those who censure it should themselves be censured',[2] he suggests; and this is in fact the tactic he adopts. In so doing he seeks to give the appearance of being diplomatic and fair-minded, but essentially he is having recourse to a well-known and well-tried courtroom stratagem, much favoured by the Ancients: loudly denigrate your client before establishing his innocence: or again, for maximum effect build up the opposition first and then demolish it. The Apologia thus falls into two roughly equal parts. In the first Bernard deplores the suggestion that his Order should see fit to criticize another. Damned as they would be for the sin of pride, where would be the point of the white monks' austerities? There must be a more comfortable way of going to hell. As for him personally, he has the greatest respect for the black monks and has always been on excellent terms with individuals

42

and communities.[3] *In any case, why the rivalry? The Church has need of both Orders; and here Bernard addresses himself to the theme of plurality in unity, and finally to the primacy of the spiritual virtues of charity and humility over the outward and penitential observances. Having made his own position clear and berated the zealots in his own camp for Pharisaism, he feels free — indeed morally obliged — to weigh into the opposition. The second part is thus devoted to a mordant attack, not on the Cluniac way of life — God forbid! — but only on their failure to live up to their own high ideals. In a series of short chapters he turns his fire-power on a number of abuses, concluding with the hope that all monks who have their Order's good at heart will be grateful to him for his honest concern.*

The Apologia is a finely wrought example of a literary genre based on classical models and assiduously practised in the Middle Ages, particularly by monastic reformers.[4] *It did not and was never intended to give an accurate picture of life in a typical black monk monastery of the time. No doubt it contained enough truth for it to hurt as well as amuse, for Cluny had recently and dramatically slipped from its former pinnacle. But by the time the Apologia appeared, Peter the Venerable, one of the most attractive personalities of the century, was abbot of Cluny and did not need Bernard to put him right, though it may be that Bernard's strictures strengthened his reforming hand.*[5]

Bernard protests in his pamphlet that he does not want to create scandal. In fact he succeeded in doing just that: the quarrel was pursued in some eleven tracts composed during the course of the next hundred years, and the continuing polemic did nothing to improve relations between the Orders. If Peter the Venerable did not cease to love him, lesser men found it hard to turn the other cheek after the first had been well slapped.

Ultimately, however, if the debate between Cîteaux and Cluny has an abiding interest, it is because the issues are wider than the immediate context, wider even than the Benedictine Rule of which each claimed to be the faithful interpreter. Each generation of Christians has to live out the tension between the poverty, the self-emptying of God incarnate and the majesty, the fullness of God transcendent. Either they emulate the first or they devote their creative gifts to glorifying the second. Cistercians and Cluniacs fought a pitched battle over the issue in terms of their own day, but, since the tensions, attitudes and temptations are endemic, St Bernard's critique has lost nothing of its relevance.

* * *

AGAINST DETRACTORS

V, 10   I have a point at issue here with certain members of our Order who are said to be running down other Orders and trying to establish their own righteousness instead of submitting to the right-
Rom. 10:3 eousness of God, and this in despite of the saying: 'Do not pass judgement prematurely, before the Lord's coming: he will bring to light what is hidden in darkness, and reveal the secrets of men's
1 Cor. 4:5 hearts.' Now I have stated most clearly that these men, if they are in fact behaving thus, are not of our Order nor indeed of any other, inasmuch as those whose lives are 'ordered', but whose words are arrogant, make themselves into citizens of Babylon, meaning chaos; yes, truly, into sons of darkness, of hell itself, where there is no
Job 10:22 order, the dwelling-place of everlasting dread. And so to you, brothers, who trust in your own righteousness and look down on others, even after hearing the Lord's parable of the Pharisee and the
Lk. 18:9–14 publican, to you I say this: I have heard it said you are boasting that you alone among men are righteous, or at least holier than the rest, that you are the only monks to live according to the Rule; others honour it rather in the breach.

11   First, what business have you with another's servants? Whether
Rom. 14:4 they stand or fall concerns their master. Who has set you up as
Lk. 12:14 judges over them? In the next place, if, as is said, you stand upon your Order, what sort of order is it that has you peering and prying so diligently after the motes in your brothers' eyes before
Mt. 7:3–4 each of you has removed the beam from his own? You who glory
Rom. 2:23 in the Rule, why do you undermine it? Why do you go against the Gospel in judging prematurely and against St Paul in judging another's servants? Surely the Rule accords with the Gospel and with Paul? Else the Rule is wrong, and so no rule at all. Listen and learn what order is, you who run counter to it in finding fault with other Orders: 'Hypocrite, first cast the beam out of your own eye and then you will see clearly to cast the mote out of your brother's.'
Mt. 7:5 Which beam, you want to know? What about the long, large beam of pride, pride that makes you think yourself something when you
Gal. 6:3 are nothing, that has you foolishly vaunting your fancied soundness,

and taking others groundlessly to task about their motes while carrying a beam yourselves? 'I thank you, God,' you say, 'that I am not as other men, unjust, extortioners, adulterers.' Carry on and add: detractors. As motes go it is no smaller than the rest. Why, then, when you list the others so carefully, do you pass that one over? If you think it is a non-existent or trivial fault, listen to the Apostle: 'Nor will detractors inherit the kingdom of God.' And hear God himself fulminating in the Psalm: 'I will rebuke you and place you face to face with yourself' – the context leaves no doubt that he is addressing a detractor. And how right that the detractor should be wrenched round and made to look himself in the face, he who has spent his time prying into the faults of others rather than contemplating his own. — Lk. 18:11 / 1 Cor. 6:10 / Ps. 49:21

VI, 12   But, you reply, what about those who wear furs, who eat meat or animal fat when in perfect health, and three or four cooked dishes a day, all of which things the Rule forbids;[6] who don't do the manual work that it prescribes;[7] and who alter this, add that or subtract the other as they see fit – in what way are they keeping the Rule? These things exist; there's no denying it. But give heed to the rule of God with which St Benedict's is certainly not at odds. 'The kingdom of God is within you', that is to say, not in outward things like clothing and food for the body, but in the virtues of the inner man. Which is why St Paul says that the kingdom of God is not food and drink, but righteousness and peace and joy in the Holy Spirit; and again, that the kingdom of God does not consist in talk but in virtue. You traduce the Fathers therefore in this matter of outward observances, and, by forgetting that spiritual institutions are greater than any Rule, you strain out the gnat while swallowing the camel. What sophistry! It is your greatest concern that the body should be clothed as stipulated, and yet you break that same Rule in leaving the naked soul without its garments. When so much zeal is employed to furnish the body with the tunic and cowl that are supposed to make the monk, why is there not the same concern to attire the spirit in piety and humility? Sublime in our tunics we shudder at the thought of furs – as though humility wrapped in furs were not better than pride draped in a tunic. God, after all, made Adam and Eve garments of skin, John wore a leather girdle round his waist in the desert, and Benedict himself[8] in his hermitage wore animal skins rather than a tunic. — Lk. 17:21 / Rom. 7:22 / Rom. 14:17 / 1 Cor. 4:20 / Mt. 23:24 / Gen. 3:21 / Mt. 3:4 / Mk. 1:6

Having filled our belly with beans and our mind with pride, we condemn rich foods, as though it were not better to eat a modicum of fat as need requires than to stuff oneself to belching point with flatulent pulses. Remember that it was not meat but
Gen. 25:34 lentils that got Esau his reproof, not meat but fruit that was
Gen. 3:17 Adam's downfall, while Jonathan was condemned to death for
I Sam. 14:29 tasting not meat but honey. On the other hand, no harm came to
I Kgs. 17:6 Elijah from eating meat, Abraham found favour by serving meat
Gen. 18:8 to the angels, and God ordered animals to be offered to him in sac-
Ex. 20:24 rifice.

Again, it is better to use a little wine for one's infirmity than to slake one's thirst greedily with water. Paul, after all, advised
I Tim. 5:23 Timothy to take a little wine, and the Lord himself drank it and
Mt. 11:19 was even called a drunkard; he gave it, too, to his apostles to
Lk. 7:34
Mt. 26:27–8 drink, and established in wine the sacrament of his blood. Con-
Jn. 2:1–10 versely, he would not have water drunk at the marriage feast, and punished the people severely for their complaining at the waters of
Num. 20:1–13 Meribah. As for David, he feared to drink the water he had longed
2 Sam. 23:16– for, and those of Gideon's men who from greed had lain flat on
17 their bellies to drink from the river were not judged worthy to go
Jud. 7:5 into battle.

Lastly, how should we pride ourselves on manual work when
Lk. 10:41–2 Martha was rebuked for working and Mary praised for sitting quiet. As for Paul, he states openly that manual work is of some avail, but
I Tim. 4:8 godliness is all-availing. Best of all is the work to which the Prophet
Ps. 6:7 referred when he said: 'I labour in my groaning', and again: 'I think of God and I am ravished. I am exercised and' (lest we should think
Ps. 76:4 of this exertion as physical) 'my spirit faints'. Clearly the work referred to is spiritual, since it is the spirit and not the body that is wearied by it.

VII, 13 'What then?' you exclaim. 'Do you so press the inward and spiritual side that you condemn the outward and bodily practices which the Rule enjoins on us?' Not at all. It is rather a matter of
Mt. 23:23 doing the one and not neglecting the other. In general, if there has
Lk. 11:42 to be a choice, it is better to omit the bodily rather than the spiritual exercises; for even as the soul is superior to the body, so are the spiritual exercises more beneficial than the physical. So when you smugly find fault with others for their neglect of the practices which you observe, you are surely the greater transgressor, for while you

keep the minutiae of the Rule, you turn your back on the higher gifts which Paul describes as earnestly to be desired. When you run down your brothers while vaunting your own virtue, you lose humility, and charity when you trample them in the dust, both without doubt among the higher gifts. Granted, you wear yourself out with constant hard work, and use the austerity of the Rule to do to death whatever is earthly in you; and you do well. But what if the brother who in your view labours less hard has yet performed some of that bodily work which is of limited value, while being richer than you in all-availing godliness? Which of you, I should like to know, keeps your common Rule better? Surely, the better man? And who is better, the humbler or the wearier monk? Is it not he who has learned from the Lord to be meek and humble of heart, and who has chosen with Mary the better part, which shall not be taken away from him? *1 Cor. 12:31* *Col. 3:5* *Mt. 11:29* *Lk. 11:42*

14   To be blunt: neither you nor he keep the Rule as you reckon it should be kept by all who profess it, that is, to the letter without admitting of any dispensation. He may indeed, in the matter of outward observance, offend in many particulars; it is none the less impossible that you should not offend in one, and, as you know, he who offends in a single point is guilty of all. But if you accept the possibility of dispensation, then without question both of you keep the Rule, but differently: you more strictly, he perhaps more prudently. I am not saying that outward observances should be neglected, nor that the monk who shunned their practice would become spiritual overnight, but rather that the spiritual virtues, for all they are higher, are acquired and preserved with difficulty, if at all, without the external exercises, for, in the words of Scripture: it is not the spiritual that comes first but the physical, and then comes the spiritual. Thus Jacob was unfit for Rachel's much desired embraces until he had knowledge of Leah. And again we read in the Psalm: 'Raise a song and sound the timbrel', meaning take up spiritual things, but practise first the physical. The man best placed is he who toils with discretion and relevancy on either front. *Jas. 2:10* *1 Cor. 15:46* *Gen. 29:16–30* *Ps. 80:3*

15   If this is to be a letter, it is time I finished it. I have taken up the pen and rebuked as vigorously as I could those monks of ours whom you, Father, complained of as having criticized your Order, and have cleared myself at the same time, as it behoved me, of any unfounded suspicion on this count. However, I feel bound to add a

few remarks. Because I give our own men no quarter, I might seem to condone the behaviour of certain monks of yours – conduct which I know you disapprove of, and which all good monks must necessarily avoid. I refer to abuses that, if they exist in the Order, God forbid should ever be a part of it. Certainly no order can contain an element of disorder, for disorder and order are incompatible. So long, therefore, as I attack in the men I censure not the Order they belong to but their vices, I shall be seen as arguing for the Order and not against it. In doing this I have no fear of offending those who love the Order. On the contrary they will surely thank me for hunting down what they themselves detest. Any who might be displeased would prove by their refusal to condemn the vices that corrupt it that they did not have the Order's good at heart. To them I make the Gregorian rejoinder: better that scandal erupt than that the truth be abandoned.[9]

AGAINST SUPERFLUITY

VIII, 16   It is said, and quite rightly, that the Cluniac way of life was instituted by holy Fathers; anxious that more might find salvation through it, they tempered the Rule to the weak without weakening the Rule. Far be it from me to believe that they recommended or allowed such an array of vanities or superfluities as I see in many religious houses. I wonder indeed how such intemperance in food and drink, in clothing and bedding, in horses and buildings can implant itself among monks. And it is the houses that pursue this course with thoroughgoing zeal, with full-blown lavishness, that are reputed the most pious and the most observant. They go so far as to count frugality avarice, and sobriety austerity, while silence is reputed gloom. Conversely, slackness is called discretion, extravagance liberality, chattering becomes affability, guffawing cheerfulness, soft clothing and rich caparisons are the requirements of simple decency, luxurious bedding is a matter of hygiene, and lavishing these things on one another goes by the name of charity. By such charity is charity destroyed, and this discretion mocks the very word. It is a cruel mercy that kills the soul while cherishing the body. And what sort of charity is it that cares for the flesh and neglects the spirit? What kind of discretion that gives all to the body and nothing to the soul? What kind of mercy that restores the servant and destroys the mistress? Let no one who has shown that sort of mercy hope to obtain the mercy promised in the Gospel by him who is the truth: 'Blessed are the merciful, for they shall receive mercy.' On the contrary, he can expect the sure and certain punishment which holy Job invoked with the full force of prophecy on those whom I call 'cruelly kind': 'Let him be no longer remembered, but let him be broken like a sterile tree.' The cause – and a sufficient cause for that most proper retribution – follows at once: 'He feeds the barren, childless woman and does no good to the widow.' Mt. 5:7

Job 24:20

Job 24:21

17 Such kindness is obviously disordered and irrational. It is that of the barren and unfruitful flesh, which the Lord tells us profits nothing and Paul says will not inherit the kingdom of God. Intent on satisfying our every whim it pays no heed to the Sage's wise and warning words: 'Have mercy on your own soul and you will please God.' That is indeed true mercy, and must perforce win mercy, since one pleases God by exercising it. Conversely it is, as I said, not kindness but cruelty, not love but malevolence, not discretion but confusion to feed the barren woman and do no good to the widow – in other words, to pander to the desires of the profitless flesh while giving the soul no help in cultivating the virtues. For the soul is indeed bereaved in this life of her heavenly Bridegroom. Yet she never ceases to conceive by the Holy Spirit and bring forth immortal offspring, which, provided they are nurtured with diligent care, will rightfully be heirs to an incorruptible and heavenly inheritance. Jn. 6:64 / 1 Cor. 15:50 / Sir. 30:24 / 1 Pet. 1:4

18 Nowadays, however, these abuses are so widespread and so generally accepted that almost everyone acquiesces in them without incurring censure or even blame, though motives differ. Some use material things with such detachment as to incur little or no guilt. Others are moved by simple-mindedness, by charity or by constraint. The first, who do as they are bidden in all simplicity, would be ready to act differently if the bidding were different. The second kind, afraid of dissension in the community, are led, not by their own pleasure, but by their desire to keep the peace. Lastly there are those who are unable to stand out against a hostile majority that vociferously defends such practices as pertaining to the Order and moves swiftly and forcibly to block whatever judicious restrictions or changes the former try to bring in.

IX, 19   Who would have dreamed, in the far beginnings of the monastic order, that monks would have slid into such slackness? What a way we have come from the monks who lived in Anthony's day! When one of them paid on occasion a brotherly call on another, both were so avid for the spiritual nourishment they gained from the encounter that they forgot their physical hunger and would commonly pass the whole day with empty stomachs but with minds replete. And this was the right order of precedence – to give priority to what is nobler in man's make-up; this was real discretion – making greater provision for the more important part; this indeed true charity – to tend with loving care the souls for love of whom Christ died.

As for us, when we come together, to use the Apostle's words, it I Cor. 11:20 is not to eat the Lord's supper. There is none who asks for heavenly bread and none who offers it. Never a word about Scripture or salvation. Flippancy, laughter and words on the wind are all we hear. At table our ears are as full of gossip as our mouths of festive fare, and all intent on the former we quite forget to restrain our appetite.

ON MEALS

20   Meanwhile course after course is brought in. To offset the lack of meat – the only abstinence – the laden fish dishes are doubled. The first selection may have been more than enough for you, but you have only to start on the second to think you have never tasted fish before. Such are the skill and art with which the cooks prepare it all that one can down four or five courses without the first spoiling one's enjoyment of the last, or fullness blunting the appetite. Tickle the palate with unaccustomed seasonings and the familiar start to pall, but exotic relishes will restore it even to its preprandial sharpness; and since variety takes away the sense of surfeit, one is not aware that one's stomach is overburdened. Foodstuffs in their pure and unadulterated state have no appeal, so we mix ingredients pell-mell, scorning the natural nutriments God gave us, and use outlandish savours to stimulate our appetite. That way we can eat far more than we need and still enjoy it.

To give but one example: who could itemize all the ways in

which eggs are maltreated? Or describe the pains that are taken to toss them and turn them, soften and harden them, botch them and scotch them, and finally serve them up fried, baked and stuffed by turns, in conjunction with other foods or on their own? What is the purpose of all this unless it be to titillate a jaded palate? Attention is also lavished on the outward appearance of a dish, which must please the eye as much as it gratifies the taste buds, for though a belching stomach may announce that it has had enough, curiosity is never sated. Poor stomach! the eyes feast on colour, the palate on flavour, yet the wretched stomach, indifferent to both but forced to accept the lot, is more often oppressed than refreshed as a result.

ON DRINK

21   What can I say about the drinking of water when even watering one's wine is inadmissible? Naturally all of us, as monks, suffer from a weak stomach, which is why we pay good heed to Paul's advice to use a little wine. It is just that the word *little* gets overlooked, I can't   1 Tim. 5:23 think why. And if only we were content with drinking it plain, albeit undiluted. There are things it is embarrassing to say, though it should be more embarrassing still to do them. If hearing about them brings a blush, it will cost you none to put them right. The fact is that three or four times during the same meal you might see a half-filled cup brought in, so that different wines may be not drunk or drained so much as carried to the nose and lips. The expert palate is quick to discriminate between them and pick out the most potent. And what of the monasteries – and there are said to be some – which regularly serve spiced and honeyed wine in the refectory on major feasts? We are surely not going to say that this is done to nurse weak stomachs? The only reason for it that I can see is to allow deeper drinking, or keener pleasure. But once the wine is flowing through the veins and the whole head is throbbing with it, what else can they do when they get up from table but go and sleep it off? And if you force a monk to get up for vigils before he has digested, you will set him groaning rather than intoning. Having got to bed, it's not the sin of drunkenness they regret if questioned, but not being able to face their food.

ON THOSE WHO TAKE THEIR EASE IN THE
INFIRMARY WITHOUT BEING ILL

22   I have heard a laughable story – laughable, that is, if it is true –
from a number of people who claim to be certain of the facts, and I
see no reason not to repeat it here. I am told that healthy and strong
young men are opting out of the common life and taking up
quarters in the infirmary without being in any way infirm; and this
to enjoy the meat that the Rule in its wisdom allows to the
genuinely weak and ailing in order to build up their strength.[10] In
this case, of course, the purpose is not to restore a body weakened
by illness but to satisfy the wanton whims of the flesh.

I ask you, is it a sensible strategy, when the flashing spears of a
furious enemy are all about you and their darts are flying on every
side, to throw down your arms as though the war were already over
and won, and either embark on a protracted lunch or snuggle down
unarmed in a soft bed? Is this not cowardice, my brave warriors?
While your comrades mill around in gore and carnage, you are
enjoying the finest fare or catching up on your morning sleep.
Others keep watch round the clock, anxious to redeem the time
Eph. 5:16 because the days are evil, while you sleep the long nights through
and pass your days in idle chatter. Are you perhaps crying 'Peace',
Ez. 13:10 when there is no peace? How can you feel no shame at the fierce
reproach in the Apostle's words: 'You have not yet resisted to the
Heb. 12:4 point of shedding your blood'? Can you not even rouse yourselves at
the thunder of his fearful threat: 'When people say, "There is peace
and security", then sudden destruction will come upon them as
travail comes upon a woman with child, and there will be no
1 Thess. 5:3 escape.'

What a comfortable therapy! You bandage yourselves before
receiving a wound, bewail the sound limb, ward off the undealt
blow, rub ointment into the unbruised skin and stick a plaster where
there is no cut.

The final touch is this: in order to distinguish between the hale
and the sick, the latter are made to carry a walking-stick. Since they
are neither pale nor drawn, the stick is needed to support the
Pretence of illness. Ought we to laugh or cry at such absurdities? Did
Macarius live like that? Is that what Basil taught or Anthony began?

Is that the life the Fathers lived in Egypt? And lastly, what of their own founding fathers and teachers – Odo, Majolus, Odilo and Hugh,[11] the glory of their Order – did they take that course or hold with its taking? No, these were holy men, and being holy were of one mind with the Apostle in his affirmation: 'If we have food and clothing, with these we shall be content.' But as for us, we must have food to glut us, and are content with nothing less than finery.

1 Tim. 6:8

ON COSTLY AND OSTENTATIOUS CLOTHING

X, 24 As regards clothing, today's religious is less concerned with keeping out the cold than with cutting a good figure; so he is after refinement rather than serviceability, and seeks, not the cheapest article, as the Rule prescribes,[12] but the one that can be displayed to the best advantage. Alas, poor wretched monk that I am, why have I lived to see the monastic order come to this? – the order that preceded every other in the Church; indeed the Church grew out of it.[13] Nothing on earth was liker to the angelic orders, nothing closer to the heavenly Jerusalem, our mother, whether it were for the grace of chastity or for the fervour of charity. It was founded by the apostles, and those whom Paul so often calls the saints were its first members. And because none among them kept anything back for his own use, distribution was made to each as he had need, not to gratify individual childish whims. And it is obvious that, where need was the one criterion, there was no room for the useless, the exotic or the showy. 'As he had need' are the words; as regards clothing, the need was the dual one of staying covered and keeping warm. You don't suppose that anyone there was furnished with silks and satins[14] to wear, or mules to ride worth two hundred pieces of gold? Do you imagine that, where distribution was according to need, the beds were spread with catskin coverlets or multicoloured quilts?[15] I do not think myself that they would have bothered overmuch with the quality, colour and style of their clothes: they were too intent on living in harmony, achieving unity and progressing in virtue, which is why the company of believers is described as being of one heart and soul.

Gal. 4:26

Acts 4:32, 35

Acts 4:32

25 Where is this zeal for unanimity nowadays? Our energies are directed outward and, turning our backs on the true and lasting

Lk. 17:21 values of God's kingdom, which is within us, we look abroad for the hollow comfort afforded by trifles and fancies, losing thereby not only the inward vigour of the old religious life but even its outward semblance. Take the habit itself, which used to betoken humility: it grieves me to say that on the backs of our contemporaries it has become a sign of pride. They have trouble finding anything locally that is good enough to wear. Knight and monk today cut cloak and cowl from the one bolt. There isn't a secular dignitary – no, not the king, nor the emperor himself – who would turn up his nose at our clothing, provided cut and style were adapted to his use.

26   Religion is in the heart and not the habit, I hear you say. Quite so. Consider this, then: when you want to buy a cowl, you traipse from town to town and trail round the markets, visiting every booth. You turn the merchant's premises upside down, unrolling the huge bolts of cloth, fingering, peering, holding the lengths up to the light and rejecting anything coarse or faded. But if something takes your eye with its quality or sheen, you will pay any price to ensure you get it. Tell me, do you act thus quite unthinking, or is this the heart speaking? When, instead of buying, as the Rule enjoins, the cheapest you can find, you seek out with infinite pains the most distinctive and therefore costliest article, do you do this in all ignorance or by design? There are no surface vices that do not spring from our hidden depths. The heart's frivolity is worn without, and extravagant attire mirrors the vanity within. Soft clothing is a sign of moral flabbiness: the body would not be decked out with such care had not neglect first left the soul unkempt and bare of virtues.

ON THE NEGLIGENCE OF SUPERIORS

XI, 27   Considering that the Rule bids superiors look to the shortcomings of their charges,[16] and that the Lord threatens through the Prophet to hold the pastors accountable for those who die in their
Ez. 3:18 sins, I find it amazing that abbots permit these kinds of behaviour. One possible reason, if I dare suggest it, is that one cannot administer a confident rebuke unless one's own position is secure. It is only human nature to be lenient in respect of liberties that one allows oneself. So say I, and shall be called presumptuous for it, but it is the

truth for all that. Ah, how has the light of the world been dimmed Mt. 5:14
and the salt of the earth lost its savour! When those whose life Mt. 5:13
should trace a path of life for us to follow set us instead an example Ps. 15:11
of pride, it is indeed a case of the blind leading the blind. Mt. 15:14

ON MOUNTING ONE'S HIGH HORSE

Leaving the rest aside, what evidence is there of humility when one
solitary abbot travels with a parade of horseflesh and a retinue of
lay-servants that would do honour to two bishops? I swear I have
seen an abbot with sixty horses and more in his train. If you saw
them passing, you would take them for lords with dominion over
castles and counties, not for fathers of monks and shepherds of souls.
Moreover, napery, cups, dishes and candlesticks have to be taken
along, together with packs stuffed full, not with ordinary bedding,
but with ornate quilts. A man cannot go a dozen miles from home
without transporting all his household goods, as though he were
going on campaign or crossing the desert where the basic necessities
were unobtainable. Surely water for washing one's hands and wine
for drinking can be poured from the same jug? Do you think that
your lamp will fail to burn and shine unless it stands in your very Jn. 5:35
own candlestick, and a gold or silver one at that? Can you really not
sleep except on a chequered blanket and under an imported coverlet?
And is a single servant not capable of loading the packhorse, serving
the food and making up the bed? And lastly, if we must travel with
these retinues of men and beasts, can we not mitigate the evil by
taking the necessary provisions instead of battening on our hosts?

ON THE PLACE OF PICTURES, SCULPTURE,
GOLD AND SILVER IN MONASTERIES

XII, 28   But these are minor points. I am coming to the major abuses,
so common nowadays as to seem of lesser moment. I pass over the
vertiginous height of churches, their extravagant length, their inordinate width and costly finishings. As for the elaborate images that
catch the eye and check the devotion of those at prayer within, they
put me more in mind of the Jewish rite of old. But let this be: it is

all done for the glory of God. But as a monk I ask my fellow monks the question a pagan poet put to pagans: 'Tell me, O priests, why is there gold in the holy place?'[17] 'Tell me, O poor men,' say I – for it is the meaning, not the measure that concerns me – 'tell me, O poor men, if poor you are, what is gold doing in the holy place?' It is one thing for bishops but quite another for monks. Bishops are under an

Rom. 1:14 obligation both to the wise and the foolish. Where people remain impervious to a purely spiritual stimulus, they use material ornamentation to inspire devotion. But we who have separated ourselves from the mass, who have relinquished for Christ's sake all the world's beauty and all that it holds precious, we who, to win Christ,

Phil. 3:8 count as dung every delight of sight and sound, of smell and taste and touch, whose devotion do we seek to excite with this appeal to the senses? What are we angling for, I should like to know: the admiration of fools, or the offerings of the simple? Or have we perhaps, through mixing with the Gentiles, learned their ways and

Ps. 105:35-6 taken to worshipping their idols?

To put it plainly: suppose that all this is the work of cupidity, which is a form of idol-worship; suppose that the real objective is not yield but takings. You want me to explain? It's an amazing process: the art of scattering money about that it may breed. You spend to gain, and what you pour out returns as a flood-tide. A costly and dazzling show of vanities disposes to giving rather than to praying. Thus riches elicit riches, and money brings money in its train, because for some unknown reason the richer a place is seen to be the more freely the offerings pour in. When eyes open wide at gold-cased relics, purses do the same. A beautiful image of a saint is on show: the brighter the colours the holier he or she will be considered. Those who hasten to kiss the image are invited to leave a gift, and wonder more at the beauty than at the holiness they should be venerating.

Instead of crowns one sees in churches nowadays great jewelled wheels bearing a circle of lamps, themselves as good as outshone by the inset gems. Massive tree-like structures, exquisitely wrought, replace the simple candlestick. Here too the precious stones glimmer as brightly as the flames above.

What is this show of splendour intended to produce? Tears of

Ecc. 1:2 contrition or gasps of admiration? O vanity of vanities, but above all insanity! The walls of the church are ablaze with light and colour, while the poor of the Church go hungry. The Church revets its stones in gold and leaves its children naked. The money for feeding the destitute goes to feast the eyes of the rich. The curious find plenty to relish and the starving nothing to eat. As for reverence, what respect do we show for the images of the saints that pattern the floor we tread beneath our feet? People often spit on angels' faces, and their tramping feet pummel the features of the saints. If we care little for the sacred, why not save at least the lovely colours? Why decorate what is soon to be defaced? Why paint what is bound to be trodden on? What good are beautiful pictures where they receive a constant coating of grime? And lastly, what possible bearing can this have on the life of monks, who are poor men and spiritual? And yet perhaps the poet's well-known line can be countered by the Prophet's words: 'Lord, I have loved the beauty of your house and the place where your glory dwells'. Very well, we will   Ps. 25:8 tolerate such doings in our churches on the grounds that they harm only the foolish and the grasping and not the simple-hearted and devout.

29   But what can justify that array of grotesques in the cloister where the brothers do their reading, a fantastic conglomeration of beauty misbegotten and ugliness transmogrified? What place have obscene monkeys, savage lions, unnatural centaurs, manticores, striped tigers, battling knights or hunters sounding their horns? You can see a head with many bodies and a multi-bodied head. Here is a quadruped with a dragon's tail, there an animal's head stuck on a fish. That beast combines the forehand of a horse with the rear half of a goat, this one has the horns in front and the horse's quarters aft. With such a bewildering array of shapes and forms on show, one would sooner read the sculptures than the books, and spend the whole day gawking at this wonderland rather than meditating on the law of God. Ah, Lord! if the folly of it all does not shame us, surely the expense might stick in our throats?[18]

30   This is a rich vein, and there is plenty more to be quarried, but I am prevented from carrying on by my own demanding duties and your imminent departure, Brother Oger. Since I cannot persuade you to stay, and you do not want to leave without this latest little book, I am falling in with your wishes: I am letting you go and shortening my discourse, particularly since a few words spoken in a spirit of conciliation do more good than many that are a cause of

From *The Life of Malachy the Irishman*

St Bernard's Life of Malachy the Irishman was written as a tribute to a man the abbot had known, albeit briefly, and loved. It is an expression of loss, but above all a celebration, and there was in Bernard's eyes a great deal to celebrate in Malachy's life and death. They were almost exact contemporaries, and Malachy had been a great reforming bishop of the kind dearest to Bernard's heart: a man who lived the Gospel as well as preaching it; who despised possessions and went about on foot; who faced down the great and was a father to the poor.

They met first in 1139, when Malachy travelled to Rome and halted both going and coming to spend a few days at Clairvaux. Abbot and prelate were instantly drawn to one another. Malachy, already living a monastic life at Down, sought permission from Innocent II to resign his bishopric and enter Clairvaux. Not surprisingly it was refused, and Malachy duly reshouldered his burden but left his heart at Clairvaux (he also left four of his disciples to be formed in Cistercian ways and later return with others to found the monastery of Mellifont).

In 1148, in a second attempt to obtain the pallium for Ireland, this time from the Cistercian pope Eugenius, Malachy set out again for Rome. On one occasion, when asked by his followers where and when he would wish to die, he had answered: at Clairvaux, on the feast of All Souls. He arrived at the abbey as the first signs of autumn touched the woods. He would go no further, for although neither Bernard nor his own companions believed it at the time, it was the end of his journey.

These final pages of the Life illustrate the extraordinary and subtle skill with which Bernard could weave an independent narrative almost entirely from texts and references culled from Scripture. Far from breaking the flow of his prose, the biblical content carries it forward as it were on a flood-tide.

*   *   *

MALACHY'S LAST VISIT

Malachy was received by us, although he came from the west, like
Lk. 1:78 the day star from on high visiting us in its dawning. Ah! how the
radiance of that sun filled our house with added glory! How joyful
the feast-day that dawned on us at his coming! What gladness, what
Ps. 117:24 rejoicing in this, the day which the Lord gave! As for me, trembling
and weak though I was, with what swift, springing strides I ran to
meet him! How happily I rushed to kiss him! With what blithe arms
I hugged this grace sent to me from above! With what an eager face
and spirit, my father, I brought you into my mother's house and
S. of S. 3:4 into the chamber of her who conceived me! What festive days I
spent with you, but oh, how few! And how did our traveller in turn
greet us? Most cheerful and courteous was his manner towards all,
Ps. 132:1 and unbelievably gracious. How good and how pleasant a part he
played as a guest among us, whom he had come from the ends of
Mt. 12:42 the earth to see – not even to hear, but to show us a Solomon! It
was we who heard his wisdom, we who enjoyed his presence and
have it with us still.

Four or five days of this festival of ours had passed when he was
seized with a fever and took to his bed, and we too were with him
Prov. 14:13 there. So the end of our joy was grief, tempered though, for the
fever seemed, for the time being, slight. You should have seen the
brothers scurrying to and fro, as eager to give as to receive. For who
did not delight in seeing him and still more in waiting on him? Each
was sweet and brought its benefits. It was an act of kindness to do
him service, repaid with advantage to oneself in thanks brought
Lk. 10:40 back. Everyone helped punctiliously with all the serving: searching
out medicines, applying poultices, frequently urging him to eat.
And his response: 'This serves no purpose. Yet for love of you I will
do whatever you bid me.' For he knew that the time of his passing
was at hand.

When the brothers who had come with him confidently insisted
that he ought not to despair of life – since no signs of death appeared
in him – he replied: 'This is the year when Malachy must leave the
body,' adding: 'See, the day is drawing near which, as you full well

know, I always wished to be the day of my departing. I know 2 Tim. 4:6
whom I have believed, and I am sure that I, who have already a part 2 Tim. 1:12
of my desire, shall not be disappointed of the rest. He who in his Ps. 77:30
mercy has brought me to the place I asked for will not deny me the
time that I wanted just as much. As regards this poor body, here is
my resting-place; as for the soul, the Lord will provide, who saves Ps. 131:14
all those who put their trust in him. There is no small hope laid up Ps. 16:7, 36:40
for me on that day on which so many benefits accrue from the Col. 1:5
living to the dead.[1]" 2 Tim. 4:8

This day was not far off when these words were spoken. Meanwhile, he asked to be anointed with holy oil. The whole community
turned out, that it might be done with solemnity, but he would not
let the brothers come up to him: he went down to them (he was
lodged on the first storey of the upper house). He was anointed and
received the viaticum, and then, commending himself to the brothers' prayers and the brothers to God, he went back to his bed. He
came all the way down from the upper storey on his own feet and
climbed back up the same way, and yet he said that death was at the
gate. Who could believe this man was dying? Only himself and God
could know it. His face seemed no paler, no thinner. His brow was
unlined, his eyes were not sunken, his nostrils not pinched, his lips
not contracted, his teeth not discoloured, his neck was not wasted or
gaunt, his shoulders were not bowed, nor had he lost flesh on the
rest of his body. Such was the grace of his body, such the glory of
his face, that they did not fade, even in death. As he had been in life,
so he appeared in death, just like his living self.

So far we have raced along, but here we shall pause awhile, for
Malachy's race is run. He is at rest; we too will rest with him. 2 Tim. 4:7
Besides, who runs gladly towards death? And yours especially, holy
Father, who can relate it? Who wants to hear about it? Yet we loved
one another in life, and in death we shall not be divided. Brothers, 2 Sam. 1:23
let us not abandon in death him whom we followed in life. From
Ireland he hastened hither to die; let us also go and die with him. It Jn. 11:16
must indeed be told, just as we needed to witness it.

All Saints' Day was at hand, a universal feast; but as the old
saying has it, music in mourning is like a tale out of time. We were Sir. 22:6
there and we sang, but without heart. Weeping we sang, and
singing, wept. But Malachy, although he did not sing, did not weep
either. What should he weep for, he who was approaching the

threshold of joy? To us who were left was left the grief; Malachy
alone kept festival. What he could not do in body, he did in spirit,
as it is written: 'The thought of man shall give you praise, and the
Ps. 75:11 residue of thought keep holiday for you.' As his bodily faculties
failed and tongue and voice fell silent, it remained for him to hallow
the day with mental jubilee. Why should he not keep festival with
the saints, he who was on his way to join them? He was offering to
them what would soon be due to himself. Yet a little while and he
would be one of them.

By nightfall, when we had somehow brought the day's celebra-
tions to their close, Malachy had drawn near, not dusk, but dawn.
For surely it was dawn to him, for whom the night was nearly over
Rom. 13:12 and the day at hand? As the fever mounted, a burning sweat from
within began to break out all over his body, so that, passing as it
Ps. 65:12 were through fire and water he might be brought to a place of ease.
Now was his life despaired of; each of us blamed his own lack of
discernment, for no one doubted now that Malachy would be
proved right. We were summoned and came. Looking up at those
who stood round him, he said: 'I have ardently longed to eat this
Lk. 22:15 passover with you. Thanks be to God in his goodness: I have not
Ps. 77:30 been disappointed of my desire.' Here you have a man untroubled
in the face of death and, even before he was dead, certain of life.
Amazing? No. When he saw that the night he had been waiting for
had come, the night that was to be his dawn, he seemed to exult in a
sort of triumph over its darkness, as though he were crying: 'I shall
not say; "Perchance the darkness will cover me," for this night shall
Ps. 138:11 shine bright about me in my delights.' And then these tender words
of comfort: 'Take care of me and I shall not be unmindful of you, if
so I may. And so it shall be, for I have believed in God and
Mk. 9:22 everything is possible to one who believes. I have loved God, I have
1 Cor. 13:8 loved you, and love never fails.' Then looking up to heaven, he said:
Jn. 17:11 'O God, keep them in your name, and not these only, but all who
through my words or ministry have given themselves to your
service.' Then laying his hands on each and blessing every one, he
Jn. 2:4 bade us leave him for a while, for his hour had not yet come.

We went, and we returned towards midnight, for it is said that
Jn. 1:5 light shines in the darkness at that hour. The house was full; the
whole community was present, and a gathering of abbots too. With
Col. 3:16
Eph. 5:19 psalms and hymns and spiritual canticles we accompanied our friend

on his journey home. In the fifty-fourth year of his life, in the place and at the time he had chosen beforehand and foretold, Malachy, bishop and legate of the holy Apostolic See, taken up as it were by the angels from our hands, fell happily asleep in the Lord. And truly did he fall asleep. His peaceful face was the sign of a peaceful end. And though all eyes were fixed on him, no one was able to pinpoint the moment of his passing. When dead we thought him alive, when living, dead, there being no dividing line between the two states. His face had the same glow, the same serenity that commonly appear in a man asleep. You might say that death, far from diminishing these qualities, greatly intensified them. He was not changed, but he himself changed all of us. In a wonderful way the sounds of grieving were stilled; sorrow was turned to joy; singing banished lamentation. Voices were raised to heaven as he was carried out and borne shoulder-high by abbots into the oratory. Faith has conquered, affection triumphs, the mutable attains finality; all things are performed in due order, and all are grounded in reason. Acts 7:60

cf. Jas. 4:9

1 Jn. 5:4

And in truth where is the reason in mourning Malachy overmuch, as though his death were not precious, as though it were not the port of death and portal of life? Our friend Malachy sleeps, shall I then mourn? Mourning is sustained by custom, not by reason. If the Lord has given sleep to his beloved, such a sleep as encompasses a heritage of the Lord, the reward of sons, the fruit of the womb, which of these seems to call for tears? Shall I weep for him who has passed beyond weeping? He leaps for joy, he triumphs, he has been taken in to share in the joy of his Lord; and I, shall I lament him? I desire these things for myself, I do not begrudge them to him. Ps. 116:15
Jn. 11:11

Ps. 126:2–3

Matt. 25:21

Preparations meanwhile were made for the funeral rites, the sacrifice was offered for him and all that was customary was done with the utmost piety. There was a boy standing some way off whose arm hung dead at his side, more of a hindrance than a help to him. When this was brought to my notice, I nodded to him to come forward and, taking his withered hand I placed it on the bishop's and life was restored to it by the contact. In truth the gift of healing lived in Malachy's dead body, and his hand quickened the boy's hand as Elisha quickened the Shunamite's dead son. The lad had come from a long distance, and the hand he had brought hanging at his side he carried healthy home again. Matt. 12:10

2 Kgs. 4:18–37

Now that the rites were all completed, in that same oratory he

Three Sermons on the Song of Songs

The eighty-six sermons on the Song of Songs, a series begun in 1135 and left unfinished at his death in 1153, are St Bernard's crowning work and have been described as the supreme example of monastic theology. The twelfth century saw a small flush of commentaries on the Song of Songs, drawing on a tradition that harked back through Gregory the Great to Origen. From earliest times the Old Testament love poem had invited allegorical interpretation and had been seen initially as representing the relationship between God and his people, Christ and his Bride, the Church, and, more frequently as time passed, between the Word and the believing soul. It is this latter aspect that St Bernard treats of mainly, though by no means exclusively.

Bernard used the freedom afforded by the sermon form to creative advantage, never tying himself too closely to the text, but using it as a springboard to explore his understanding of the soul's relations to the Word, of the awakening and growth of a loving response to a God who is love, and of much more that seemed germane to him at the time of writing. His objective was not to theorize but to further and strengthen the spiritual life of his readers by drawing on and sharing his own experience of all that advances and hinders the soul in its quest for God.

Love, for Bernard, is of its nature God-given and therefore good. It has, however, as a consequence of sin, become misdirected; hence the need, not to root out emotions and feelings, but to re-centre them and set them in order, establishing a hierarchy of good, better, best and conforming one's life and actions to it. Since the highest form of love is directed to something utterly beyond, it cannot hope for consummation in this life, except as a fleeting foretaste of a union to come. At the same time the soul's own desire is subject to fluctuation, waxing and waning in intensity. This experience of essential instability is explored by Bernard through the theme of the alternating presence and absence of the Bridegroom in the Song. To come to any understanding of what he is trying to say it is necessary to move with him into a symbolic mode which has become largely unfamiliar, and to accept, free from erotic connotations, the bridal imagery of the Old Testament, by no means restricted to the Song of Songs. It may at first seem alien, but the rewards are great.

Although written by a monk for monks, St Bernard's Sermons on the Song reached a wider audience from the start, one of the first such works to be translated into the vernacular in response to a growing demand. Other translations have followed, several into English. Bernard is always hard to translate because he was such a consummate wordsmith, but there are also intractable problems of vocabulary. He had a wide range of terms at his disposal – to cite only amor, dilectio, caritas, affectus, affectio – with a general meaning of love. Sometimes he uses them specifically, at others almost interchangeably. To attempt greater differentiation by introducing psychological terminology inhibits the flow of the English. I have settled for a version that reads, I hope, easily, while regretting the loss of finer·shades of meaning. I have made a few small cuts to eliminate untranslatable wordplay or otherwise accommodate the reader.

*   *   *

SERMON 50

1   I dare say, brothers, that you are expecting a discussion of the next verse, thinking we dealt fully with the one we expounded the other day. However, I have something else in hand. I have some scraps from yesterday's banquet still to set before you, which I gathered up *Jn. 6:12* lest they should be lost. Lost they will be if they are offered to no one, and if I wanted to keep them for my own enjoyment, I should be the one to perish. Nor do I want to deprive you, knowing your hunger for such things, especially since these particular morsels are from the dish of love, sweet and full of flavour for being delicate and tiny. Besides, to cheat anyone of love is to fly in the face of love itself; which brings me to my subject: 'He has set love in order in *S. of S. 2:4* me.'

2   Love can be a matter of doing or of feeling. Regarding the first, I believe that mankind has been given a law, an explicit commandment. But as to feeling, nobody can love to order, let alone in the measure required. To love in deed is therefore a command to be

carried out; a loving heart is received as a gift, in recompense. That in our present life love may, by divine grace, be born in our hearts and grow, I do not deny; but I firmly believe that its coming to full maturity is reserved to future bliss. So how is it that something impossible of achieving came to be commanded? If, on the other hand, you prefer to believe that the command was given with reference to love as an emotion, I will not dispute that, provided you grant me in return that it cannot be fulfilled in this life by anyone, nor ever could, save to a minimal degree. Who would dare to claim for himself what Paul admitted he had not attained? He who laid this precept on us was not unaware that its weight exceeded our strength, but he saw in this very imbalance the best way of drawing men's attention to their shortcomings, so that they might know exactly what goal they had to strive for with the strength they had. So he did not, by commanding the impossible, make men into transgressors: he made them humble, so that every mouth might be silenced and the whole world brought under the judgement of God, for by keeping the Law no human being will stand justified before him. Taking this commandment into our hearts and feeling our own inadequacy, we shall call to heaven and God will have mercy on us, and we shall know in that day that he saved us not because of any upright actions of our own, but in virtue of his mercy.

Phil. 3:13

Rom. 3:19–20

Titus 3:5

3   This is what I should say if we were agreed that the command applied to love as an emotion. In fact, it seems to apply more to love expressed in action, manifestly so indeed, because after saying, 'Love your enemies', the Lord at once added, 'Do good to those who hate you.' And it is written again: 'If your enemy is hungry, feed him; if he is thirsty, give him drink.' All this is a matter of doing, not of feeling. But listen to what our Lord commands us regarding our love of himself: 'If you love me,' he says, 'keep my commandments.' Here too, with the injunction to observe his commandments, the emphasis is on doing. It would have been pointless advocating actions if our love for him had been a purely emotional thing. This is how you must also understand the precept bidding you to love your neighbour as yourself, although it is not expressly stated. For in fact, do you not consider yourself to be fulfilling the commandment about loving your neighbour if you observe perfectly that which the law of nature enjoins on every human being, namely: 'Do as you

Lk. 6:27
Rom. 12:20

Jn. 14:15

Mt. 22:39

Tobit 4:16   would be done by', and again, 'Always treat others as you would
Mt. 7:12   like them to treat you'?

I am not suggesting that we should be devoid of feeling, with active hands but arid hearts. Among the great and grievous human evils listed by the Apostle, I have found heartlessness enumerated Rom. 1:31   too.

4   But there is an affective response bred of the flesh, another ruled by reason and yet another seasoned with wisdom. The first consists of those natural inclinations that Paul says are not and cannot be Rom. 8:7   subject to the law of God. The second he shows on the contrary as Rom. 7:16   acknowledging that the law of God is good. Plainly the emotion that conflicts and the emotion that accords with the divine law are alien to one another. The third again is far removed from the other Ps. 33:9   two, for it both tastes and sees that the Lord is good, and purges us of the first while crowning the second. Our natural inclinations entice but degrade; love that is governed by reason is arid but enduring; while the third brims over with delights. Doing pertains to the second, and here it is that charity resides. I refer here not to Col. 4:6   infused charity, seasoned with the salt of wisdom, whose rich increase fills the soul with the abundance of God's sweetness, but rather to that active love, which, if it does not as yet refresh the soul with a foretaste of bliss, yet fans to a fierce flame our love of love itself. 'Let us not love,' he says, 'in words or mere talk, but in deed 1 Jn. 3:18   and in truth.'

5   You see how cautiously he makes his way between our disordered inclinations and our feelings of affection, distinguishing equally from each the active love that saves. He will accept no feigned profession, nor on the other hand does he demand that one should have banqueted at wisdom's table. Let us love, he says, in deed and in truth; that is to say that our impetus to good should come from the dynamism of truth rather than from the flush of that full-flavoured love. 'He has set love in order in me.' Which kind of love, do you suppose? Each, but in inverse order. For love which is lived puts lower things first, love which is felt, higher. For example, in a mind whose affections are well-ordered the love of God is unquestionably placed before the love of men. Such a mind prefers among men the fine to the frail, heaven to earth, eternity to time and the soul to the body. However, in well-regulated actions, often, if not always, the opposite prevails. For it is our neighbour's care that weighs heaviest and most frequently upon us; we are at greater pains to help the weaker brothers; justice and urgency ensure that we are more intent on achieving peace on earth than attaining the glory of heaven; and anxiety over temporal interests allows us little freedom of mind for those that are eternal. Finally, we attend almost continuously to our physical aches and pains, neglecting the care of our souls; in fact it is just those weaker parts of the body that we surround with greatest dignity, putting as it were into practice the Lord's words: 'And the last shall be first and the first last.' Who doubts that a man at prayer is speaking with God? And yet how often, at love's bidding, are we torn away to attend to those who need our practical help and advice! How often does devout quiet dutifully give way to the turmoil of business! How often does conscience prompt us to lay down our book and sweat instead at manual labour! How often, and quite rightly, do we forgo celebrating mass to attend to administrative duties! It is a preposterous order, but necessity knows no law. Active love follows its own order as laid down by the Father of all. Being kindly and just and no respecter of persons, it begins with the last, for it does not weigh relative values but sees only the needs of men. _{1 Cor. 12:23} _{Mt. 20:16}

6   But affective love follows a different order, putting first things first. Being itself the wisdom which sets on all things their true value, it loves most that which is naturally best, the less good less and the worst least. The truth of charity creates the first order, the charity of truth demands the second. For love is true when those are served first who are in greater need; and inversely, truth is loving if in our hearts we keep its rational order.

If then you love the Lord your God with all your heart, with all your soul and with all your strength, and if, transported by fervour in a bound beyond that love of love with which active charity is content, you are set wholly alight by divine love, received in the fullness of the Spirit (and to which the former love serves only as a step), then assuredly you have a knowledge of God. It is true that you do not know him adequately, or as he is, which lies utterly beyond the scope of any creature, but you know him according to your own capacity. Next, you will know your own self as you are when you perceive that there is nothing whatever in you to love, save only in so far as you are God's, since you have poured all your capacity for loving into him. I repeat, you will know yourself as you are when the very experience of the love and affection that you bear yourself reveals to you that there is nothing in you deserving of your love, unless it be on his account without whom you yourself have no existence.

Mt. 22:39
Mk. 12:31 **7** Now as for the neighbour whom you are to love as yourself, if you want to know him as he is, it must perforce be in the way that you know yourself, for he is of the same stuff as you. And since you only love yourself because you love God, you love also as yourself all who love God as you do. An enemy, being of no worth inasmuch as he does not love God, you cannot love as yourself who do love God. You will love him, however, so that he may learn to love.

8 Give me the man who loves God above all else and with his whole being; who loves himself and his neighbour in the measure in which they both love God; his enemy as one who will perhaps one day love God; his natural parents tenderly as nature prompts, his spiritual parents – namely his teachers – unreservedly as gratitude requires.[1] And in this way he reaches out to the rest of God's creation with an ordered love, looking down on the earth and up to heaven, dealing
1 Cor. 7:31 with this world as though uninvolved, and distinguishing with an inward refinement of the soul between what is to be merely employed and what enjoyed, paying passing attention to the transient, and that only as need requires, while embracing all things eternal with a desire that never flags. Give me, I say, a man like that and I dare to proclaim him wise. Such a man takes all things as they really are, and is able with truth and confidence to boast: 'He has set love in order in me.' But where is such a man and when shall these things be? Weeping, I ask: how long shall we have the fragrance without the savour, we who glimpse our heavenly home from an unapproachable distance and are left sighing for it and hailing it from afar? O Truth, homeland of wanderers and the end of exile! I see you, and yet, detained still in the body, I may not enter in, nor am I worthy of admittance, grimed as I am with sin. O Wisdom, you who span
Wisd. 8:1 the universe with power, beginning and preservation of all that is,
Ibid. you who order our affections without coercion, distilling your blessing, so govern our acts that our present obligations are discharged, and dispose our affections to reflect the eternal values of your truth, so that each one of us may safely glory in you and say: 'He has set love in order in me.' For you, O Christ, are the power

and wisdom of God, the Bridegroom of the Church, our Lord and I Cor. 1:24
God blessed for ever more. Amen.

SERMON 57

1   'My beloved speaks to me.' Consider the gradual approach of   S. of S. 2:10
grace and mark the steps by which the divine Bridegroom conde-
scends. Notice the single-mindedness and the perception of the
Bride, her sharp-eyed watching for the coming of the Bridegroom,
the loving scrutiny she gives by turns to everything pertaining to
him. As for him, he is coming, hastening, drawing near, he is here,
he looks at her, he speaks with her. Not one of these moments
escapes the Bride's intent observation or catches her unaware. He
comes to her in angelic messengers, he hastens in the patriarchs, he
draws near in the prophets, he is present in the flesh, the miracles
convey his caring look, the apostles his address to her. To put it
another way: in his love and eagerness to pardon we see his coming,
his hastening in his ready help, and his approaching in his self-
abasement; he is present to those living here and now, looks forward   Phil. 2:8
to coming generations, and speaks to us in his persuasive teaching
about the kingdom of God. Thus it is that the Bridegroom comes,   Acts 19:8
bringing blessings with him and abundance of salvation, while all   Isa. 33:6
that pertains to him is brimming with delights, with joy unmeasured   Job 22:26
and the mysteries of salvation. She, meanwhile, who loves, is awake
and watching. And blessed is she whom the Lord finds watching.   Lk. 12:37
He will not pass her by, nor leave her in his wake, but will stay and
speak with her, and his words will be of love, the words of one
beloved. Thus, 'My beloved speaks to me'; and rightly beloved, he
who comes with words of love and not of censure.

2   For indeed she is not one of those whom the Lord accuses with
justice of knowing how to read the face of the sky but not detect the
signs of his coming. No, the Bride is so perceptive and far-sighted,   Mt. 16:4
so tirelessly watchful, that she has spotted him from afar, seen him
leaping in his haste, her sharp eyes have spied him bounding over   S. of S. 2:8
the proud to draw near to her, who is lowly, humbling himself to
do so. And when at length he was standing there, hiding behind the
wall, she sensed his presence none the less and was aware of him   S. of S. 2:9
gazing in through the windows and the lattices. And now, in   Ibid.

recompense for her pains, her conscientious care, she hears him speaking. Plainly, if he had just looked and not spoken, that silent look might have been seen as one of displeasure rather than of love. After all, he looked at Peter without saying a word, and perhaps it Lk. 22:61-2 was just that silent gaze that made Peter weep. The Bride, however, does not weep. When, after the look, she merits an address, she glories in her happiness, exclaiming: 'My beloved speaks to me!'

You will remark that the Lord's look, unchanging in itself, does not always produce the same effect but, according to the deserts of those he looks on, strikes fear into some while conveying comfort and confidence to others. He looks on the earth, we read, and it Ps. 103:32 trembles, whereas he looked on Mary and poured out his grace on her. 'He has looked', she says, 'on the lowliness of his servant, and Lk. 1:48 behold, from now onwards all generations will call me blessed.' These are not the words of one fearful or anxious, but of someone rejoicing. Just so did he look on the Bride here, and she did not tremble, nor did she weep like Peter, for her mind was not set, like Phil. 3:19 his, on earthly things. The Bridegroom put joy in her heart, bearing Ps. 4:7 witness in his words to the love with which he looked on her.

3 Listen to the words he speaks to her, words not of anger but of S. of S. 2:10 love: 'Arise, my love, my dove, my fair one and come away!' A conscience thus addressed is a happy one indeed. Which of us, do Lk. 19:44 you think, is so wide awake to the time of his visitation, so intent on watching each movement of the approaching Bridegroom, that at Lk. 12:36 his knock he will open on the instant? This text applies, it is true, to the Church, but not to the exclusion of the individual: each one of us, who together form the Church, is called to share in these blessings of his. Indeed we are all called without distinction to enjoy 1 Pet. 3:9 blessings by inheritance.

4 Why then are we still depriving ourselves of our paternal heritage, forgetful of every assurance that has been given us? What are we making of Paul's testimony that the Spirit himself bears witness with Rom. 8:16 our spirit that we are sons of God? In what way are we sons, if we have no share in the inheritance? Our very poverty speaks accusingly of negligence and nonchalance on our part. For if one of us were, in the words of the Sage, to turn at dawn with all his heart to the Lord Sir. 39:6 who made him and plead in the presence of the Most High, and at the same time make it his chief desire to prepare, as Isaiah says, a Isa. 40:3 way for the Lord and make straight a highway for his God; if he

were a man who could say with the Psalmist, 'My eyes are ever
towards the Lord' and 'I keep the Lord always before me', would he
not for that reason receive a blessing from the Lord and mercy from
the God of his salvation? He will indeed be frequently visited and he
will never be ignorant of the hour of his visitation, however secretly
and covertly his spiritual visitor may come, as might a reticent
lover. The clear-sighted and prudent soul will catch sight of him a
long way off and in due course discover all the signs that the Bride,
as we have said, has discerned with as much precision as skill in the
coming of the Bridegroom, for he himself says: 'Those who seek me
early shall find me.' She will recognize the longing that makes him
hasten; she will sense at once when he is close and when he is
actually at hand. Her happy eyes will catch his gaze as it falls on her
like a ray of sunlight through the windows and the fissures in her
wall. Then she will hear expressions of joy and love, hear herself
called 'My love, my dove, my fair one.'

5   Who is there wise enough not only to understand these things
but to distinguish between them and define each one, and then
render them comprehensible to others? If you are looking to me for
this, I personally would rather listen to an expert, versed and
practised in such matters. But since such persons modestly prefer to
shroud in silence what they have learned in silence, and judge it safer
to keep their secret to themselves, I, who am obliged by my office
to speak and have not the refuge of silence, will relate whatever I
have learned directly or from others, keeping to what most of us can
hope to experience and leaving higher things to those able to grasp
them.

If, therefore, I were to be urged by some other person or
prompted inwardly by the Spirit to safeguard righteousness and
maintain equity, I should certainly take any such salutary counsel as
a sign that the Bridegroom was at hand, and as an aid in preparing
myself to receive his visitation as I ought. I find corroboration in the
Psalmist's words: 'Righteousness will walk before him', and again
where he says to God: 'Righteousness and justice are the foundation
of your throne.' And I should be favoured with the selfsame hope if
the counsel were one of humility and patience, and most of all if it
concerned the pursuit of holiness and peace and the search for purity
of heart, since Scripture teaches us that holiness befits the Lord's
house, that his dwelling-place is in peace, and again that the pure in

Ps. 24:15
Ps. 15:8
Ps. 23:5

Prov. 8:17

Hos. 14:10

Ps. 84:14

Ps. 88:15

Ps. 92:5
Ps. 75:3

Mt. 5:8   heart shall see God. So any prompting that came to me in respect of these or other virtues would, as I have said, be a sign to me that the Lord of virtues was about to visit my soul.

Ps. 140:5 **6**   Again, if a good man were to criticize and rebuke me in kindness, I should have the same reaction, knowing that the rebuke of a righteous man is not to be despised, for it undoes sin, heals the heart and prepares a path for God to enter the soul. But one neglects at one's peril any word at all that reinforces piety, virtue and good

Ps. 49:23   conduct, since this is the path which shows us God's salvation. For if the word sounds sweetly to you, and if, having overcome any repugnance, you listen eagerly, you may believe that the Bridegroom is not merely coming but hastening, eager himself. For his desire creates yours, and, because you are quick to open to his word, he

1 Jn. 4:10   himself makes haste to enter, for he first loved us, not we him. Again, if you hear a fiery discourse and if it scorches your conscience with the memory of sin, call to mind the scriptural saying; 'Fire goes

Ps. 96:3   before him', and you will not doubt that he himself is near – and
Ps. 33:19   indeed the Lord is close to the broken-hearted.

    7   If what you have heard not only fills you with remorse, but if you also turn wholly to God, vowing and maintaining your oath to keep his upright judgements, you should know that he himself is now present, especially if you feel a consuming love for him. For we read of him both that fire goes before him and that he is himself a fire,

Dt. 4:24   for Moses says of him that he is a devouring fire. Yet the two are different, for the fear that precedes has heat, but not love; it burns, but does not melt down; it moves, without carrying away. The Lord sends it before him only to awaken and prepare you, giving you an insight into what you really are, which will heighten the contrast with what, by his grace, you shortly will be. The fire that is God, on the other hand, consumes without pain, its burn is balm, its

Ps. 119:4   desolation, joy. It is a red-hot coal that cauterizes vices so that it may apply in turn its salve to the soul. You must therefore understand that the Lord is present both in the transforming power of virtue and in the enkindling flame of love. For the right hand of the Lord

Ps. 117:16
Ps. 76:11   works virtue, but this change of the right hand of the Most High
2 Cor. 6:6   takes place only in fervour of spirit and love unfeigned, such as allows us to say: 'My heart grew hot within me, and as I mused a

Ps. 38:4   fire burned.'

    8   If, then, when the stain of sin and the rust of vice have been burned off in this fire, and your conscience lies unclouded and serene, you experience a sudden unusual expansion of the mind and an impression of light flooding the intellect and giving you a new understanding either of the Scriptures or of the mysteries (the one in my view bestowed for our delight, the other for strengthening our neighbours), this, without any doubt, is the eye of the Bridegroom looking on you, and then, as Isaiah says, your light shall rise like the sun and your darkest hour be as the noonday. Not through   Isa. 58:10 open doors, but through narrow fissures only – at least while the decrepit wall of our body stands – shall this ray of dazzling light pour itself into our souls. You will err if you hope for more, however far you advance in purity of heart, since the master of contemplation says that now we see only reflections in a mirror, but then face to face.   1 Cor. 13:12

9   This look of infinite kindness and compassion is followed by a voice quietly and gently presenting to the mind the Father's will. This voice is love itself, forever engaged in commending to us by invitation and persuasion all that pertains to God. And lastly, the Bride hears that she must arise and hasten, without a doubt to enrich other souls.

It is a part of true and pure contemplation that it now and then fills a mind already set ablaze with divine fire with such a passionate desire to win others to the love of God that it gladly and readily exchanges the quiet of contemplation for the stress of preaching. Later, the desired end achieved at least in part, the soul returns to contemplation, its fervour fuelled by the memory of so profitable an interruption, and, having savoured another taste of contemplation, hurries back as readily as before to reap a fresh harvest.

But the soul often hesitates uneasily amid this toing and froing, becoming deeply anxious lest the tug of its inclinations should lead it to favour one side more than the other and deviate from God's will to some slight degree. Perhaps Job was suffering from something similar when he said: 'When I lie down I say: when shall I arise? And then again I look for the evening.' In other words, when I am   Job 7:4 quiet I accuse myself of neglecting my work, and busy, of having disrupted quiet. A holy man may be painfully torn between fruitful work and the quiet of contemplation. He is always straining to do what is right, yet forever repenting of what he sees as failures, and moment by moment anxiously seeking out the will of God. The only remedy or refuge in this situation is prayer, in which we plead with God that he in his goodness may increasingly show us what, when and how much he wants us to do. We have here, as I understand it, three things, namely preaching, prayer and contemplation, which are presented to us in the three words that the Bridegroom addresses to the Bride. 'My love', he calls her, and rightly, since she wins riches for him by preaching, counselling and ministering with tireless zeal. Yet still she moans, dovelike, bewailing her faults in prayer and ever entreating the mercy of him who calls her deservedly his dove; and rightly too 'My fair one', since, resplendent with love, she enfolds herself in the beauty of contemplation whenever leisure and opportunity allow.

10 But let us also see if it is possible to dovetail into this threefold blessing of a single soul another three-in-one: three persons living in a single house who were close friends and intimates of the Saviour. I speak of Martha who served, Mary who sat and listened, and Lazarus as it were groaning beneath the stone and pleading for the grace of resurrection; and this in relation to the Bride's attention and skill in descrying the tracks of the Bridegroom. There is no hiding from her when or how swiftly he will come, so vigilant is she, no taking her by surprise, whether she be far off, or close, or present. And it is this vigilance that has won her his look to reassure her, his words of love to gladden her, and the sound of his voice to fill her with all joy.

Lk. 10:38–40
Jn. 11:1 ff.

Jn. 3:29

11 To this I have added, somewhat boldly, that every soul among us, if it watches like the Bride, will, like her, be greeted as beloved, consoled as a dove and embraced as fair. Everyone shall be deemed perfect in whose soul these three endowments are found in due order and degree, enabling him to lament his faults, rejoice in God and advance with all his power the good of others – pleasing, in short, to God, wary of self and useful to the community. But who can combine these three? Would that they were in every one of us, and if not all in each, then at any rate one quality per person; and in those who today are seen to have them, may they be long preserved! We have indeed a Martha, just like the Saviour's friend, in those who faithfully manage the daily running of affairs. We have a Lazarus too, as it might be a plaintive dove: namely, the novices who, having just died to their sins, lie groaning from these still-open wounds in fear of judgement – lie like the wounded in the grave,

1 Pet. 2:24

who believe, as these do, that they are no more remembered, until   Ps. 87:6
at Christ's bidding the crushing slab of fear is raised and they can
breathe again in the hope of pardon. We have also a contemplative
Mary in those who, with the passage of time and God's helping
grace, have attained to a better and happier state where, taking
forgiveness as already granted, they are less preoccupied with gazing
inward at the sorry spectacle of their sins, and can take endless
delight in meditating day and night on the law of God. Sometimes,   Ps. 1:2
even, while in ineffable joy they look with unveiled face upon the
glory of the Bridegroom, they are changed into his likeness from
one degree of glory to another, as by the Spirit of the Lord.   2 Cor. 3:18

Now why he bids the Bride arise and hasten we shall consider in
another sermon. May he be present then and deign to reveal to us the
reason of that mystery, he who is the Bridegroom of the Church, Jesus
Christ our Lord, who is above all, God blessed for ever more.

SERMON 74

1   'Return, my beloved, be like a roe or a young stag on the
mountains of Bethel.' Return, says the Bride. Clearly the one whom
she is calling back is not there. He has been there, however, and not
long since, for she appears to be calling him back in the very act of
his leaving. This untimeliness indicates how greatly she loves him
and how lovable he is. Who then are these devotees of charity, these
tireless practitioners of dalliance, the one pursued and the other
goaded on by restless longing? I remember promising to apply this
passage to the Word and the soul, but to do it at all worthily I
confess that I shall need the help of the Word himself. Perhaps my
apprehension – or better, any profit you may possibly derive – will
help excuse my boldness.

Return, says the Bride. Very good. He was leaving, he is called
back. Who will unlock for me the mystery of the mutability of
God? Who will give me a fitting explanation of the coming and
going of the Word? Surely there cannot be inconstancy in the
Bridegroom? Where can he come from and whither go again, he
who fills heaven and earth? How can he move in space, who is   S. of S. 2:17
spirit? And finally, what kind of movement can be attributed to him
at all, who is God unchanging and unchangeable?

Mt. 19:12 **2**   Let him understand who can. As for us, as we proceed with prudence and simplicity in the expounding of this holy and mystical text, let us follow the mode of Scripture, which expresses in human
1 Cor. 2:7 language the secret and hidden wisdom of God and infiltrates into our affections the God it bodies forth; and, by analogy with things material and familiar, feeds into our minds the unknown and invisible things of God, as though proffering a precious draught in a common cup. So let us too, following scriptural usage, say that the Word of God, God himself, the Bridegroom of the soul, both comes to the soul and departs again at his pleasure, provided we realize that what is described is an inward perception of the soul and not an actual movement of the Word. For example, when the soul feels an inflowing of grace, it recognizes his presence; when it does not, it complains of his absence and seeks his return, saying with the
Ps. 26:8 Psalmist: 'My face has sought you; your face, Lord, will I seek.' Why should the soul not seek him? Having lost so dearly loved a Bridegroom, she will be unable even to think of anything else, let alone desire it. All she can do is painstakingly seek him when he is absent and call him back when he leaves. That is how the Word is recalled: namely, by the desire of the soul, but of a soul which is his, on which he has once bestowed his grace. Does not desire have a voice? Indeed it does, and a powerful one, for the Lord heard the
Ps. 9:38 desire of the poor. So it is that, when the Word departs, the soul emits an unbroken cry, the cry of its unceasing desire, as it might be a long-drawn-out 'Return' until he comes.

3   Show me now a soul that the Word – the Bridegroom – habitually visits, a soul that familiarity has rendered bold, that has tasted just enough to acquire a hunger, that contempt for all else has left at leisure for the Bridegroom, and I will unhesitatingly assign to it the voice and name of Bride and would not judge our text inapplicable to it. For she who is introduced as speaking is certainly like that. The fact that she recalls the Bridegroom is proof that she has merited his presence, although not the fullness of his grace; otherwise she would not have called him back but merely called him. 'Return' implies a recalling. It may be that was why he withdrew himself, to be called back more eagerly and clasped with greater urgency. For once or twice on earth he made as if to go on, not because he wanted to, but to hear them say: 'Stay with us, for it is nearly
Lk. 24:28–9 evening and the day is far spent.' And on another occasion, when

the apostles were out on the Sea of Galilee and hard-pressed in their rowing, he came walking on the water as though he was going to pass them by. This was not in fact his intention; he wanted to test their faith and get them to call on him. As it was, they were terrified and cried out, thinking it was a ghost. This kind of pious pretence, contrived entirely for our good, which the Word incarnate sometimes used on earth, the Word as spirit constantly and caringly employs on the spiritual level with the soul that is devoted to him. He wants to be caught and held as he passes by, and recalled when he is leaving. For this Word is not irrevocable: he comes and goes as he sees fit, visiting in the morning and, of a sudden, testing. His going is designed to profit us, his return is always of his own free will. The one and the other are weighty with judgement, but he alone knows the underlying reasons. *Mk. 6:48* *Mk. 6:49* *Job 7:18*

4   Such changes in the soul connected with the coming and going of the Word are well established and confirmed by his own words: 'I am going away and shall return', and again, 'In a short time you will no longer see me, and then a short time later you will see me again.' Oh, that short time! How long a short time can be! O loving Lord, do you call it short, the time when we do not see you? Saving the respect I owe my Lord's words, it is a long time – unconscionably long. Yet each of these estimates is true: the time is as short as our merits and as long as our longing. Both senses are illustrated in the Prophet's words: 'If it tarries, wait for it: it will surely come, it will not delay.' How will it not delay if it tarries, unless it is more than we deserve, yet less than we desire? But the soul that loves the Lord is carried away by its longing, borne forward by the pull of its desire; choosing to forget its small deserving, it shuts its eyes to God's majesty and opens itself to bliss, sure of its salvation and dealing confidently with him. Without fear or shame it recalls the Word and trustingly asks for its former delights, calling him, with its accustomed liberty, not Lord but Beloved. 'Return, my beloved, be like a roe or a young stag upon the mountains of Bethel.' But more of this later. *Jn. 14:28* *Jn. 16:16* *Hab. 2:3*

5   First I must ask you to bear with me in a little foolishness. I want to tell you, as I agreed, something of my own experiences, pointless as that is. My purpose in speaking out is to be of use to you, and any benefit you gain will mitigate my foolishness; if none, it will stand exposed. I confess that the Word has come even to me – I speak as a *2 Cor. 11:1* *2 Cor. 12:1*

2 Cor. 11:17   fool – and frequently too. But often as he came, I never once sensed the moment of his entry. I knew when he was there, I recalled his having been, and sometimes I have had a premonition of his coming; but that is all. As to where he came from into my soul or whither he went on leaving it, or how he made his entrance and departure, I confess my ignorance to this day. Perhaps he did not enter in at all, not coming from without? On the other hand he did not come from within me, for he is good and I know that there is no good in me. I have mounted higher than myself, but the Word was higher still. I have explored with care the depths below me and found him to lie deeper yet. If I turned my gaze outwards, I discovered him beyond; if inwards, he lay further in. And then I knew that what I had read was true: that in him we live and move

Acts 17:28   and have our being; but blessed is the man in whom he is, who lives for him and who is moved by him.

Rom. 11:33 **6**   Seeing that his ways are so wholly inscrutable, you may well ask
Heb. 4:12 how I knew that he was present. He is alive and active, and, as soon as he entered in, he roused my drowsy soul. He quickened and
S. of S. 4:9
Ez. 36:26 softened and ravished my heart, which lay inert and hard as stone.
Jer. 1:10 He began to root up and tear down, to build and to plant, to water the dry places and light up the dark corners, to unlock what was tight shut and fan dead embers to a blaze, to make the crooked
Isa. 40:4 straight and level the rough ground, so that my soul might praise
Ps. 102:1 the Lord and all that is within me bless his holy name. So on the occasions when the Word – the Bridegroom – has visited me, he has never made his entry apparent to my hearing, sight or touch. None of his movements has been perceptible to me, nor was it through any of my senses that he penetrated into my inmost being. Only the stirrings of my heart, as I said before, betrayed his presence. I discovered his saving power as vices took to flight and my natural inclinations were subdued; the critical exposure of my secret faults enabled me to marvel at the depth of his wisdom; in the change and renewal of the person that I was, I glimpsed a facet of his beauty; the amendment of my life, however slight, served as a touchstone for his kindness and compassion; and when I surveyed the whole I bowed
Ps. 150:2 down in awe before his immeasurable greatness.

  7   It is true that, as soon as the Word departed, all this activity began to die down, as though the flame had been pulled away from under a bubbling pot. The subsequent feeling of chill, inertia and depression is to me the sign of his departure, and my soul is perforce cast down until he comes again and signals his return by rekindling as before the heart within my breast. With such experience of the Word, is it surprising if even I adopt the words of the Bride to call him back when he has left, since my yearning, though not indeed so strong, is similar to hers. For as long as I live, that word 'Return' for calling back the Word will be close to my lips. And as often as he slips away I shall seek to draw him back, nor shall I cease to clamour in his wake, entreating him with all the longing of my heart to give me again the joy of his salvation and restore himself to me. I assure you, my sons, that everything is stale when the only thing that pleases is not there. And this I pray, that he may not come empty-handed but full of grace and truth, as is his way and as he did before; in which case he might show himself to me as a roe or a young stag, since truth has the keen sight of the roe, and grace is light of heart and foot like the stag. *Ps. 41:6, 12; 42:5*

Ps. 50:14

Jn. 1:14

8 My need is of both: truth from which I cannot hide and grace from which I do not want to. If either were lacking, the visitation would be less than perfect, for the stringency of truth alone might be found harsh, while grace without truth could be so elating as to appear lax. Truth is bitter without a flavouring of grace, just as religious sentiment without the curb of truth is volatile, intemperate and often extravagant. How many have failed to profit from grace received because they did not accept an equal measure of truth? In consequence they have luxuriated in the enjoyment of grace while paying scant respect to truth, and instead of regarding the steadfast mettle of the roe have given themselves over wholly to the light-footed gaiety of the stag. And because their revelling was selfish, grace was withdrawn from them. Such as these might have been told – too late – 'Go then and learn what this means: Serve the Lord with fear and rejoice in him with trembling.' The Psalmist once said in his prosperity: 'I shall never be moved', but when he suddenly sensed that the Word had turned his face from him, he was not merely moved but dismayed, and learned in sorrow that he needed the counterweight of truth to balance the gift of devotion. The plenitude of grace resides neither in grace alone nor in truth alone. What is the use of knowing what you ought to do if you are not also given the will to do it? And what if you want to, but are yet unable? How many have I known who were worse off once they knew the truth, since they no longer had the excuse of ignorance, *Mt. 9:13*

Ps. 2:11

Ps. 29:7–8

and were left knowing, and still not doing, what the Word was urging them to do.

9 This being the way things are, neither gift suffices without the other; singly, indeed, they bring no benefit at all. How so? Whoever knows what is right and fails to do it commits sin. And again: the servant who knows his master's will and does not carry it out will be well flogged. So much for truth; what about grace? It is written: 'After the sop, Satan entered into him.' This is Judas who, after accepting the gift of grace, did not walk in truth with the master of truth — or better, with Truth himself — and thus made room in himself for the devil who had nothing to do with truth but was a liar from the beginning, which is why he was told: 'You lost wisdom through your beauty.' Personally, I want no beauty that might deprive me of wisdom.

10 You would like to know what beauty it is that is so hurtful and destructive? Yours. Perhaps you still don't understand? I will spell it out. Your own individual beauty. It is not the gift that is to blame, but the use you make of it. For if you notice, it was not beauty that deprived Lucifer of wisdom, but 'his' beauty and unless I am mistaken the beauty of an angel is the same as that of a soul: namely, wisdom. For without wisdom what is either but raw, unordered matter? Yet with it, Lucifer was not merely ordered, but beautiful. He lost his beauty, however, by making selfish use of it. It is possession that is the root cause. Because he was wise in his own eyes, because he did not give God the glory or render grace for grace, because he did not follow after wisdom in sincerity of heart but abused it for his own ends, he lost it. To put it more exactly: that constituted the losing, for this sort of possession is itself loss. We read that if Abraham had been justified by works, he would have had something to boast about, but not before God. Then I am certainly not safe. I have lost whatever I have that is not lodged in God. For what is so utterly lost as that which is cut off from God? What is death but to be deprived of life? There is no loss but severance from God. Woe to those who think themselves wise and believe themselves enlightened! Of them it is written: 'I will destroy the wisdom of the wise, and the cleverness of the clever I will thwart.' They will lose wisdom because their own wisdom lost them first. What is there left for them to lose who have lost themselves? And are they not truly lost whom God ignores?

Margin references: Jas. 4:17; Lk. 12:47; Jn. 13:27; 2 Jn. 1:4; Eph. 4:27; Jn. 8:44; Ez. 28:17; Mt. 15:16; Prov. 26:5; Jn. 9:24; Rom. 4:2; Isa. 5:21; 1 Cor. 1:19

For the foolish virgins – who are only foolish, as far as I know, in claiming to be wise – have been made fools; and these, I repeat, are doomed to hear God say: 'I know you not.' And those too who have misused for their own prestige the grace of working miracles will hear the Lord declare: 'I never knew you.' It follows with perfect clarity that not only is grace of no benefit where sincerity is lacking, it is in fact prejudicial, and both are in the Bridegroom's hand; for, as John the Baptist said, grace and truth came through Jesus Christ. If, therefore, the Lord Jesus (who is God's Word, the Bridegroom of the soul) were to knock at my door bringing either grace or truth alone, he would be coming not as Bridegroom but as judge, and God forbid that that should happen! May he not enter into judgement with his servant! May he enter in peace, bringing joy and gladness; yet let him be grave too, and with the sterner countenance of truth restrain my bumptiousness and purify my joy. May he enter light-foot like a stag, leaping over my offences to put them out of sight, but also soft-foot like the roe, looking with eyes of pity and forgiveness. Let him come in festive splendour, bounding down the mountains of Bethel, yet gentle too and kind, as one proceeding from the Father, who will not disdain to be and to be called the Bridegroom of the soul who seeks him: he who is above all, God blessed for ever more. Amen.

Mt. 25:2
Rom. 1:22
Mt. 25:12
Mt. 7:23
Jn. 1:17
Rev. 3:20
Ps. 142:2
Ps. 85:5
Jn. 15:26

From *On Consideration*

The treatise On Consideration *was written during the last four years of St Bernard's life. Although its burden was directed to one man, it achieved the widest circulation of any of the abbot's works and passed into print with its popularity undimmed, enjoying – rare distinction – the esteem both of Calvin and the Curia. Bernard was responding to a request from Eugenius III, who had soared from Clairvaux to the Apostolic See via the abbacy of St Anastasius in Rome, and who felt in need of counsel. Under the cover of a letter of advice, his former superior allowed his reflection to range over many topics, from the evils besetting the Curia to the nature of the Trinity. The thread on which they are strung is the concept of consideration: the conscientious search for truth in one's own circumstances and beyond.*

The work is divided into five books:

Book I. Bernard warns against overactivity and complacence. He sees particular dangers for Eugenius in the abusive legislation, centred on Rome, to which all causes led.

Book II. Bernard proposes to Eugenius four subjects worthy of consideration: himself (man and office), and things beneath, around and above him. The Pope is first encouraged to examine himself against Bernard's high ideal of the universal pastor.

Book III. Beneath him are the faithful. His responsibility extends to all mankind, and his duty is to spread the Gospel and to govern the Church as a faithful and humble steward.

Book IV. Around him are the clergy, the people of Rome and the Curia. Eugenius is instructed in how to govern his household (seen as badly in need of reform) and in how to delegate.

Book V. He is invited to look above him and to consider the nature of faith, the angels, the being of God (Trinity in unity), the person of Christ, the dual aspect of eternal life, and finally the 'length, breadth, height and depth of God'.

The dominant theme of the De consideratione *is the paradox at the heart of spiritual government, the tension between the absolute standards of the Gospel and the compromises enjoined on the office-bearer by responsibility. Bernard, as already in the* Apologia *(rhetorical flourishes apart), shows himself an exponent of the median way. His zeal for reform never outran the prudence of the pragmatist in him, and the enduring popularity of this, his last work, is a tribute to his gift for distilling general truths from particular situations so that the relevance of his work is constantly renewed in different times and circumstances.*

*　　*　　*

THE DANGERS OF BEING TOO BUSY

I, II, 2　　Do not be overconfident of retaining your present dispositions. There is nothing so firmly established in the soul that neglect and time will not weaken. Callus forms on an old and neglected wound, and this deadening of the tissues prevents their proper healing. In any case, severe, relentless pain cannot be borne indefinitely. If there is no other way of getting rid of it, it has to yield to itself: it is relieved either by a cure or the stupor of inurement. What will habit not pervert? What is not dulled by repetition or worn away by constant use? For how many has the bitter taste that once.sent a shudder through them been regrettably transmuted by habituation into something sweet? Listen to Job deploring this: 'The things my soul refused to touch are now, in my distress, become my good.' Job 6:7 Something seems to you unbearable; in time, if you persist, you will decide that it is not so very burdensome; a little later you will find it trifling, and later still not notice it at all; again a little later you will even take pleasure in it. So it is that the heart becomes gradually hardened and then proceeds to hate what is good. That is the way of it. There must, as I said, be a swift end to severe, continuous pain, either by healing or through insensibility.

3　　It is precisely this that I have always feared for you and still do: namely, that having put off remedial action and desperate with pain, you will be overwhelmed by your trial and sink for good. I am afraid, I say, lest, beset by such a host of occupations and despairing of seeing an end to them, you set your face and thus gradually free yourself from any sensation of a pain that you ought properly to be

feeling. Far wiser to disengage yourself in time from these trammels than to allow them to take you in tow and, ineluctably, lead you step
Jn. 21:18 by step where you do not want to go. Where's that, you ask? To hardness of heart. And don't go on to ask what that is. If it hasn't made you shudder, it is yours already. The only hard heart is the one that does not shudder at itself for its own lack of feeling. Why ask me, anyway? Ask Pharaoh. No one hard of heart ever attained to salvation save perhaps the man whom God took pity on, removing his heart of
Ez. 36:26 stone, as the Prophet tells us, to give him a heart of flesh. What then is a hard heart? It is a heart that is not riven by remorse, softened by kindness or moved by entreaties. It does not give way to threats, and scourging further hardens it. It is ungrateful for kindnesses received, untrustworthy in counsel, harsh in judgement, shameless in causing scandal, fearless in the face of danger, inhuman as regards mankind, and heedless in respect of heaven. Oblivious of the past, it neglects the present and makes no provision for the future. Of the past it retains nothing, save only the memory of wrongs it has suffered; the present is wholly wasted; it has no vision of nor thought for the future, unless perhaps to settle scores. To sum up all the evils of this dreadful bane, it
Lk. 18:4 is a heart which neither fears God nor reverences man.

See where these accursed occupations are bound to drag you if you carry on as you have begun, that is to say, giving yourself wholly to them and saving nothing of yourself for you. You are wasting time and, if I may play Jethro to your Moses, you, like him, are wearing
Ex. 18:18 yourself out in foolish labour over things which are nothing but an
Ecc. 1:14, 17 affliction of spirit, the dissipation of your mental energies and an
Job 8:14 expense of grace. And what does it yield you in the end but cobwebs?

* * *

Bernard imagines the Pope defending himself with the words of Paul: 'I
1 Cor. 9:19 *made myself the slave of all, to win as many as I could.'*

* * *

SOME FAIRLY TIMOROUS ADVICE

I, v, 6 Here is my answer to that and my advice. If you give your life and knowledge wholly over to action and reserve nothing for
1 Cor. 11:22 consideration, shall I commend you? Not for that, I won't. Nor do I

believe anyone would who had heard Solomon's words: 'A man with few commitments will grow wise.' Action itself certainly gains nothing from a lack of prior consideration. Again, if you want to live wholly for others, like Paul who became all things to all men, I salute your humanity, but only on condition it be all-inclusive, and how can it be that if it excludes yourself? You too are a man. If your humanity, therefore, is to be entire and whole, you too must be clasped in your all-embracing arms. Else what does it profit you, as the Lord said, if you win every human life and lose your own? In view of the fact that all have you, make sure you are one of the haves. Why should you alone be cheated of your reward? How long will you be a breath of wind that passes and does not return? How long before you receive yourself in turn among the rest? You are under obligation both to the wise and to the foolish; are you the only one to whom you deny yourself? Fool and sage, slave and free man, rich and poor, male and female, old and young, clerk and lay, just and wicked: all have a like share in you, all drink at the public fountain of your heart, and will you stand apart and thirst? If the man who squanders his portion is accursed, what of the one who renders himself wholly destitute? Certainly let your streams of water flow in the public squares; let men and beasts of burden and cattle slake their thirst; by all means water even the camels of Abraham's servant; but make sure you drink with the rest of the water from your well. The stranger, says Scripture, is not to drink from it. Well, are you a stranger? To whom are you not a stranger if you are a stranger to yourself? In a word, if someone treats himself badly, whom will he treat well? So remember, I don't say always or even often, but just sometimes remember to restore yourself to yourself. Along with the crowds, or at least in their wake, see that you too make use of yourself. What could be more liberal than that? I say this by way of concession, not as my strict opinion. I think indeed that I am more liberal than the Apostle in this matter. More, then, than you should be, you reply. I don't deny it. But what matter if his standard is the right one? You, I am quite confident, will not be content with my timid and tentative instruction, but will go well beyond it. And it is surely more fitting that you should soar beyond than I presume too far. I feel, too, that it is safer for me, in view of the majesty of your office, to risk being too timid rather than overbold. And perhaps our words to the wise should always fulfil

Sir. 38:25

1 Cor. 9:22

Mt. 16:26

Ps. 77:39

Rom. 1:14

Prov. 5:16

Gen. 24:14
Prov. 5:17

1 Cor. 7:6

Prov. 9:9

the scriptural injunction: Give a wise man opportunity and he will become still wiser.

EXALTED FOR WHAT PURPOSE?

II, VI, 9 There is no disguising the fact that you have been set above other men; we must now carefully consider why. Not, I believe, to lord it over them; for the prophet, when similarly exalted, was told to uproot and break down, to demolish and scatter, to build and to plant. Which of these has a ring of pride to it? It is the yokel's sweat that is the usual metaphor for spiritual labour, and we, therefore, if we are to think much of ourselves, should feel that a burden of service has been laid on us, not the privilege of lordship bestowed. You who teach others, teach yourself by repeating: 'I am not greater than the Prophet, and, if perchance I have as much power, there is no comparison between our deserts.' Consider yourself to be like one of the prophets. Is that not enough for you? Too much, indeed. But by God's grace you are what you are. Be then what a prophet is — are you more than a prophet? If you are wise, you will content yourself with the measure that God has meted out to you, for anything more than this comes from evil. Learn from the prophets' example to govern not so much for the sake of giving orders as to tackle the moment's need. You will find that it is a hoe, not a sceptre, that you want for doing a prophet's work, and that the latter has not been raised aloft to play the king but to grub up weeds. Don't you suppose that you too may find something to work at in your Lord's field? Plenty indeed and to spare. The prophets were plainly unable to clear the ground completely: they left something for their sons, the apostles, to do, and these, your fathers, left a job for you. Nor will you manage to do it all. You will certainly leave something for your successor, and he for his, and so on to the end of time. A last point: labourers, around the eleventh hour, were taxed with idleness and sent into the vineyard. Your predecessors, the apostles, were told that the harvest was indeed great but the labourers were few. Claim for yourself the inheritance of your fathers, for if you are a son, you are an heir as well. To prove yourself an heir, wake up to your responsibility and don't lie back in indolence, lest it be said to you too: 'Why have you been standing here idle all day long?'

Jer. 1:10

Mt. 11:9
2 Cor. 10:13
Mt. 5:37

Mt. 20:6-7

Mt. 9:37
Gal. 4:7

Mt. 20:6

10   Much less should you be found pillowed in pleasures or puffed
up with pomp. Nothing like this falls to your lot under the testator's
will. On the contrary, if you content yourself with its provisions,
you will inherit care and toil rather than glory and riches. Does   Ps. 111:3
Peter's chair appeal? It is a watch-tower from whose height you will
strain your eyes, while the title of bishop speaks to you not of
lordship but of ministry. Why should you not be set on a pinnacle
that permits an overall view, since you have been made the universal
watchman? I can assure you that this prospect stimulates to battle-   Ez. 33:2
readiness and not to leisure, and, when leisure is ruled out, what
opportunity is there for glorying? Yours is certainly no place for
leisure, ridden as you are by responsibility for all the churches. For   2 Cor. 11:28
what else did the holy Apostle transmit to you? 'What I have,' he
says, 'I give you.' And what is that? I know one thing: it isn't gold   Acts 3:6
or silver, since he himself says, 'Silver and gold have I none.' If you   Acts 3:6
should happen to have any, do not use it for your own gratification,
but according to the needs of the moment. In that way you will be
using it as though you were not handling it. As regards our spiritual   1 Cor. 7:31
welfare, gold and silver are neither good nor bad: to use them is
good, to abuse them, bad, to worry about them, worse, to pursue
them, shameful. It may be that you can lay claim to them on some
other ground, but not on that of apostolic right, for the Apostle
could not give you what he had not got. What he had, he gave:
responsibility, as I said, for the churches. Not lordship? Listen to his
own words: 'Not lording it among the clergy, but being examples
to the flock.' And in case you should suppose the words sprang only   1 Pet. 5:3
from humility and were not based on truth, here is the Lord's own
warning in the Gospel: 'The kings of the Gentiles lord it over them,
and those in authority over them are called Benefactor.' And he
adds: 'Not so with you.' It is clear: lordship is forbidden to the   Lk. 22:25–6
apostles.

THE MANY MODES OF CONTEMPLATING GOD

V, XI, 25   You may perhaps find it somewhat irritating if I still
persist in asking: what is God? The question has after all been asked
so often, and you may also doubt whether the answer is to be
found. I tell you, Father Eugenius, God alone can never be sought in

Isa. 45:19 vain, not even when he cannot be found. You may know this from
personal experience. If not, believe one who does – not me, but the
holy man who said: 'You are good, O Lord, to those who hope in
Lam. 3:25 you, to the soul that seeks you.' So, what is God? With respect to
creation, its end; to election, salvation; to himself, he alone knows.
What is God? All-powerful will, all-benign power, eternal light,
immutable reason, blessedness supreme. Creator of beings to partake
of him, he quickens men to perceive him, disposes them to desire
him, enlarges them to receive him, justifies them that they may
deserve him, fires them with zeal, fertilizes them that they may bear
fruit, directs them in the way of justice, moulds them to kindness,
contempers them to wisdom, strengthens them to virtue, visits them
with consolation, enlightens them with understanding, preserves
them unto immortality, fills them with felicity and keeps them safe
in his encircling arm.

THAT GOD IS NO LESS THE PUNISHMENT OF THE PROUD THAN THE GLORY OF THE HUMBLE

v, XII, 25 What is God? The torment of the wicked no less than the
glory of the humble. He is the changeless and inflexible principle of
Wisd. 8:1 rational justice, which spans the universe and must of necessity bring
to naught any perversity colliding with it. How could anything
gross and misshapen dash itself against this principle and not be
shattered? Alas for anything with which this rectitude might come
into collision: it cannot yield, for it is fortitude as well. What can be
more hateful and frustrating for hostile wills than to be ever striving,
ever in conflict, yet in vain? Woe to all wills in confrontation,
which harvest only the bitter fruit of their own animosity; for what
doom can be so bitter as to be ever wanting what will never be, and
ever rejecting what must come to pass? What is so accursed as a will
enslaved to the point where it must still choose or refuse, but can do
neither without being wrong or wretched? It fails eternally to gain
what it wants, and what it does not want it must none the less
eternally endure. How wholly in keeping, that a will which never
desires what it should, should never attain what it desires! Who
ensures that this is so? The righteous Lord our God, who with the

crooked shows himself perverse. There can be no meeting between right and wrong, straight and crooked.[1] They confront one another, though not to their mutual hurt: only one suffers injury, and in no way can that be God. It is hard for you, we read, to kick against the goad – hard, that is, for the kicker, not the goad. In the same way God is the punishment of the depraved, for he is light, and what is so loathed by lewd and dissolute minds? Indeed, all doers of evil hate the light. But will they not be able to turn aside, I ask? Absolutely not. The light shines everywhere, even if not for all. It shines in the darkness and the darkness does not comprehend it. The light sees the darkness, for with it seeing and shining are the same, but it is not seen in return by the darkness, for the darkness does not comprehend it. Being seen, it is confounded, and failing to see, receives no consolation. Those in darkness are not only seen by the light, they are also seen in the light. By whom? To their greater confusion, by all who are blessed with sight. Yet out of that multitude of spectators no look is so unaccommodating to a darkened conscience as its own. There is no eye in heaven or earth which it would sooner escape or is less able to. The darkness is not hidden from itself. It sees itself, although it sees nothing else. The works of darkness follow the dark and there is nowhere it can hide from them, not even in darkness. Here is the worm that does not die, the memory of things past. Once it has worked its way in, or better, been begotten there by sin, it clings tenaciously and there is no dislodging it again. It never ceases gnawing away at the conscience, and sustained by this inexhaustible source of food it lives for ever. I have a terror of this biting worm, this death undying. I have a terror of falling into the hands of the living death, the dying life.

26   This is the second death, which never gives the *coup de grâce* but is forever killing. Who will grant them to die once and for all, that they may not be eternally a-dying? Those who say to the mountains, 'Fall on us', and to the hills, 'Cover us', what do they want but to finish with death or pass beyond it, by courtesy of death itself? To sum up in the words of Scripture: they will call on death and it will not come. Let us be quite clear about this. It is agreed that the soul is immortal and can never exist without its memory, or else it would no longer be the soul.[2] While the soul persists, then, so does the memory. But what kind of memory? In this case one soiled with vice, made hideous with crimes, swollen with vanity, matted and

Marginal references:
2 Sam. 22:27
Ps. 17:27
Gal. 5:17

Acts 9:5

Jn. 3:20

Jn. 1:5

cf. Rom. 13:12
Rev. 14:13
Isa. 66:24; Mk. 9:43, 45, 47
Wisd. 11:13

Heb. 10:31
Rev. 20:14

Lk. 23:30

Job 3:21

Nine Letters

We still have nearly 550 letters from the stream that St Bernard sent out to a wide array of recipients on an equally wide range of subjects. Some consist of a few lines, others have the length and weight of a short treatise. The majority were prompted by a perceived need to remonstrate, correct, conciliate or redress a wrong, or written in response to a request. To that extent they are business letters and, as such, addressed to those able to influence events. They are also much more, for Bernard was so powerful a personality and so natural a writer that he poured into his correspondence whatever aspect of himself was foremost at the time. He could be, as John of Ford says of him, 'terrible as an army with banners'; he could show himself irritable, defensive, sublime, affectionate, humorous and surprisingly gentle. He tried to leave no letter unanswered, however humble the writer,[1] and was never too busy to recommend to the mercy of the drover any toad caught under the harrow of Church or State.

The letters that contribute most to the portrait of the man while requiring least historical context are those that have as their chief purpose the fostering of personal relationships. The following fall in the main within this category. Where dates are known, the order is chronological, but the placing of Letters 506, 536 and 540 is guesswork. The numbering is that used in SBO 7 and 8.

LETTER 536

The recipient is unknown, though William of St Thierry has been suggested. The bishop was probably William of Champeaux, Bishop of Châlons, who kept open house for the monks of Clairvaux. A conversation between friends is shown to be the germ of a biblical commentary that was to attain its fullest expression in St Bernard's Third Sermon on the

Circumcision (see J. Leclercq, 'Études sur saint Bernard et le texte de ses écrits', AC, IX (1953), pp. 55–62).

* * *

To Brother G., greetings from Brother Bernard, styled Abbot of Clairvaux.

Regarding the interpretation I defended recently while talking about the text of the Gospel with the lord bishop and yourself: I don't want you to write it up until you have first talked it over with me once again. And if by chance you have already made a fair copy, don't give it to anyone to read until I have seen it. Pondering later on what we said at the time, I realized that, intent as we were on discovering the moral sense, we had in certain places strayed in error from the facts of the story, and I now consider myself to have pointed this out to you as well. The first mistake is that there are not, as we thought, fifty days between the Nativity of the Lord and the Purification of the Blessed Virgin, but only forty. Then we said that Mary and Joseph were on their way to Jerusalem when the child was born, and this was incorrect. And lastly, as for the eight days leading up to the Circumcision for which we developed the moral sense: counting forward from the day on which the child was, as it were, born, that is to say the moment when the intention became firmly fixed in the heart,[2] the circumcision took place not on the eighth but on the ninth day after. The other points, as far as I can judge, are correct and these can easily be put right.

As for the rest, you should know that we were very upset at your leaving us without the escort promised to you, though no one but yourselves could properly be held responsible for this. Farewell.

LETTERS 73 AND 74

Foigny was founded from Clairvaux in 1121, and Rainald was its first abbot. The two letters given here were clearly written within a relatively short time of his leaving the security of the mother house.

* * *

[To Rainald, Abbot of Foigny, c. 1122–1123]

You wring your hands, Rainald, my dearest son, over your many troubles, and move me with your affectionate complaints to do the same. It is impossible for me not to grieve when you are sad, or hear about your trials and worries without becoming troubled and worried myself. In fact, since I both foresaw and, if you remember, warned you of the very ills you now complain of having met with, I think you might have borne with a lighter heart what you knew of in advance, thus sparing me the bother of it all. I suffer quite enough as it is from your absence, missing the sight of you and the very great comfort of your company, so much so that I almost regret having sent you away. True, it was charity that made me send you; yet, however great the need may have been, because I cannot see you I bewail you as lost as well as gone. So when on top of this you use your faint-heartedness as a stick to beat me with, when you ought to be a staff for me to lean on, you pile grief on grief and add another torment to the first. And if it is a sign of affection for me to hide none of your problems from me, it is hard of you all the same to make a display of them to one so fond as I. What need is there to inflict more worry on someone anxious enough already, or give a further wrench to my fatherly heartstrings, sore as they are from your absence? I have shared my burdens with you as a son, a much needed and faithful helper. Give a thought to how you should carry your father's load. If your shouldering of it, instead of relieving me, weighs me down more, you burden yourself without unburdening me.

This burden of ours is souls – the souls of the weak; for those who are in sound health do not need to be carried and are therefore not a burden. You should know it is those of your flock whom you find depressed, faint-hearted or grumbling that are the very ones of whom you are father and abbot. It is in dispensing comfort, counsel and reproof that you do your job and shoulder your burden, and, in the carrying, you heal those whom you carry. If there is someone so hale that he helps you more than you help him, you should recognize that you are not his father but his fellow, his comrade, not his abbot. So why do you complain that the company of those around you is more of a burden than a solace to you, when it is you and you alone who are given to be a comfort to all of them, because

2 Cor. 2:3

you are healthier and stronger than they – the one who, by God's grace, is capable of being a solace to all while needing the comfort of none? A final point: you will be as rich as the load you carry; and the more help you receive, the smaller will be your reward. So make your choice, whether you want those who help you by being a burden, or those who burden you by being a help. The first win merit for you, the latter do you out of it; for never doubt that those 2 Cor. 1:7 who share in the labour will have a part in the reward. Now that you know you have been sent to help and not to be helped, recognize yourself as representing the one who came, not to be Mt. 20:28 served, but to serve.

There was much that I wanted to write by way of consolation, but it became unnecessary, for what is the use of filling a dead page with a glut of words when the living voice is there to speak? Once you have seen the prior, I am sure you will feel I have written enough and your spirit will revive in his presence. You will no longer need written consolation when you have been buoyed up by his spoken words of comfort. And do not doubt that in and through him I have sent my spirit, which you begged me in your letter to send you if I could, for, as you know, he and I are of one mind and will.

*   *   *

[To the same]

I hoped, dearest friend, that, if you kept your troubles from my knowledge, I should obtain some easing of my anxiety for you. Indeed I remember having written to you among other things in a previous letter that, if it was a sign of your affection for me to keep none of your problems from me, it was none the less hard of you to make a display of them to one so fond as I. But I must admit that the very thing I thought would lighten my cares has left me feeling more weighed down than ever. Before, I only felt, or grieved over, or feared what you actually told me about. Now there is no imaginable evil that I do not fear for you. In fact, in the words of your favourite Ovid:

When have I not feared worse dangers than befell me?[3]

Being sure of nothing, there is nothing I do not suspect, and I often have to contain real sorrow for purely imaginary ills. He who has once given his affection is no longer his own master. He fears he knows not what, worries more intensely and about more matters than he wants to, sympathizes reluctantly and pities in spite of himself. And since you see, my son, that neither my careful precautions nor your kind discretion have been of any avail to me, I beg you now to hide nothing of what is going on around you, lest, in thinking to spare me, you make me more uneasy. Be sure to return, when you conveniently can, those little works of mine you borrowed.

LETTER 90.

The first of four surviving letters written between 1124 and 1139 to Oger, a Canon Regular of Mont-Saint-Éloi near Arras, who was an intimate of St Bernard's, a scholar who shared his friend's reforming zeal and to whom Bernard submitted the first draft of his Apologia.

* * *

[To Oger, Canon of Mont-Saint-Éloi]

I have written a short letter in reply to yours, glad of a pretext for matching your brevity. And truly, what does true and, as you truthfully say, eternal friendship gain from the expenditure of empty, fleeting words? However you multiply and vary the words and phrases and expressions with which you demonstrate and commend your love to me, I have the firm impression that you say less than you feel, and you would not be wrong if you thought the same of me. When your letter came into my hands, it found the sender already in my heart. As I write mine, I am certain of your presence and sure that, when you read it, I shall be close to you. We labour over the letters we so frequently exchange, we tire out messengers with carrying them to and fro – yet is the spirit ever wearied by loving? Let us give up what cannot be done without effort, and concentrate on what assiduous practice makes ever easier. Let us rest our brains from composition, our lips from speaking, our hands from writing and our messengers from scurrying back and forth, but let our minds never rest from meditating day and night on the

Ps. 1:2   law of the Lord, which is the law of love. For the more we rest from that activity, the less reposed we are, and the busier in that respect, the calmer in all others. Let us love and be loved, in the first profiting ourselves, in the second benefiting those we love. For we certainly rest in those whom we love, and we prepare in ourselves a resting-place for those who love us. Moreover, to love someone in God is to have charity, and to make oneself lovable for God's sake is to serve charity.

But what am I doing? I who promised to be brief will be taken for an example of verbosity. If you want to know about Brother Guerric,[4] or rather, because you want to, he does not run aimlessly,

1 Cor. 9:26 or box as one beating the air; but knowing as he does that the result
Rom. 9:16 depends not on the boxer, nor on the runner, but on God's mercy, he begs you to ask on his behalf that the Lord who enables him now to box and run may grant him too to conquer and to reach the goal.

Convey my heartfelt greetings to your abbot, dear to me not only on your account but for the good that I have heard of him. I shall meet him with great pleasure at the time and place you have arranged. I must tell you that for a short while now the hand of the

1 Sam. 5:6 Lord has been heavy on me; I was pushed hard and was close to
Ps. 117: 13 falling. In fact the axe was laid to the root of the barren tree of my
Mt. 3:10 body and I was already in fear of being felled, but thanks to your prayers and those of my other friends the kind Lord has spared me this time, but only in the hope of promised fruit to come.

LETTER 540

The recipient has not been identified, but was clearly held in affection by Bernard despite the disapproval of his monks and his own misgivings.

★　　★　　★

To his beloved brother and friend G., a monk, in the hope that he may be changed for the better.

I am sending you back your dogs and whatever I have belonging to you, on account of our brothers who take it very ill that I ever accepted anything from you and are acutely anxious that I should not keep them. They loathe the thought of any intimate connection with you on account of your deplorable way of life, which they saw for themselves and put to the test.

And, to tell the truth, it weighs very much on me that I accepted them, but because of your scandal I was unable to refuse. I beg you, therefore, dearest friend, to have pity on your soul and not to waste your days in this make-believe, nor, while currying favour now, store up wrath for yourself on the day of wrath ahead. I implore you, too, and warn you not to deceive souls for whom Christ died. And any such who come to you from the world and whom you take into your care you are most certainly deceiving, since you have never taken good care of your own soul.

I have perhaps used harsher language than you wished to hear, but you should know that it proceeds from charity, and, if charity does not abide in you, my words will not be without profit to you. Farewell.

LETTER 506

A kid-glove relationship? The use of the more formal second person plural suggests a lack of real intimacy, which makes William of St Thierry an unlikely recipient.

*　　*　　*

To his W., Brother Bernard.

Just as I portrayed myself in the letter, so I am, except in so far as the hand proved inadequate to express the heart's feelings. There is absolutely nothing that you need fear from me, nor ever was. As for me, if ever I was in fear of you, I no longer am. I do not ask for my friend back, being wholly confident that I have him, and cannot therefore receive what I have not lost. I clasp him tight, ensconced in my inmost heart, and there is no one who can tear him from my breast. My old friend is as new in my embrace, for true friendships Dt. 32:39 do not age, else they were never true. I will hold him and I will not let him go, until I have brought him into my mother's house and into the chamber of her who conceived me. When I speak of him as S. of S. 3:4 at leisure, I am not implying that he is idle, but happy. It is obvious that his is no leisurely leisure, but a zealous pursuit of all that is good, richly conducive to salvation. Alas for me, who have so many irons in the fire, I am an exile from the realm of the spirit, unworthy of holy leisure, a stranger to the blessings of repose. However, since you consider me worthy, I am yours and shall be while I live. The sermons you ask for were not ready; they will be put in order and you shall have them soon.

LETTERS 147 AND 387

Ten of St Bernard's letters to Peter the Venerable survive, as also a number of the latter's replies. No one could fail to love the Abbot of Cluny, and his affection and esteem for Bernard were great enough to span the rift opened between the orders and to smooth, on occasion, his friend's ruffled feathers. The Nicholas mentioned in the second letter is Bernard's secretary, dear to both men until the intimacy turned the young monk's head. Secretaries have many uses, not least as scapegoats: sharpness in Bernard's letters is common enough and cannot always have been the fault of the scribes. The first letter dates from the spring of 1138, the second was written between 1149 and 1150.

✱   ✱   ✱

To his most reverend lord and father, Peter, Abbot of Cluny, all the devotion of his Bernard.

Lk. 1:78   May the day star from on high visit you, best of men, because you have visited me in a foreign land and comforted me in my place of
Ps. 118:54   exile. You have done well in caring for the poor and weak. I have
Ps. 40:2   been away, and away a long time, yet you, a great man busy with great matters, have remembered my existence. Blessed be your holy angel, who inspired your kind heart with the thought! Blessed be our God, who prompted you to act! See! I have something to boast of among strangers: a letter from you, and one in which you pour out your soul to me. I pride myself that you keep me not only in remembrance but in favour. I pride myself in the privilege of your
Ps. 144:7   love, and am refreshed by the abundant goodness of your heart. Not
Rom. 5:3   only that: I take pride in my hardships, if I have been held worthy to suffer them for the Church. These assuredly are my glory, lifting
Ps. 3:4   up my head – the triumph of the Church; for if we shared in the

labours, we shall share in the consolation. We were required to toil and suffer with our Mother, lest she should complain of us, saying: 'Those who were close to me stood aside, and those who sought my life did me violence.' Thanks be to God who has given her the victory, crowned her efforts with success and consummated her labours. Our sorrow has turned to joy and our mourning to the music of the lyre. Winter is past, the rain is over and gone, the flowers appear on the earth, the time of pruning has come, and the unproductive branch, the rotten limb has been lopped off. He, the impious one, who made Israel to sin,[5] has been swallowed up in death and gone down into the pit. He had made, as the Prophet says, a treaty with death and struck a pact with hell, and so, in the words of Ezechiel, he has been utterly destroyed and is gone for ever . . .

2 Cor. 1:7

Ps. 37:12
1 Cor. 15:57
Wisd. 10:10
Jn. 16:20
Job 30:31
S. of S. 2:11–12

1 Kgs. 14:16

Isa. 28:15

Ez. 28:19

The time is coming for me to return to my brethren, and, provided life keeps me company, I hope to visit you on the way. I commend myself meanwhile to your holy prayers. My greetings to Brother Hugh, the bursar, and to all those round you, as well as to the rest of the holy congregation.

Gen. 18:10

* * *

To his most reverend father and dearest friend, Peter, by the grace of God Abbot of Cluny, Brother Bernard, styled Abbot of Clairvaux, salutation in him who is our true health and salvation.

How I wish I could send you my inner self in the same way as I send this letter; then without a doubt you would read with the greatest clarity what the finger of God has inscribed in my heart and engraved on my very bones about my love for you. What? Am I beginning to commend myself to you afresh? God forbid! My soul has been fused with yours for a long time now, and an equal measure of love has placed two unequal people on one footing. How could my lowliness consort with your sublimity if you had not condescended out of regard for me?[6] From then on low and lofty intermingled, so that neither could I be lowly without you nor you lofty without me. I say all this because my Nicholas, who is yours as well, swept by a wind of agitation, has agitated me in turn, maintaining that he had seen a letter of mine, addressed to you, that contained some acrimonious words. Believe me who love you:

cf. 2 Cor. 3:2–3
2 Cor. 3:1
Gen. 34:3
1 Sam. 18:1

Ps. 47:8

nothing which might offend your holy ears has dawned in my heart or passed my lips. Pressure of business is to blame. When my secretaries do not fully grasp my meaning, they put an excessive edge on their style, and I haven't time to check what I have told them to write. Forgive me this once: whatever I do about other letters, I shall look through yours, trusting no eyes or ears but mine. You will hear everything else more clearly and fully from our common son. Give him your ear as you would to me who love I Jn. 3:18 you, not merely in word or speech, but in deed and truth. Greet that holy throng of yours from me and ask them to pray for their servant.

LETTER 266

Suger, Abbot of Saint-Denis, a great builder and patron of the arts, and long the chief counsellor of Louis the Fat, was also a frequent recipient of St Bernard's letters. They had not always been close. Suger has been suggested as the abbot in the Apologia *who was seen travelling with sixty horses and more in his train. Certainly he lived in the grand style, but between the publication of the* Apologia *in 1125 and a long letter written to him by Bernard in 1127 there was a dramatic conversion: Suger reformed his life, that of his monks, and subsequently other monasteries. Bernard congratulated him warmly on the change, and between the two men a friendship grew. Suger died on 13 January 1151.*

* * *

To his very dear and intimate friend Suger, by the grace of God Abbot of Saint-Denis, Brother Bernard, wishing him the glory that is Ps. 44:14 from within and the grace that comes from above.

Have no anxiety, man of God, about stripping off that man who is I Cor. 15:47 made of earth, the one who presses you earthwards and would indeed press you down to the regions under the earth. He it is who plagues and burdens and makes war on you. What need have you of earthly garments, you who are on your way to heaven and have a Sir. 45:9 robe of glory to put on? The robe is ready, but will not be given to a man still clothed. It is to cover our nakedness, not for wearing over our own clothes. And so bear patiently with being found naked and unclothed, or, better still, accept it gladly; for God himself wishes man to be clothed, but it must be done when he is naked, not already clad. God's part in man will not return to God until that part which is of the earth, and is earth, has first gone back to earth. For these two are at war with one another, and there will be no peace until they are parted each from each; and if there were peace, it would not be the peace of the Lord, not peace with the Lord. You are not one of those who cry 'Peace' when there is no peace. You are waiting for that peace which passes all understanding; the righteous are waiting for you to receive your reward; the joy of your Lord awaits you.

And I, dearest friend, have an intense desire to see you first, and so receive your dying blessing. Since man's course is not in his own control, I dare not promise what I am not sure of keeping, but what I do not yet see my way to doing I shall do my best to bring about. Maybe I shall come and maybe not. But whichever it is, I have loved you from the first and ever shall. With confidence I declare that I cannot lose a friend whom I have thus loved to the end. One with whom I am joined soul to soul in an indissoluble union and with an unbreakable bond will not be lost to me, he will go before. But remember me when you come to the place to which you are preceding me, that it may be granted me to follow you swiftly and rejoin you there. Be sure meanwhile that your dear memory will never fade for me, even though we who mourn you lose your presence. Yet God is still able to give you to us in answer to our prayers and preserve you for those who need you: of this there is no doubt.

cf. 2 Cor. 5:2-4

Gen. 3:19

Ez. 13:10
Phil. 4:7
Ps. 141:8
Mt. 25:21

Jer. 10:23

WILLIAM OF ST THIERRY

William of St Thierry, friend and biographer of St Bernard, was his elder by a few years and by no means his intellectual inferior; yet he fell at their first meeting so totally under the spell of the younger man's charisma, reverencing him as a disciple does a master, that posterity took him at his own estimate and either neglected his writings or ensured them a borrowed fame by attributing them to the saint. It is only in this century that he has been rescued from Bernard's slipstream, where he would happily have remained, and been valued for what he is: a profound thinker and a master of the spiritual life.

A native of Liège, he came from the ranks of the lesser nobility, the class that yielded so rich a crop of Cistercian recruits. He may well have studied under Anselm at Laon before entering the Benedictine abbey of St Nicasius at Reims. In or shortly before 1120 he both met Bernard at Clairvaux and was elected abbot of St Thierry, in the neighbourhood of Reims. The combination of events set up tensions within William that were later reflected in the friendship. Already a zealous promoter of monastic renewal, he found at Clairvaux and in Bernard the incarnation of his ideal, and had from the time of their first meeting one desire: to live at Clairvaux with his friend. This Bernard was adamant in refusing. He was very strongly of the opinion that responsibilities, however unwelcome, should not be sloughed off – many of his letters are on this subject. He may also have shrunk from the thought of having so ardently devoted a spirit as William under the same roof. Bernard needed friendship, but liked it on his own terms: free from emotional demands and sensitive to the pressures on him. William obediently remained fifteen years at St Thierry, struggling with his urgent wish for a more contemplative life. Finally, and without Bernard's prior knowledge, he joined a group of monks leaving the monastery of Igny to found a daughter house at Signy in the Ardennes, and there, garbed at last in the white habit, he lived until his death in 1148. The rift, if rift there was, was certainly bridged, for the two men were in close contact over the condemnation of Abelard, and William's veneration for Bernard is plain on every page of the *Vita Prima*, on which he was working during the last three years of his life.

If William was only latterly a member of the Order and wrote many of his best-known works as a black monk at St Thierry, he was a Cistercian in spirit from the time of his first visit to Clairvaux. It was the Benedictine William who first pressed Bernard into writing the *Apologia*, to which so many of his brethren took exception. The fact that his earliest work, *On Contemplating God*, was by 1165 to be resituated under the Bernardine umbrella proves how closely William's vision from the outset corresponded to the Cistercian ideal, without, however, his being in any way derivative. He was, on the contrary, a markedly original thinker whose principal works give an idea of his range and achievement: *On Contemplating God*; *On the Nature and Dignity of Love*; *On the Nature of Body and Soul*; *Commentary on the Epistle to the Romans*; *Meditations*; *Commentary on the Song of Songs*; *The Mirror of Faith*; *The Enigma of Faith*; *A Letter to the Brethren at Mont Dieu* ('The Golden Epistle'). Philosophically speaking, it is the most solid body of work to emanate from a Cistercian environment. William combined the twelfth-century passion for ideas with an ardent love for Christ embodied in the Church, which offered a counterweight, lacking in Abelard, to the uninhibited ranging of the intellect. In fact, in William the two currents – intellectual/metaphysical and affective/mystical – which had hitherto in Christian tradition flowed in a common bed but were so soon to divide, were still perfectly intermingled. The formulae *amor ipse notitia est* and *amor ipse intellectus est* (love is knowledge, love is understanding), which William made his own, epitomize this.

The Cistercians did not write about the love of God without giving much thought to the nature of man. Self-knowledge was widely seen in the twelfth century as a prerequisite to the knowledge of God. William's writings reflect a marked interest in human psychology, seen always as a key to spiritual understanding. He saw its relevance vouched for by both the Ancients and the Bible: 'The answer of the Delphic Apollo, "Man, know yourself", was famous among the Greeks. The same thing was said by Solomon, or rather Christ, in the Song of Songs: "If you do not know yourself, go forth." '[1]

The *Meditations* are not William's best-known work; that title must go to his wonderful treatise on the solitary life, written for the Carthusians at Mont Dieu, with whom he entertained very close relations. But a meditation does not have to be amputated or dismembered as would a longer composition, and this is a very great advantage. The *Meditations* also reflect the main themes of William's spirituality: the contrast between his wretchedness and God's majesty; the redeeming power of Christ, who is himself the bridge, the door of heaven; the spirit as the bond of love between the Father and the Son; William's yearning for the face of God, the fullness of contemplation, ever longed for and never attained. It is not certain when they were written: although they are highly personal, the internal evidence is not conclusive. There are thirteen in all, and it is likely that William wrote them over a number of years before gathering them together. The *Meditations* survive in a single manuscript, truly a lone voice speaking out of the sea of silence in which so much has sunk for good.

Three Meditations

MEDITATION II

The soul presents itself to God, desiring to receive his
light and, with a mind detached from sensory perceptions,
to meditate upon the Holy Trinity.

'Come to him and you will be illumined, and your faces will not
be confounded.' I am, I am confounded, Lord, I am thrown into a
black pit of confusion as often as I turn to you and find the door of
vision closed to me; it is almost as though I heard those fearful
words: 'Truly, I say to you, I know you not.' And because of my
longing illumined by you, my heart's hurt and my mental
disarray are such as to plunge me into total darkness, where it almost
seems that it would have been better for me if I had not come
at all. For who is there to console me if you would have me
desolate? I will have no solace, none, that is not you yourself or sent
from you. Let them all perish from the earth! 'Woe to him who is
alone', says Solomon. And woe to me who am indeed alone if you
are not with me or I with you. Twice and thrice blessed do I hold
myself, O Lord, if I feel you with me, but self-disgust and loathing
fill my soul whenever I feel that I am not with you. As long as I am
with you, I am present to myself; I am not wholly me when I am
not with you. Woe to me each and every time that I am not with
you, without whom I cannot even be. I should not be able to subsist
in any way at all, either in body or in soul, without the indwelling
of your power. Were it not for the presence of your grace in me I
should neither desire nor seek you; nor should I ever find you unless
your mercy and goodness came to meet me. But when in these ways
I am with you, I feel your grace at work within me, and then I am

Ps. 33: 6

Mt. 25:12

Ecc. 4:10

glad I am, and am alive: my soul gives praise to the Lord. If, Ps. 33:3 however, you are present to me, working for my good, and I am absent, either in thought or feeling, then the very benefits with which your grace surrounds me seem to me like burial rites punctiliously performed over a corpse.

And if from time to time I sense you passing by, you do not pause for me but carry on your way, leaving me like the Canaanite woman crying in your wake. And when I have importuned you to Mt. 15:22-3 weariness with shouting out my needs, you reproach the sullied conscience of the creature that I am with past depravity and present impudence and drive your dog from your table – or let it take itself off – unfed and famished and stung by conscience' lash. Should I, in that case, come back again? Yes, surely, Lord. For even the whelps whipped from their master's house return at once and, keeping watchful guard over the place, receive their daily bread. So I, thrown out, come back; shut out, I yelp, and whipped off, fawn. A dog cannot live without man's companionship, and nor can my soul without the Lord its God. Open to me therefore, Lord, that I may come to you and be illumined by you. You dwell in your heavens Ps. 2:4 and have made darkness your hiding-place, even the thick clouds dark with water; you have wrapped yourself with a cloud, as the Ps. 17:12 Prophet says, so that no prayer may pass through. As for me, I have Lam. 3:44 rotted on the ground and encased my heart in a weight of thickest Ex. 8:14 mire. The stars of your sky do not shine for me; the sun is darkened; Hab. 2:6 the moon does not give its light. In psalms and hymns and spiritual Mt. 24:29 canticles I hear your mighty works proclaimed. Your words and Eph. 5:19 deeds blaze out at me from the Gospels. The good examples set by your servants ceaselessly assault my eyes and ears. I am shaken with terrors and taunted with the sure and certain promises of Scripture that they are forever thrusting before my eyes and dinning into my deaf ears. But bad habits combined with a profound lethargy of mind have hardened me. I have learned to doze full in the sun's splendour. More, I have grown used to doing so, and to not seeing what is coming towards me. In the midst of the sea I no longer hear its roaring, nor, dead at heart as I am, do I hear the heavens' Ps. 30:13 thunder.

How long, O Lord, how long? How long till you rend your Ps. 12:1 heavens and come down, till you shake me out of my stupor and Isa. 64:1 consume me in your wrath, so that I may be other than I am, so that

I may know that you rule over Jacob and to the utmost ends of the earth, and may return, at least at eventide, to prowl like a hungry dog about your city – a part of which still sojourns on the earth, but which in the main rejoices already in heaven – and perhaps meet with some who will receive the weary traveller into their habitation, since I have no couch of my own on which to lay my head?

Sometimes I hear the voice of your spirit, a passing whisper like the faintest breeze, and I understand it to say, 'Come to him and you will be illumined.' I hear and I am roused from my torpor. As I shake myself awake, I feel a certain wonder; I open my mouth and draw a deep breath; then I give my spiritual faculties a good stretch to rid them of their lethargy before stepping out of the darkened recesses of my consciousness into the light of the sun of righteousness rising upon me. But when I want to turn my sleep-filled eyes towards it, they are dazzled by the unaccustomed light, used as they are to darkness. And as reason blinks its eyes beneath trembling lids at the inhabitual splendour, with the hand of exercise I wipe away as best I can the rheum of their prolonged sleep.

If, by your gift, I discover the fount of tears, which will well up swiftly in the valleys of the humbled and contrite soul, I wash the hands of work and the face of prayer. Then, as the hawk spreads its wings towards the south to feather them, I raise my outstretched hands to you, O Lord, and my soul lies before you like a land without water; like a dry and trackless waste I appear before you in your holy place, that I may see your power and your glory. And when, O Sun of Righteousness, I lift to you my mind's eyes – reason's apperception – I suffer the common fate of those drunk with sleep, or with poor eyesight: namely, to see two or three where there is only one, until by dint of looking they begin to understand that the fault is in their eyes and not the object. For the first mental pictures that meet my soul, newly awakened from its dependence for its pleasures on the senses and what can be apprehended by them, are the very ones that darken and confuse it. Its exclusive preoccupation with the sensible having dulled its powers of perception, there is now nothing else that it can conceive or grasp. So when, aroused from the sleep of negligence, I suddenly raise my eyes to God, of whom the Law says, 'Hear, O Israel, the Lord your God is one God'; when I fix my inward gaze full upon him to whom I turn for light, to whom I offer worship or entreaty: it is God as Trinity who

Ps. 58:14

Lk. 16:9
Mt. 8:20

1 Kgs. 19:12

Mal. 4:2

Jer. 9:1

Job 39:26

Ps. 142:6
Ps. 62:3

Dt. 6:4

comes to meet me, a truth which the Catholic faith, bred in my bones, instilled by practice, commended by yourself and by your teachers, presents to me. But my soul, which must always visualize, perceives this given truth in such a way that it foolishly fancies number to reside in the simple being of the Godhead, which is beyond all number, and which itself made all that is by number and measure and weight. In this way it allots to each Person of the Wisd. 11:21 Trinity as it were his individual place and, praying to the Father, through the Son, in the Spirit, pictures itself as passing from the one to the other through the third. And thus the mind, baffled by the one, is diffracted among the three, as though there were three bodies that must be differentiated or united.

When the imagination, that is the visualizing faculty of the mind, rejects this representation of the Trinity or struggles against its imposition, faith comes and remonstrates, reason with faith's help distinguishes, authority condemns, and all that is within me cries out what was said above: 'Hear, O Israel, the Lord your God is one God.' For while faith and reason and authority teach me to reflect on the Father, the Son and the Holy Spirit individually, they still decree that nothing should enter my reflection that would either, through the concepts of time, place or number, seem to make division of the substance, or alternatively indicate confusion of the Persons. Indeed, they affirm the oneness of the Trinity in a way that precludes solitude, and so define the threefold unity as to exclude from the being of the Godhead plurality of number.

Your grace, O Lord, which gives us what we have of merit, knowledge, virtue, gives us too our knowledge, however scanty, of ourselves and you. That same grace makes us subject to humility, humility to authority, authority to faith; faith instructs reason, reason by means of faith refines, or else demolishes and discards, our mental images. It is not reason, however, that leads faith to under-standing; rather, through faith it looks for understanding from above, even from you, the Father of lights from whom comes every good and perfect gift. This is not that understanding which is Jas. 1:17 acquired by the exercise of reason, or results from intellectual processes: it is drawn in response to faith from the throne of your greatness and formed by your wisdom. In all things like its source, Wisd. 9:10 on entering the mind of the believer it embraces reason and conforms it to itself, while faith is quickened and enlightened by it.

So it is that the soul that is about to pray to its God stands
quaking and bewildered, bearing its own self ever in its hands after
the manner of an offering. It fears what it knows and is bewildered
by the unfamiliar; it sets out to find you carrying the sign of its faith
in you, but without finding as yet to whom it may present it.
Neither knowing nor yet wholly unaware, it is your face, O Lord,
your face that it is seeking. It abominates as idols the phantasms of
yourself it conjures up; it loves you as faith represents you to it, but
the mind's eye is unequal to its task. Aflame with longing for your
face, before which it would offer the sacrifice of its righteousness
and duty, its oblations and burnt offerings, it is the more distraught
when it finds itself put off. And the failure to win at once the
radiance of faith from you in whom it trusted leaves it at times so
nonplussed that it almost loses faith in its own belief and is on the
verge of hating itself, for want, as it seems to it, of loving you. Far
be it from my soul not to believe in you for whom it frets with
longing, or to love you not, for whom it yearns to the point of
spurning all that is, itself included! How long, O Lord, how long?
Unless you light my lamp, unless you lighten my darkness, I shall
not be delivered from these straits, nor, save it be in you, my God,
shall I ever scale this wall.

Ps. 118:109

Ps. 50:21

Ps. 17:28–9

MEDITATION VI

The soul contemplates the joy of the blessed, and also
heaven, which is God, and the ark of the covenant,
which is Christ's humanity.

'I saw in heaven an open door,' says St John, 'and the first voice,
which I had heard speaking to me like a trumpet, said, Come up
hither.' O Lord who made heaven and earth, you cursed the earth in
the sin and work of Adam, and condemned all his descendants, its
inhabitants, to live under a curse, since they suffer the abiding
penalties of the ancient malediction. Moreover, by forsaking your
commandments they add to the burden daily, even as it is written:
'Cursed are they who depart from your commandments.' I am
weary of all these curses new and old, by which I am forced to pay
for the spoils I did not take, and dunned, with compound interest,

Rev. 4:1

Gen. 3:17

Ps. 118:21

for those I did. If only I could find the stairway and the door standing open, how gladly, how eagerly I would flee our earth for the heaven that you purged once for all of pride when you cast the proud one out, and have since kept for yourself. For there, I am told, is found none of the many ills from which I suffer here. There is no morning and no evening there – neither morning with its fleeting joys nor evening with its lingering griefs – and you know with what delight I should say farewell to that. Instead there is one continuous day, free from all disturbance or distraction, for celebrating the never-ending vision of your glory. They say that neither fire nor hail nor snow nor ice nor stormy winds ascend there, all of which, at your bidding, harass us here below. Death has no entrance there, nor has corruption, whether of body or of soul; destructive passions of all kinds are banished utterly; there virtue alone is found, and happiness and joy, and charity delighting in its proper object without mistrust of losing it. Isa. 14:12
Lk. 10:18 Ps. 29:6 Zach. 14:7 Ps. 148:8

I hear too that that festal day is splendid with the praise of the rejoicing angels, glorious with the crowns of the apostles and martyrs and of all good men who from the dawn of time found favour in your sight. There the Church is gathered in one body and has established for this festive day her everlasting dwellings. When on earth, as happens, we see two or three gathered together in your name and you in the midst, their unity strikes us as so good and so pleasant, so rich in the oil of the Holy Spirit, that all can see they enjoy the blessing you ordained. If thus on earth, how much more so in heaven, where you have assembled your saints who recorded your covenant with sacrifices, and where the heavens you made declare your righteousness. Mt. 18:20 Ps. 132:1–3 Ps. 49:6

That beloved disciple of yours was not the only one to find the way to heaven, nor was it only to him that the open door was shown. You proclaimed it clearly to all, not through some herald or prophet but in person, saying: 'I am the door, if anyone enters by me he will be saved.' You then are the door, and open, it seems, from what you say, to all who wish to enter. But what does it avail us earthbound folk to see an open door in heaven? Paul gives us the answer: he who ascends is also he who descended. And who is this? Love. Love in us, Lord, ascends to you on high, because love in you descended here to us. You loved us, therefore you came down to us; by loving you we shall climb where you are. But you who yourself cf. Rev. 4:1 Jn. 10:9 Eph. 4:10 1 Jn. 4:9

declared, 'I am the door', by your own self I beg you, open yourself to us, that we may have a clearer view of the house that you admit to, and learn when and to whom you are open. That house, as we have said, is heaven, where the Father dwells, of whom it is written, 'the Lord has his throne in heaven'. And no one comes to the Father but by you who are the door.

Ps. 10:5
Jn. 14:6

O author of all that is, including place and time, you are neither moved by time nor contained by place. You are not borne up bodily by the heavens lest you fall, nor does your dwelling there prevent your filling heaven and earth – everywhere present, if that can be said of one who is not confined to place, everywhere in your entirety, if wholeness can be predicated where there is no division. Yet you yourself taught us to say: 'Our Father, who are in heaven.' And this way of thinking has such a universal hold that all mankind, including Jews and pagans, affirm that God dwells in heaven. But those who are in error derive one meaning from these terms, while those who profess the truth infer another. Thus the same words can mediate the truth to those with understanding, while still allowing those whose beliefs prevent their grasping or perceiving the reality of things to form a more or less tolerable idea. So it is that the Prophet who speaks of 'our God in heaven' adds a little later, 'who dwells in Jerusalem'. I implore you, therefore, answer those who are striving to reach you, those who chase breathlessly after you. 'Master, where do you dwell?' Swift comes the reply: 'I am in the Father and the Father in me.' Elsewhere you say: 'In that day you will know that I am in the Father and the Father in me', and again, 'I in them and you in me, that they may become perfectly one.' Your dwelling-place, therefore, is the Father, and the Father's, you. Nor is that all: we too are your dwelling-place and you are ours. Since, therefore, O Lord Jesus, you are in the Father and the Father in you, O highest and undivided Trinity, you are your own abode, you are your own heaven; and just as you have no source of being you need no place in which to be save of and in yourself.

Mk. 6:9

Ps. 113:11
Ps. 124:1

Jn. 1:38
Jn. 14:10–11
Jn. 14:20
Jn. 17:23

And when you dwell in us, we are assuredly your heaven. Not that we furnish you with an abode: you, on the contrary, keep us in being that we may have you dwelling in us. But for you the heaven of heavens is your eternity, where you are what you are in your own self, the Father in the Son, the Son in the Father, together with the unity that makes you one, namely the Holy Spirit, not coming from without to form the bond between you, but there by virtue of his coexisting. The same Holy Spirit is the author and ordainer of the unity that makes us one in one another and in you, so that we, who were sons of wrath by nature, are made sons of God by grace, *Eph 2:3* as the apostle says: 'See what love the Father has given us that we should be called the children of God: and so we are.' By a gift *1 Jn. 3:1* indeed, namely the Holy Spirit. A little further on he adds: 'Beloved, we are God's children now; it does not yet appear what we shall be, but we know that when he appears we shall be like him, for we shall see him as he is.' But whereas the birth of the Son from the *1 Jn. 3:2* Father is of another and eternal mode, our birth as sons of God is an adoption that proceeds from grace. The former is not the product of unity, nor does it create it: it is itself unity in the Holy Spirit. The latter has no autonomous existence, but is brought into being by the Holy Spirit in as much as it is stamped with the divine likeness; and though it falls short of the unity that pertains to the Godhead, it is yet beyond that which we can humanly aspire to. For it is the Holy Spirit who is the seed of that birth, of which the same John says: 'Whosoever is born of God does not commit sin, for God's seed abides in him, and therefore he cannot sin.' *1 Jn. 3:9* This likeness will be conferred on us by the vision of God, when we shall not merely see that he exists but shall see him as he is; and this is precisely the likeness with which we shall be like him. Whereas for the Father to see the Son is to be what the Son is, and vice versa; but for us to see God is to be like God. This unity, this likeness is that very heaven where God abides in us and we in God.

You indeed are the heaven of heavens, O truth supreme, who are what you are, who have your being of yourself, for yourself, and are sufficient unto yourself. In you is neither lack nor excess; no discordance, no confusion, no evolution, alteration nor any shadow of change, no need, no death. Rather is there perfect harmony, utmost clarity, total plenitude and fullness of life. No vileness in your creature can degrade you, its ill will cannot harm you nor error lead astray – you who have preordained for all the righteous their abodes of virtue or of blessing, to which they needs must come whatever the force or drag of circumstance, and have fixed bounds for the wicked in their evil that none can overpass, however much *Job 14:5* he might desire it.

O Lord, this height, this depth, this wisdom and this might, are
these the heaven to which you are the door? Yes, clearly, it is so.
Which is why, according again to John, when the door was opened,
Rev. 11:19 the ark of the covenant was seen in heaven. And what does the ark
of the covenant seen in heaven signify but, to use the words of Paul,
the dispensation of the mystery hidden for ages in God who created
Eph. 3:9 all things? You are yourself the ark of the covenant. In you has been
hidden down the ages the mystery fulfilled in these latter days, to
which from the beginning of the world all the saints and prophets
have borne witness, through the Law, through prophecies, by
wonders and by signs. You are the ark covered on all sides with
Heb. 9:7 pure gold, for the fullness of God's wisdom found its resting-place
in you and encompassed you totally with its glory. In you is the
Ibid. golden urn holding the manna, the holy and immaculate soul in
Col. 2:9 which the fullness of the deity dwelled bodily; and Aaron's rod that
Heb. 9:4 budded, the dignity of the eternal priesthood; and the tables of the
Ibid. covenant, by which the world is made the heir of your grace and
the nations co-inheritors, members of the same body and partakers
Eph. 3:6 of your promise. Above all these are the glorious cherubim, the
Heb. 9:5 plenitude of knowledge.[2] Their being above does not signify the
pre-eminence of knowledge, but rather its need to be borne up and
underpinned by the others; and, in that the cherubim overshadow
Heb. 9:5 the mercy seat, they bear witness to the incomprehensibility of the
mysteries of your atoning grace.

Col. 1:26 These riches, hidden down all the ages in the recesses of your
heaven, you disclosed at the ages' end to a hungering world by
opening in heaven the door that is yourself. You opened it when
Titus 2:11–12 your grace appeared to all men, teaching us; when your goodness
and loving-kindness appeared, saving us not because of any upright
Titus 3:5 actions done by us, but in virtue of your mercy. Then through that
open door all the goodness and sweetness of heaven streamed down
upon the earth. Then all the kindness you harboured towards us, O
God, who did not spare your own Son but delivered him up for us
Rom. 8:32. all, was plain for all to see. For when you made your salvation
known to the world and revealed your righteousness in the sight of
Ps. 97:2 the nations, making it over to us in the blood of your only Son, he
paid out to you for our salvation the spotless obedience that comes
from love, while giving to us the love that springs from that
obedience. Then it was that you blessed our earth, and from then on

it began to yield its increase. From that day on, the high road to Ps. 84:1, 13 your heaven lay open wide, the high road trodden by the feet of the apostles and martyrs and of all the saints, who, strong in your example and the grace of your charity, have set themselves at naught for love of you and have not feared to lay down their lives for your sake.

These unsearchable riches of your glory, Lord, lay hidden in you in the secret depths of heaven until the soldier's lance opened the side of your Son, our Lord and Redeemer, on the Cross, and the sacraments of our redemption came flowing out. So now it is not, like Thomas, a Jn. 19:34 finger or a hand that we may thrust into your side, but we may enter Jn. 20:27 whole through that open door, O Jesus, into your very heart, the sure seat of mercy, and even to your holy soul filled with all the fullness of God, full of grace and truth, our treasury of comfort and salvation. Jn. 1:14 Open, O Lord, the door in your ark's side, that all your own who are to be saved may enter in and escape the flood submerging all the earth. Open to us your body's side, that those who long to see the Gen. 7:6 secrets of the Son may enter and receive the sacraments that flow from it, and the price of their redemption. Open the door of your heaven, that your redeemed may see the good things of the Lord in the land of the living, they who labour still in the country of the Ps. 26:13 dying. And seeing, may they long, and burn, and run to you who are the way by which they go, the truth to which they go, and the life for which they go – the way being the imitation of your Jn. 14:6 lowliness; the truth, the reflection of your purity; and the life, life eternal.

All these things you have become for us, merciful Father, sweet Lord, dearest Brother. You are the way, the truth and the life for us who are your little ones, to whom you said: 'Little children, I shall be with you only a little longer'. We are your servants, to whom Jn. 13:33 again you said: 'You call me Master and Lord, and you do well, for so I am'; your brothers, to whom you sent word to go where they Jn. 13:13 would see you. O good Father, dearest Brother and sweet Lord – Mt. 28:10 good you are, and dear and sweet, you in whom goodness utterly abounds – open yourself to us, that from you even to us your sweetness may flow out and fill us. Open yourself to me, O you who are the door, that once in a while I may pass through and, though undeserving as yet of the full reality, may enter in longing into the wondrous tabernacle, the very house of God. Now and Ps. 41:5

then you have opened your servant's ear, that he might hear on rare occasions the sound of exultation there and the shout of those who Ps. 41:5 feast; but there was no going further. Wherefore you are deservedly cast down, my soul, and rightly are you disquieted within me; yet put your trust in God, for I shall praise him still, my saviour and my Ps. 41:6 God. Open to me, Lord, so that I, a stranger in your land and not yet worthy of enrolment as its citizen, may be granted the favour of occasional and fleeting visits thither, that I may look upon your glory and never leave except I be thrown out. If I am found worthy to ascend more often, to linger longer, to return again, your citizens will come to know me, they who, like all the inhabitants of heaven, know no suffering, but rejoice with a joy no words can utter and in which all share. Nor will they take me for a stranger if, now and then, somewhere within your house you bid me take my rest.

Lord, my heart frets with longing for you and I can find no rest for it apart from you. This is why, when I am cast out of heaven, I am so weary of my life that I sometimes have a mind to go down alive into hell (ah, may that never be my dying fate!) to see what is happening there too. But when I find it written on the very Ps. 6:6 threshold that there is none in hell who gives you praise, I curse the place and hurry hotfoot back. Within I hear weeping and gnashing Mt. 8:12 of teeth: O Lord, let it not befall me to make that descent! On you, Ps. 122:1-2 O Lord, my eyes are ever trained, on you who dwell in the heavens, and on your dwelling-place, Jerusalem your city, whence you came down to us, bringing at your coming so wonderful an exemplar of its life. Inspired by which, eagerly, ardently and often I run back there. If I find you, the door, standing open, I enter in and all is well with me for the duration of my stay. But if I find it shut, I beat a disorderly retreat, and, prevented from looking on your glory, I am sent home wretched to endure my own familiar poverty. If only I may see, if only I may persevere, if only I may one day hear 'Enter Mt. 25:21 into the joy of your Lord', and may so enter that I never leave! You Ps. 88:9 are mighty, Lord, and your truth is all about you. Fulfil what you began and give what you promised.

MEDITATION IX

William's soul takes issue with its thoughts and reflections.

* * *

The wretchedness that is in me, Lord, is at once so impenetrable and so extensive that I can neither examine it in detail nor survey the whole in all its amplitude. For even now, when I wish to speak and listen to you, O Lord my God, the fog of it blankets me, as it so often does, and prevents my seeing you clear or hearing you plain. So it is that I am forever finding myself cast out of doors by my own conscience. Is it not a case of 'let the wicked be taken away lest he see the glory of God'? And when I struggle on without the light cf. Isa. 26:10 of understanding, groping my way towards my goal, the impulse of my ardent longing is blunted and broken, and from your heights I fall back into my depths – from you to me, and from me lower still. And once the driving force of my best effort is exhausted, like so much dust thrown up off the face of the earth I am turned into the Ps. 1:4 plaything of the winds, blown this way and that by the fantasies of thought, and whim, and feeling, as multitudinous as the faces of men, of moments in time, of links in the chain of events. So while your face is ever bent on me in purposeful goodwill, I in my wretchedness am always gazing down at the dull earth, and yet so blind withal and lapped in darkness that I do not know how to reach your presence – nor can I, save in as much as there is no hiding from the face of truth, which sees through all things whatsoever their condition. And so, leaving my gift before the altar, I take Mt. 5:24 myself angrily in hand, rise up, and, lighting the lamp of the word of God, in wrath and bitterness of soul I enter the darkened house of Ez. 3:14 my conscience, seeking to identify the source of this murk, this hateful fog that comes between me and the light of my heart.

At once – imagine this! – a plague of flies erupts in front of my eyes and virtually chases me out of my own private domain, the house of my conscience. I enter, however, as of right, only to be met by a swarm of thoughts so insolent, so indisciplined, so diverse and disorderly that the human heart that spawned them is powerless to sort them out. However, I prepare to sit in judgement on them. I order them to stand in front of me so that I can identify the particular features and the general type of each, in order to assign to each its place in my household. But before I can make them out and distinguish between them, they scatter and, constantly switching places, seem to mock their would-be judge. In growing anger with myself I stand up, preparing to wield my sovereign power more harshly. I call on other thoughts to tender their assistance – thoughts that I used to find so sure and stable, those that I drew from the Saviour's wells. Let him be the judge and prosecutor, and the witness too. I separate out the unclean and most abominable as not deserving an audience: they can be condemned unheard and pay the due penalties of penance. The idle and troublesome I brush away like so many annoying flies. To busy thoughts related to my work I grant temporary admittance: they can be given a reasoned hearing and sent about their business, with proper times and places allocated to them. Those that my conscience has condemned accept their sentence without a murmur. The idle thoughts, seeing that I am in earnest, take flight or lose their zest, fearful of disturbing the business in train. The officious ones, seeing themselves neglected and of little use now that their occasions have been dispensed with, retire, embarrassed to find themselves accounted among the idle.

Isa. 12:3

Having thus dispersed for a while the thick mist of my thoughts, I turn my attention to their source, in order to impose some discipline on my feelings. In the solitude to which I have fled, I find that carnal affections are denied both access and outlet. Were I to discover the contrary, I should confess my wretchedness and view my frailty with the deepest suspicion. But love, the prince of my affections, by the grace of him who strengthens me, intent on making room for the one affection that I seek, brings the rest of the mob into bondage under himself. He gives them laws and standards of behaviour and fixes bounds that may not be transgressed.

Phil. 4:13

Job 14:5

Now that the murk is quite dispelled, I turn a clearer gaze on you, O light of truth, and, having shut all else out, I shut myself up alone with you, and hiding myself in the covert of your presence I speak with you in a more intimate and homely way, opening all the nooks and crannies of my conscience to you. Having thus thrown off the garment of skin that you made to cover Adam's shame, I present myself before you, naked as you created me, saying: 'Here I stand, not as you made me, Lord, but as I have made myself by cutting myself off from you. Behold my wounds, new and old. I

Gen. 3:21

Gen. 2:25

keep nothing back, I set it all before you, your benefits and my
betrayals, all. You created me in your own image, you put me in — Gen. 1:27
your own paradise, you gave me a chosen place in the company of — Gen. 2:15
your sons, and even from my boyhood with its tarnished innocence
the light of your countenance set a seal upon me. As for me, I fled — Ps. 4:7
the paradise that you had given me, and in its stead I found myself a
sewer and wallowed in it. The seal of your countenance remained
ever dear to me, but my deeds disowned it, for I wasted my youth
in pursuing my own desires and chasing after the heart's vain
fancies; in fact I nearly embarked on the way of the dog.[3] But if the
body paid no heed to you, my spirit loved you still. And when I
fled that way of life, it was to you I fled, and you plucked me from — Ps. 142:9
the whirlpool of the world. I made a pact with you: I vowed and
resolved to observe your righteous statutes. Whereupon, opening — Ps. 118:106
wide the arms of your mercy, you folded me in them, and, as I lay
there in sweet repose, I saw the Day of Man and longed for it. You — Jer. 17:16
sent me out, whether I would or no, and yet I was not dismissed.
And if I happened to forget my God, if I stretched out my hand
towards forbidden fruit, at once the secret tormentors of my conscience set about their inward work of breaking the bones of my
soul with the rod of your discipline, while sinners belaboured my
back without. So it went on for a long time, with me falling, rising, — Ps. 128:3
dying, reviving, while you supported and sustained me. When at
last I failed in mind and body, and called to you out of the belly of
hell, on the instant you were at my side. You stretched forth your — Jon. 2:3
hand and brought me up out of the pit of my misery. You restored — Ps. 39:3
me to my former state and gave me back a joy in your salvation, — Ps. 50:14
greater than I had known before.

Thus was I, Lord, and thus I am, and all I am is here before you.
My obvious ills are plain to both you and me, but there are many
others evident to you, which blindness or forgetfulness conceal from
me. If any good remains in me, none of it is unmarred, for what the
enemy has been unable to snatch from me he has in some way
corrupted, though I myself have damaged more than he. Behold my
face of misery uplifted now to yours, O mercy of mercies! There is
no fold or corner that is hidden from you; you who are truth know
this, and I pray that what I place before you may be the truth
indeed, for there is nothing that I fear like my own self, lest,
wittingly or otherwise, I should deceive myself.

GUERRIC OF IGNY

The early life of Guerric of Igny resembles his native Picardy, a
landscape of few features shrouded in morning mist. He was certainly
a cleric, probably a canon and may have taught at the cathedral
school at Tournai. His desire for a stricter life took him eventually
to Clairvaux, first on a visit and then to stay. St Bernard gives a
progress report – 'doing well' – on a Guerric, then in the noviciate,
in a letter written no later than 1125 to his friend Oger, Canon of
Mont-Saint-Éloi.[1]

In 1138 Guerric went, already a mature man but with many
misgivings as to his own fitness for the task, as abbot to Igny, a
daughter house of Clairvaux situated between Reims and Soissons.
He served the community well, dying revered and 'full of days' in
1157. On his deathbed this most scrupulous man was visited with
remorse for an oversight: he had collected and dictated his sermons
without obtaining permission from the General Chapter. So troubled
was he that he ordered the book to be burned. Happily, there were
other copies; hence we have his liturgical sermons, fifty-four in
number, a revision, it would seem, of those delivered in chapter on
feast-days and fast-days through the year. They have won him 'a
reputation alongside Bernard, William and Aelred as one of the
'four evangelists of Cîteaux'.

Guerric's purpose in preaching was to unravel the mysteries of
Scripture, to draw out the hidden core – what he calls the spiritual
kernel in the hard shell of the literal meaning – and present it to his
monks as nourishment for their spiritual life. His sermons are
permeated with the theme of light. The theology of light is characteristic of the Cistercian Fathers, but one can say that for Guerric above
all others God was perceived as the 'Father of lights'. His disposition
is gentle and his style often elegiac; he has none of the cutting edge

of Bernard. He writes with tenderness of the motherhood of God
and of the individual's sharing in the motherhood of Mary, conceiv-
ing Christ in the soul and nourishing him that he may be formed in
us and we in turn conformed to him. His concern as an abbot was to
waymark the path to holiness for the brothers in his charge, but his
real preference in commenting on Scripture is for the allegorical
level, where he can follow the many threads to their point of union
in Christ.

Three Sermons

THE SECOND SERMON FOR ADVENT (NO. 2)

'Behold, the king is coming; let us run to meet our Saviour.'[2] Solomon expresses it very well: 'As cool water to a thirsty man, so is good news from a distant land.' This is good news indeed that announces the Saviour's coming, the reconciliation of the world and the joys of the world to come. How beautiful are the feet of those who proclaim peace, the bringers of good tidings! And many they are, not one. Many in number, yet one in spirit, a long line of messengers have come to us from the beginning of time with one voice and one gist between them: 'He is coming, yes, he is coming!' And where, you ask, did they come from, these messengers? From a distant land, as Scripture tells us, from the land of the living, which is cut off by a deep divide from this land of the dying, for between us and them a great chasm is still fixed. It was from there that the prophets – and angels too – were sent to us; for if they lived here in the flesh, when the time of their sending came they were taken there in spirit to hear and see the burden of their message to us here. To the soul athirst for God such tidings are indeed a cooling drink and a draught of saving wisdom, and the herald of the Saviour's advent or his other mysteries proffers to such a soul water drawn for him with joy from the Saviour's wells. And the soul, which has drunk of the same spirit as Elizabeth, replies to the messenger, be it Isaiah or another of the prophets, in Elizabeth's words: 'Why should I be honoured with a visit from my Lord? For behold, when your greeting reached my ears the spirit within me leaped for joy, longing to run to meet God its saviour.'

And we too, brothers, ought in truth to hasten with leaping spirits to meet the coming Christ and salute him now already from

Prov. 25:25

Isa. 52:7

Ps. 26:13, 141:6

Lk. 16:26

Isa. 12:3

Lk. 1:43-4

129

afar, or at least return the greeting of him who sends greetings to
Jacob. You will not be ashamed to greet a friend, says the Sage: how
much less to return his greeting. O salvation of my countenance and
my God, how great an honour was it that you should greet your
servants, but a greater by far to save them! But your greeting to us
would not have been perfect in its saving power had you merely
sent the salutations and not delivered them in person. But this you
did indeed, not only in greeting with the kiss of peace, when you
put on our flesh, those you had saluted first with words of peace,
but in effecting our salvation on the Cross. May our spirit therefore
leap up with eager joy and hasten to meet its Saviour! Let us
worship and salute him from afar, acclaiming the approaching
Christ and crying: 'Save me, O Lord; O Lord, prosper my way!
Blessed are you who are to come in the name of the Lord! Come,
let your face shine upon us and we shall be saved. Indeed, we have
waited for you; be our right arm, a saving help in time of trouble.'
This is how the prophets and righteous men hastened with full
hearts towards the Christ who was to come, hoping, if possible, to
see with their eyes what they had foreseen in spirit. Hence the words
of the Lord to his disciples: 'Blessed are the eyes that see what you
see. For I tell you that many prophets and kings desired to see what
you see and never saw it.' Our father Abraham rejoiced that he was
to see Christ's day; he saw it – in the lower regions and was glad,
and we shall be reviled as cold and callous if our hearts do not
quicken with spiritual joy to welcome him.

We are waiting now for the anniversary day of Christ's birth,
which we shall shortly see, God willing. Scripture requires, it seems
to me, that our spirit should be so lifted up and transported with joy
that it longs to run towards the approaching Christ; and, projecting
itself into the future, it chafes at delays as it strains to see what is yet
to come. I think myself that the many passages in Scripture exhorting
us to hasten towards him refer not only to the second coming but
also to the first. How so? Because just as, at his second coming, we
shall run towards him with physical energy and joy, so do we hasten
to Bethlehem with jubilant heart and spirit. You know that at the
resurrection, having put on new bodies, according to the Apostle's
teaching we shall be caught up in the clouds to meet Christ in the
air, and so we shall be with the Lord for ever. But even here there is
no lack of clouds that will carry our spirits (provided they are not

Ps. 43:5
Sir. 22:31

Ps. 42:5

Ps. 117:25–6
Ps. 79:4, 8, 20
Isa. 33:2

Lk. 10:23–4
Jn. 8:56

I Thess. 4:16

sluggish and earthbound) to higher things, and then we shall be with the Lord if only for half an hour. Unless I am mistaken, you know from experience what I am talking about, for sometimes when the clouds have thundered, that is, when the voices of the prophets and Ps. 76:18 the apostles have rung out in the Church, your minds have been swept aloft as though borne on clouds, and on occasion been carried so far beyond that they have been favoured with some glimpse of the glory of the Lord. Then, if I am right, the truth of that word dawned clear for you, the word which God rains down from the cloud he daily appoints to bear us aloft:[3] 'The sacrifice of praise shall Ps. 103:3 do me honour: there is the path by which I will show him the salvation of God.' Ps. 49:23

It may happen, therefore, that the Lord will come to you before his actual advent; he may visit you in person before he arrives for all the world to see. For he said: 'I shall not leave you orphans: I am going away and I shall come to you.' And whether to reward desert Jn. 14:18 or ardent striving, this coming of the Lord to the individual soul is frequent in this middle time between his first and final comings, conforming us to the first and preparing us for the last.[4] Assuredly he comes to us now to ensure that his first coming will not have been in vain, and to avoid having to meet us at the last in wrath. In this middle advent he is intent on reforming our spirit of pride and patterning us anew on the humility he showed forth at his first coming, so that one day he may also transfigure our lowly body into the likeness of his glorious body which he will reveal when he Phil. 3:21 comes again. This personal visitation, which imparts to us the grace of the first advent and holds promise of the glory of the last, should be the object of our heart's desire, the goal of all our striving. And because God loves mercy and truth, he, the Lord, will give grace and glory, bestowing grace on us through his mercy and through Ps. 83:12 truth restoring glory.

Moreover, just as the spiritual advent falls in time midway between the two corporeal comings, so too in essence it partakes equally in each, poised like a mediator between the two. The first coming was hidden and humble; the last will be manifest and marvellous; this one indeed is hidden, but also wonderful. We call it hidden, not because the one who is visited is unaware, but because the Lord comes secretly. This Isaiah knew and gloried in it, saying: 'My secret is my own, my secret is my own.' But not even the one Isa. 24:16

who receives him can see him before he holds him close, as blessed Job admitted: 'If he comes to me I shall not see him, if he departs I shall not perceive his going.' Unseen and unperceived he comes and goes, he who alone, while present, is the light of the soul and mind, the light by which, invisible, he is seen and, inconceivable, perceived.

Job 9:11

For the rest, this coming of the Lord is no less wonderful for being hidden. Those who have experienced it know the rapt absorption, the blissful wonderment in which he holds the soul in contemplation at once suspended and outpoured, until from the very depths of being springs the cry: 'Lord, who can compare with you?' Would that those who have not experienced it had a real desire to do so, with this proviso: that no rash curiosity should make them into searchers of majesty, to be overwhelmed by glory. Instead, may charity move them to long for the Beloved and thus be received by grace; for the Lord who raises the meek and casts the wicked to the ground resists the proud and gives his grace to the humble.

Ps. 34:10

Prov. 25:27

Ps. 146:6
Jas. 4:6

And so, since grace marked the first coming as glory will the last, this middle advent partakes equally of grace and glory, inasmuch as through the consolations of grace we are given a foretaste of the glory to come. And as too at his first coming the God of majesty appeared of no account, and at the last he will inspire dread, so in this middle one he evokes both awe and love; but in such a way that the bounteous gift of grace, which shows him lovable, elicits in return not want of reverence but wonderment, while the awesome splendour of his glory speaks to us less of dread than of consolation. Of the first coming Isaiah wrote: 'We saw him, and he had no comeliness or beauty, wherefore we held him of no account.' And even the just man trembles at the prospect of the last, saying: 'Who will remain standing when he appears?' But of this one the Apostle says: 'And all of us, beholding the glory of the Lord, are being changed into his likeness from one degree of glory to another, as it were by the spirit of the Lord.' Utterly wonderful it is, and worthy of our love, when God who is love flows into all the faculties of the lover; when the Bridegroom embraces the Bride in oneness of spirit and she is changed into his very likeness, in which, as in a mirror, she beholds God's glory. How blessed, those whose ardent love has won for them this privilege! But blessed too are those whose holy simplicity allows them to hope for it one day. The first, already

Isa. 53:2–3

Mal. 3:2

2 Cor. 3:18

possessed of the fruits of love, enjoy relief from labour. The latter, whose merit is perhaps greater in that they have less present solace, bearing the burden and the heat of the day, look for the reward to come. As for us, brothers, who lack as yet the consolation of an experience so sublime, let us be patient until the Lord's coming, strengthened meanwhile by a steadfast faith and a pure conscience. Thus we, as happy as we are faithful, will be able to say with Paul: 'I know whom I have believed, and I am sure that he is able to guard what I have entrusted to him until that day' – until, that is, the appearing of our great God and Saviour Jesus Christ, to whom be glory for ever and ever. Amen.

Mt. 20:12

Jas. 5:7

2 Tim. 1:12
Titus 2:13

FROM THE FIRST SERMON FOR THE PURIFICATION [5] (NO. 15)

'See that you have your loins girt and lighted lamps in your hands.' We gird our loins in seeking to imitate Mary in her purification, and we light our lamps to be a visible sign to us of the joy that Simeon felt as he held in his arms the light of the world. We must be chaste of body and pure in heart to portray the purification of Mary; and if our love flames up and our deeds shine out, then with Simeon we carry Christ in our arms. It was not so much that Mary was purified as that, by fulfilling the legal rite of purification, she pointed us to its transcendent and spiritual meaning. What could there be to purify in her who conceived as a virgin, gave birth as a virgin and remained a virgin? Indeed she was wholly purified by this conception, whatever might possibly have been lacking in her purity before.

Lk. 12:35

But let us rather discuss, if you will, the lovely custom in the Church of bearing lights on this feast-day, and how it bodies forth what was done in the past and also what we should be doing now. Not that I suppose you are unaware of this, even if it has never been set out for you. Which of you today, bearing a lighted candle in his hands, does not instantly call to mind the old man who took Jesus in his arms this day – the Word clothed in flesh as the candle-flame is cupped in wax – declaring him to be the light that would enlighten the Gentiles. And Simeon was himself a lamp lit and shining, bearing witness to the light, he who came at the Spirit's prompting

Lk. 2:28 ff.
Jn. 5:35
Jn. 1:17

Lk. 2:27 into the temple, to receive, O God, in the midst of the temple your
Ps. 47:10 loving-kindness, and to proclaim him to be indeed your loving-
kindness and the light of your people. Truly, old Simeon, you did
not only bear the light in tranquil hands, your mind too was lit up;
so clear and so long-sighted was your vision of the radiance that
would dawn for the Gentiles, that even then, in the gloom of Jewish
unbelief, you saw the lambent shimmer of our faith on the horizon.
Now you can truly rejoice, for now you see what you foresaw: the
Isa. 60:3 world's shadows are scattered and the nations walk in your light,
Isa. 6:3 and all the earth is filled with the glory of that light, which, hidden,
you nursed against your breast and continued to cherish in thought.

Embrace God's Wisdom, blessed Simeon, and may all your
perceptions quicken and flame high again. Clasp God's loving-
kindness to your breast and your old age will be rich in love and
S. of S. 1:12 mercy. 'He shall lie,' says Scripture, 'upon my breast', and yet, when
I hand him back to his mother, he will remain with me, and, as he
nestles close to his mother's breasts, so shall he lie long on mine, and
his loving-kindness will fill my heart brim-full, though not to
overflowing like his mother's. For she is the one and only mother of
supernal mercy, and her breasts are wondrously filled with the milk
of mercy and loving-kindness. My thanks and praise to you, O
Lk. 1:28 Mary, full of grace, who gave birth to the mercy I received, who
prepared the candle that I took in my hands. You furnished the wax
for the light you had received, O virgin unsurpassed; mother
immaculate, you clothed the incorruptible Word in sweet unspotted
flesh. Ah! brothers, look where the candle burns in Simeon's hands;
that is the light to light your tapers from, those lamps which the
Ps. 33:6 Lord would have you holding. Go to him and you will be lit up,
not so much bearers of lamps as lamps yourselves, shining within
and without, lighting yourselves and your neighbours. May this
lamp be in heart and hand and mouth: a lamp in your heart to light
yourself, a lamp in your hands and on your lips to light your
neighbours. The light in your heart is loving faith; the lamp in your
hands is the example of good deeds; the lamp on your lips, helpful
and strengthening words. We must not only shine in the sight of
men by our deeds and words: we need to shine through prayer in
the sight of the angels and before God in sincerity of heart. We light
in the sight of the angels the lamp of pure devotion when we sing
with diligence and pray with fervour. Our lamp that burns before

God is our singleness of heart in pleasing him alone whose approval we have won.

So that you may light all these lamps for yourselves, my brothers, come to the source of light and be enlightened. Draw close to Jesus where he shines out for us in Simeon's arms, that he may light up your faith, give lustre to your deeds, power to the words you speak to others, fervour to your prayers and purity to your intentions. Then, whether it be in your prayer or in what you do or say, you will seek to please him who is the light of the living, who searches Ps. 55:13 Jerusalem by the light of his lamps, and who measures too the light Zeph. 1:12 that we give out. When all your lamps are lighted, sons of light, you will not walk in darkness, nor will you need to fear the condemnation: 'He who has cursed father or mother will have his lamp put out in deepest darkness.' In other words, the comfort of Prov. 20:20 this light will fade and fail as wave upon wave of darkness, now outer, now inner, rolls in to swamp it. But as for you for whom so many lamps are shining, you will see, when your lamp of life is doused, the light of life undying rise like the blaze of noon in your evening sky. And just when you thought your candle had burned Isa. 58:10 down, you will flame up again and your darkness will be like the noonday. You will not need the glory of the sun to light you by Job 11:17 day, nor will the moonlight shine on you, but the Lord will be your everlasting light: for the Lamb is the lamp of the new Jerusalem, to Isa. 60:19 whom be all blessing and radiance of glory for ever and ever. Rev. 21:23 Amen.

FROM A SERMON FOR AROUSING DEVOTION AT PSALMODY (NO. 54)

'You who dwell in the gardens, friends are listening; let me hear your voice.' If I am not mistaken, brothers, it is you who dwell in the S. of S. 8:13 gardens, you who meditate day and night on the law of the Lord, strolling about in as many gardens as you read books, plucking as many apples as you garner meanings. And blessed are those for whom all the apples, new and old, have been stored up; for whom, that is, the words of the prophets, evangelists and apostles have been preserved, so that the assurance of the Bridegroom to the Bride – 'All the apples, new and old, I have kept for you, my beloved' – seems S. of S. 7:13

addressed to each one of you. Let us then search the Scriptures, for you who seek in them nothing else than Christ, to whom the Scriptures Jn. 5:39 bear witness, are not mistaken in believing that you find life there. Blessed indeed are they who search his testimonies; who seek them Ps. 118:2 with their whole heart. Wonderful are your testimonies, O Lord; Ps. 118:129 therefore my soul has searched them. The search is a necessary one, not only for eliciting the hidden meanings but also for extracting the moral lessons. You, therefore, who walk in the gardens of Scripture, do not hurry careless and unreflecting on your way. On the contrary, by exploring each and every thing, draw out the spirit from the words like busy bees gathering honey from flowers. 'For my spirit,' says Jesus, 'is Sir. 24:27 sweeter than honey, my inheritance surpasses the honeycomb.'

From these gardens I have no doubt that the Bridegroom will lead you to others where rest is more sequestered and pleasure more blessed, and whose beauty is more wondrous yet. When you are absorbed in praising him with shouts of gladness and thanksgiving, Ps. 41:5 he will carry you off to the place of his wondrous tabernacle, even 1 Tim. 6:16 the house of God, the unapproachable light where he dwells and S. of S. 1:6 feeds and takes his rest at noon. If your singing and prayer has about it something of the reverential curiosity of those who asked, 'Rabbi, Jn. 1:38 where do you live?', I believe you will merit the reply: 'Come and Jn. 1:39 see.' 'They went,' we read, 'and saw and stayed with him that day.' For as long as we are with the Father of lights, with whom there is Jas. 1:17 no variation or shadow due to change, we know no night but enjoy an almost beatific day. When we fall away, we relapse into our own Ps. 89:9 darkness. Woe is me! How swiftly my days have passed away, how Ps. 101:12 quickly I have withered like grass; yet while I was in the garden with him, I throve and flourished like his paradise. With him I am a Ez. 36:35 garden of delight, without him a howling expanse of wasteland. As Dt. 32:10 I see it, the man who enters the Lord's garden becomes a garden Jer. 31:12 himself; his soul is like a watered garden, so that the Bridegroom S. of S. 4:12 says in his praise: 'A garden enclosed is my sister, my bride.' Gardens they surely are, those in whom the gardener's words come true, which he addresses to the plants his Father has set, saying: 'Listen to me, slips from the divine stock: bloom like the rose that is planted by the watercourse; give off a sweet smell of incense, blossom like Sir. 39:17-19 the lily, spread your fragrance abroad and burgeon in beauty.'

O Lord Jesus, true gardener, work in us what you want of us, for Jn. 15:5 without you we can do nothing. For you are indeed the true gardener, at once the maker and tiller and keeper of your garden, you who plant with the word, water with the spirit and give increase with your power. You were mistaken, Mary, in taking him for the gardener of that mean little garden in which he was buried: Jn. 20–15 he is the gardener of the whole world and of heaven, the gardener of the Church he plants and waters here below until, its harvest yielded, he will transplant it into the land of the living by the streams of living water, where it will fear no more the summer heat, where its leaves will be for ever green and it will never cease from bearing fruit. Blessed are they who dwell in your heavenly gardens, Jer. 17:8 Lord; through endless ages will they sing your praise. Ps. 83:5

But since the text we took as a pretext for a sermon has furnished the occasion and the matter for one, let us, if you please, see it through to the end. Those words of the Bridegroom – 'You who dwell in the gardens, friends are listening; let me hear your voice' – can be understood in two ways: either as an invitation to praise him in song and prayer, or as an encouragement to preach his word. He adds urgency by reminding us that friends are listening: the angels to the lover who prays and sings, the faithful to the preacher. The first lesson to be learned is that we should discipline heart and body to sing and pray in the sight of the angels, lest, sent away empty, they, Ps. 137:1 who had come to bear our prayers away and bring back gifts, send us in turn empty away; worse still, lest they, who had come as friends, depart as foes. The Bridegroom himself, who stands at the door and knocks, if the heart does not open to him with a correspond- Rev. 3:20 ing and fitting movement of devotion, will go away complaining and saying: 'I have paid attention and listened, but none has spoken aright. No one repents of his wickedness, saying: "What have I done?" Each one returns to his own course like a horse plunging headlong into battle.' If he prompts someone to preach, he gives Jer. 8:6 him confidence to speak, flowing from the good dispositions and attention of his listeners. They are not sceptics bent on interrupting and arguing; not rivals given to disparaging or scoffing; they do not doze or yawn out of apathy. No, they are friends, attentive and listening, whose love and merit can win for the man preaching the Gospel to them the gifts of word and spirit. Friends are good listeners. Indeed it is the mark of a friend to listen devotedly to the Bridegroom's voice. John says that the Bridegroom's friend is the one who stands by, not wandering in thought or slumped in sleep,

AMEDEUS OF LAUSANNE

Amedeus of Lausanne is one of the host of minor luminaries of their day whose light has shrunk to a barely discernible pinpoint. His life is known, like the man himself, only in outline. He came of a noble family in the Dauphiné. His father, Amédée de Hauterive, entered the Cistercian monastery of Bonnevaux in 1119. The young Amédée, aged nine or ten, accompanied his father, but after some vicissitudes was sent to be educated at the court of his kinsman Conrad, Duke of Franconia and then Emperor. At Conrad's death in 1125 he entered Clairvaux and in 1139 was elected abbot of Hautecombe in Savoy. Five years later, despite strong resistance on his part, he was made bishop of Lausanne, where he soon found himself at odds with the local lord and was once forced to flee the town. However, he enjoyed the confidence both of the Emperor and of the Duke of Savoy, administering the duchy during the latter's absence on Crusade. He died in 1159, revered by priests and people, and was soon the subject of a cult, later confirmed by Rome.

The Cistercian Order had a particular devotion to the Virgin. Their churches were dedicated to her, and her role as mother of the Saviour and the Church was celebrated in the writings of many of the fathers, notably St Bernard. Amedeus of Lausanne, following no doubt consciously in Bernard's footsteps, left eight homilies in her honour. If he lacks the Abbot of Clairvaux's depth and range, he shows himself a man of warmth and tenderness, who lets his imagination play in the garden of Scripture, happily confident that it will never wander out of bounds.

From the Fourth Homily on Mary,
the Virgin Mother

Ecc. 1:8 All things are hard, says Solomon; man cannot explain them in words. Leaving aside the way in which a vast forest can spring from one little grain, how the multitudes of humankind proceeded from the seed of Adam and Eve, and countless other things besides, who will explain the nature of the gnat? How does it spread its wings and move its legs? What of its tiny eyes and the shape of its head? How was its body formed, and the proboscis so exceedingly fine that it is sometimes invisible to the eye, yet pierced and hollow so that it can fill with sucked blood the minute body of this speck of life? O man, if your reasoning powers are unequal to examining the gnat, you should blush at searching out higher and harder matters to investigate. If you cannot fathom yourself and the shallows of your own mind, how will you rise to infinite majesty? How could a man who cannot count pronounce on arithmetic? Will he who does not know a point from a line excel at geometry? Could the person unable to emit a sound teach music? Or someone with no idea of movement make a good astronomer? In the same way, he who does not know himself cannot penetrate the depths of God.

For what is human reason compared to the divine? Not so much as a point, or even the fraction of one. For while – to state a remarkable fact – there exists a comparative relation between the eye of the gnat and the vastness of the sky, there is none between human measure and the immensity of God. What part is the finite of the infinite, the measurable of the immeasurable, the moment of eternity? As the result of what multiplication or addition will the creature be comparable to the creator? If you were to project thousands times thousands to infinity, you would have laboured in vain, and not in the remotest degree could you compare human knowledge to the wisdom of God. Hence, if God is contemplated in his essence, the substance of man will not be found, as the prophet testifies, saying: 'All the nations are as nothing before him, they are accounted by him as a sepulchre and as emptiness.' And as the Lord said to Moses: 'Say this to the sons of Israel: I AM has sent me to you'; and in affirming his essential being he deprived all others of essentiality.

Isa. 40:17

Ex. 3:14

Therefore, human insignificance, or rather human nothingness, trust in God, and may your argumentation be very solidly grounded in his almighty wisdom. Let that be your starting-point, your burden and your end. Be assured that those who cleave perfectly to their maker will not be boxed in by the law of nature, but will find firm footing above it with him who created nature. For it was not nature that imposed a law on its author but the author who gave to nature laws of his own choosing; and, when he wishes, he changes these laws, as when he turned water into wine and used clay to make blind eyes see. As also when, holding his own self in his hands, he distributed that self to his disciples to be eaten and drunk, remaining physically whole while spiritually feeding those who were eating. Thus too (and this is relevant to our subject) did he issue through the closed womb of the Virgin.

When Mary gave birth, the heavens were glad and the earth rejoiced and hell was shaken and trembled. The heavens gave him a bright and beaming star and a glorious host of angels gathered in praise and singing: 'Glory to God in the highest and on earth peace to men of good will.' The exultant earth offered him shepherds giving glory to God, and magi worshipping and presenting their gifts of gold and frankincense and myrrh. Hell's contribution from out of its turmoils was an impious king and the rage of soldiers wreaking violence on the innocent, slaughtering without pity the unweaned infants snatched from the breast. So it was that the good rejoiced and the wicked were dismayed when Mary was delivered of the one who would reward the good and mete out due requital to the wicked. She laboured and gave birth: imagine the happy smile on the face of all creation as the whole earth praised its Lord! Imagine the night sky in its beauty, all clouds swept aside and the stars saying 'Here we are!' and shining merrily. Imagine the night flooding the darkness with light and supplying brilliance in the place of murk. Before the rising of the sun, that night had shed abroad a light that eclipsed the sun's splendour, for that was the night of

Ps. 95:11

Lk. 2:14

Job. 38:35

Ps. 138:12 which the Psalmist said: 'The night will shine bright as the noonday.' And if all created things rejoiced and were glad, what must his mother's joy and happiness have been? The tongue stumbles, the heart shrinks back and the mind gapes before such an overwhelming joy as this.

Mary understands that in her are fulfilled the promises made to the patriarchs, the words of the prophets who foretold that Christ would be born of a virgin, and the hopes of our forefathers who yearned for his coming. She sees the Son of God committed to her care and rejoices that the world's salvation is entrusted to her. She hears the Lord God speaking to her and in her: 'Behold, I have
Sir. 45:4 chosen you from all flesh and have blessed you among women. I
Lk. 1:28 have committed my son to your care, I have entrusted to you my only son. Do not be afraid to suckle the one you bore, to rear the child you have brought forth. See in him not only your God but also your son. My son and yours. My son through his Godhead, yours through the manhood he has assumed.'

No human being knows with what fondness and zeal, humility and reverence, love and devotion she fulfilled this charge; it is
Ps. 7:10 known to God who tries the minds and hearts, to God who weighs
Prov. 16:12 the spirits. Often – we may imagine – forgetting food and drink, ignoring the body's needs, she would spend sleepless nights, her mind and eyes alike intent on Christ who was her whole desire, the object of her adoration. And often too she lived out the words of
S. of S. 5:2 the Song of Songs: 'I sleep but my heart watches'; for the body indeed slept, but in mind she watched, dreaming in the quiet of the night what she pondered on by day, so that, when she yielded her limbs to sleep, she would rest peacefully in the same flow of thought that had filled her waking mind. There where her treasure was,
Mt. 6:21 there too was her heart, and where her glory was, there was her
Mt. 22:37 awareness focused. She loved her God, who was her son, with all
Mk. 12:30 her heart and all her mind and all her strength: with all her heart,
Lk. 10:27 because she loved him with the full depth of her feeling; with all her mind, because her understanding was entire; with all her strength, because she carried out her charge with wholehearted intent. She saw with her eyes and dandled in her hands the word of life. Happy she to whom it was given to cherish the one who fosters and nourishes all creation, to carry the ground and stay of all that is, to suckle the child who fills the very breasts he sucks, to feed the all-

provider who gives even the birds their food! Round her neck clung the Father's wisdom and in her arms nestled the power that moves the universe. The little Jesus leaned on his mother's breast, and in her virgin lap reposed the eternal rest of the saints in heaven. Sometimes, his head supported on one or other of his mother's arms, he gazed with tranquil air on her whom the very angels long to look on, and, babbling gently, called that mother whom every spirit calls upon in need. She meanwhile, filled with the Holy Spirit, held her son breast to breast and pressed his face to hers. Sometimes she kissed his hands and arms and with a mother's freedom stole sweet kisses from his sacred lips. She never tired of feasting her eyes with looking and her ears with listening, for was he not the one whom many prophets and kings desired to see, and never saw, to hear, and never heard? In consequence she advanced ever further in love, and her ardent spirit was ceaselessly intent on the eyes of the infant God. For love of her child she feared neither toil, suffering nor danger; neither want, need, terror, death, nor the fury of a wicked king and the flight into Egypt and back. In her daily work she was supremely cheerful, prompt, obliging and devoted, no slave was humbler than she. All she did was well and actively and wisely done, for as in contemplation there was none to match her, so in the active life her like could not be found.

But where is all this leading? To the recognition that we are overmatched and happy to be so. What we have reached out towards is way above us, and we fall far short. Let us therefore return to ourselves and wash our faults with tears. Let us ask the mother of compassion, by the hidden joy and the ineffable love won for her by a unique privilege, to accord to us the benefits of a mother's tenderness and implore for our aberrations the mercy of her very own son, who lives and reigns with the Father and the Holy Spirit, God for ever and ever. Amen.

Lk. 1:41

Lk. 10:24

AELRED OF RIEVAULX

St Aelred of Rievaulx was born in 1110 in Northumbria, a province keenly aware of its own identity and past glories. Chief among these was the succession of holy men who nurtured, until the coming of the Norsemen, the Christianity brought from Iona by Aidan the Irishman in the seventh century. With these spiritual forebears Aelred felt a close kinship. His father and grandfather had been married priests at Hexham, where the bones of the abbots Acca, Eata and Alchmund lay in Wilfrid's foundation. He himself had a deep devotion to St Cuthbert, dating perhaps from school-days in Durham. His temporal allegiance lay on both sides of a still shifting border, for, though of 'fine old English stock', he had spent much of his formative years in the entourage of David I of Scotland, taken from school to be companion to the king's stepson Waltheof and the heir, Prince Henry. He was twenty-two when David made him his steward, and he was clearly marked out for high office, but life at court could not still his spiritual hunger, and a chance conversation during a journey on the king's business was enough to turn him from the road so well mapped out and send him riding down the steep track to Rievaulx.

The Cistercian abbey of Rievaulx had been founded from Clairvaux in 1132. We have Aelred's word for it that by 1143 it comprised three hundred souls, counting monks, lay brothers and hired servants, and, according to Walter Daniel, his biographer, these numbers doubled again during Aelred's abbacy. It was a huge community, therefore, over which Aelred came eventually to rule, and much of his time as abbot must have been taken up with the administrative duties that he had learned to shoulder as the king's steward. He had eight years as a choir monk, free to devote himself to prayer and the study of Scripture – a time he was often to recollect with nostalgia – before being sent to Rome on a diplomatic mission by Abbot William. On his return he was appointed novice master, and a year later was elected abbot of St Lawrence at Revesby in Lincolnshire. His tenure was short: by 1147 he was back at Rievaulx as abbot, an office he was to hold until his death almost twenty years later.

For half of that period his health was so bad that a special dispensation of the General Chapter accommodated the rigours of the Rule to his frailty. He none the less travelled extensively in England and Scotland as visitor to the four daughter houses of Rievaulx and on ecclesiastical business, which took him on occasion as far as Westminster. Abbots were also in principle obliged to attend the yearly meetings of the General Chapter; we must therefore assume that Aelred travelled to Cîteaux, while health permitted, a number of times. For a man as infirm as he, long journeys on horseback – or even in a litter – over bad roads and often in bad weather must have been arduous in the extreme, and the comforts were not always great at the other end. In the daughter house at Dundrennan in Galloway he and his suite had to sleep in an ill-thatched hovel where the abbot's bed was the only one to remain providentially dry through the unrelenting Lowland rain.

Walter Daniel tells us that Rievaulx prospered greatly under Aelred's rule. While it is true that his abbacy coincided with the period of greatest expansion of the Order, his personality was an important factor in drawing recruits. A pen portrait sketched while his memory was still fresh shows why he was not only revered but widely and deeply loved:

He did not attain to great knowledge of the liberal arts at school, but by his own efforts and the exercise of the keen and subtle mind he had, he became more cultured than many who are steeped in secular learning. He had trained his faculties in the study of the Scriptures and left behind him for posterity a lasting monument in the form of distinguished books and treatises, as edifying as they were lucidly written, for he was filled with the spirit of wisdom and understanding. He was moreover a man of the highest integrity, wise in the ways of the world, witty, eloquent, a pleasant companion, generous and discreet. At the same time no prelate of his day was as gentle and patient as he, or sympathized so deeply with the physical and moral infirmities of others.[1]

Many of these qualities are exemplified in the Life; all are amply confirmed by Aelred's own writings, beginning with his best-known work, *The Mirror of Charity*, written at St Bernard's behest during his time as novice master. The last fourteen years of his life saw the publication of four treatises on the spiritual life, a large number of sermons, including a series on Isaiah, and three short historical works: a Life of Edward the Confessor, a genealogy of the kings of England, and an account of the Battle of the Standard, an English victory over the Scots won in 1138. These writings reflect the interests of the king's man as well as the experience of the monk. Aelred left no baggage at the gate when he entered Rievaulx; he took it all with him and it underwent the same maturing and refining process as the man himself, issuing twenty years later in works of a rare spread.

He was above all a man of peace, and had the happiness in his later years of seeing the promise of a new order and stability. In 1154, after fifteen years of anarchy and civil war, Henry Plantagenet succeeded Stephen. His overriding virtue in Aelred's eyes was the descent from King Alfred that he shared with David. Legitimacy, after the Norman interregnum, was restored. The following year he saw the relics of his holy forerunners solemnly enshrined in the restored church at Hexham, and marked the event with an account of their lives. In 1163 Edward the Confessor was even more solemnly enshrined at Westminster at the instigation of the new king, Henry. All these events both marked and fostered the healing of wounds, and Aelred, whose contribution to the process had been not insignificant, could properly recite his Nunc Dimittis.

From *The Life of Aelred* by Walter Daniel

Walter Daniel tells us that he was seventeen years at Rievaulx under Aelred's rule, which would make him probably a little over forty at the time of the abbot's death. He was a man of more education than most, though there is no indication that he went further than York or Durham to acquire it. Referred to as 'magister Walterus', he had his licence to teach, yet he was an instructed rather than a learned man. He writes of his father, also a monk at Rievaulx, as dominus *Daniel, which leads Powicke to believe that he was of knightly origin. The son may have been the infirmarer at Rievaulx, and as such a monk of standing in the community. A prolific writer, all that remains of his works is a list of titles in a library catalogue, a collection of Sentences and the Life of Aelred. That Life survives in a single manuscript and was unknown, except in an unattributed sixteenth-century summary, until it was edited by F. M. Powicke.[1]*

Walter set about his task as biographer soon after Aelred's death. He had his own knowledge to draw on and the recollections of older monks, his father among them. He had also the gamut of his book learning and a gift for verbiage to fall back on when information was lacking or scant. He covers the main events of Aelred's life, touches briefly, when at all, on his diplomatic missions, and wastes no words on the administrative duties that took up so much of the abbot's time. This is a pity, as he could have told us much. On Aelred's years at the Scottish court he provides us with scarcely any hard facts but several pages of inflated prose on his subject's supernatural virtue. Taxed with exaggeration on this and other scores by 'two prelates', Walter defended himself later by claiming that all good authors used rhetorical figures, among them hyperbole, and if his critics were too obtuse to realize what he was doing, they only betrayed their own ignorance.

As a biographer, Walter's failings, in a nutshell, are too few facts and too much rhetoric. Words come pouring out of him; convoluted sentences chase their tails while he revels in the fertility of his own invention. But while we regret what he does not tell us, and sometimes the length at which he fails to do so, there is much more in which to rejoice. He knew Aelred well, and over a long period. Indeed, he would have us believe he was the abbot's closest, if not his only, companion during his last years, but the absence from the Life of any mention of Aelred's many and deep friendships makes this claim a little suspect. Walter was none the less a loyal and loving friend with ample opportunity for observation, and the more he has to say, the better he says it, now and then striking a glowing spark off the anvil of rhetoric. He has an interest in the body as well as the soul, rare in a hagiographer, and can give a vivid description of what lies close to his heart. The account of Aelred's last days is admirably clear and moving. All in all, the abbot was fortunate in his biographer.

* * *

5   While Aelred was in the neighbourhood of the city of York, where business to the archbishop of that diocese[2] had brought him, he learned, by a happily timed report from a close friend,[3] how some two years earlier certain monks had come to England from across the sea. These remarkable men, famed for their religious life, were known as white monks after the colour of their habit, for they were clothed angel-like in undyed sheep's wool, spun and woven from the natural fleece. Thus garbed, when clustered together they look like flocks of gulls,[4] and shine as they walk with the very whiteness of snow. They venerate poverty – not the penury that stems from negligence and sloth, but a poverty regulated by voluntary privation, sustained by perfect faith and rendered congenial by the love of God. So strong is the mutual love which binds them that their society is as terrible as an army with banners. Trampling the   S. of S. 6:10
flowers of the world with the foot of forgetfulness, counting riches and honours as dung, battering the face of all things mutable with   Phil. 3:8
the fist of conscience, they renounce in food, drink, act and affection the pleasures of the world and the flesh. So, in abundance as in dearth, they run in their use of this world's goods an even course between the limits of what is fitting, and always present a consistent image of discretion, using only so much and such means of sustaining life as will just take care of the body's needs without diminishing the fervour of their worship. Everything with them is fixed by weight, measure and number. A pound of bread, half a pint of drink, a dish   Wisd. 11:21
of cabbage and one of beans make up their meal. If they sup, the

remnants of the previous meal are put back on the table, except that fresh vegetables, if any are available, are served in place of the two cooked dishes.[5] They sleep girded, one to a bed, in cowl and tunic winter and summer alike.[6] They have nothing to call their own;[7] they do not even talk together,[8] and no one undertakes anything of his own volition. Their every occupation is begun, or changed, at the superior's nod.[9] Great and small, wise and ignorant, all are governed by the one law, be it at table, in procession, at communion or in other observances and rites. Differences of degree are ironed out and each is on a level with his fellows, without anyone being singled out from the generality unless it be the man whom greater holiness raises above the rest; for the only distinction that exists between them is between degrees of goodness.[10] Therefore the humbler the man, the greater he is among his brothers, and the more lowly in his own esteem, the higher he stands in the opinion and appraisal of the rest. Neither women, hawks nor dogs, save those whose ready barking helps to drive thieves away from dwellings,[11] enter the gates of the monastery. The strongest of mutual loves sweeps from their midst the bane of resentment, every growth of anger and the murky phantasms of pride, so that, in the words of Acts 4:32 the Acts of the Apostles, they are united in heart and soul by the grace and love of the Holy Spirit.

Well, then, as I have said, these most holy men, trained overseas in their spiritual wrestling-school, landed safely on English soil and built their huts near Helmsley, the principal manor of their eminent patron, the lord Walter Espec, one of the foremost barons of King Henry.[12] They sited them on the banks of the Rie, a turbulent stream which flows through a broad valley, and site and settlement took their name from that of the stream joined to the word 'valley', hence Rievaulx. High hills surround the valley, encircling it like a crown. With their motley mantle of trees they offer pleasant retreats and ensure the seclusion of the vale, their wooded delights affording the monks a kind of second Eden. Spring waters come tumbling down from the highest rocks to the valley below, and, threading their way down narrow clefts and gullies, they widen out to rivulets and rills, uniting the murmur of their softly purling voices in a sweet concert of harmonious sound. And when the branches of the lovely trees clash and part with a rhythmical soughing as the leaves flutter gently to the ground, the blissful listener enjoys a wealth of jubilant harmony and his receptive ears are charmed by so sweet a blending of tumultuous sound, where each of the myriad different notes is yet musically equal to the rest.

* * *

Moved by his friend's enthusiasm and with an urgent desire to see for himself, Aelred, on leaving York, stopped overnight at Helmsley Castle, where Walter Espec welcomed him and took him next morning to visit his new foundation. After a second night at the castle the travellers resumed their northward journey, which passed along the brow of the hill where a track led down to the monastery gate. The pull was too strong: Aelred and one companion left the king's service and entered Rievaulx to stay. Eight years later David's steward was novice master and Walter at this point introduces the story of the wayward monk, which he weaves in and out of his narrative. That many then entered the religious life with a mistaken sense of vocation is not to be wondered at. The dilemma was whether to release them under a slur (the hand once set to the plough, the dog returning to its vomit), or to accommodate them without disrupting the community. Aelred's tolerance for such men was fabled and went well beyond what most superiors would put up with.

* * *

15   There came to Rievaulx at that time a secular clerk who was eager to acquire the name and status of a monk. He was received first into the guest house and shortly after into the novices' cell, where Aelred was his teacher. This clerk was thoroughly unstable, forever wavering between one thing and the next, and would bend now this way, now that, like a reed in the wind of his changeable will. The tender-hearted Aelred was upset by this, and in his pity for the man said to God in his heart: 'Give me this soul, O Lord my God, and deign of your grace to grant what little hope he has of salvation to your unworthy servant.' Ah, the effects of virtue and the infinite power of God's mercy! Not long after, that brother, who had become difficult in the novice house and a prey to his own wrong-headedness, conceived a desire to go down into Egypt and renounce the good purpose he had already embarked on. So he came and disclosed his guilty secret to his teacher, explaining his inner turmoil and unfolding his perverse desire. 'Brother,' said Aelred to him, 'don't will your own destruction, for you won't

         Isa. 30:2
         et passim

achieve it even though you may wish it, and it is the height of folly to will the opposite of what all the saints desire. Indeed all men without exception want to be saved.' But, turning a deaf ear to the salutary warnings, he left the monastery, fatuously ignorant and foolishly untaught. Then, after passing through the outer enclosure, he wandered aimlessly all day long in the woods, and, coming just before sunset to the path by which he had left, he suddenly realized that he was back beneath the perimeter wall. His prophet, who had begged God for his soul, ran to meet him, threw his arms about his neck, kissed his face and exclaimed: 'Son, why have you treated me

Lk. 2:48 like this? I have wept many tears for you today, and I trust to God that, as I have desired of him and promised you, you will not perish.' Oh, how shall we praise you, man of mercy? For during the whole of that day he did not even tell the abbot about this aberration on the brother's part, fearing lest the holy father's severity might prove hurtful to the novice on his return, and trusting with a prophet's insight that he would benefit by coming back. And so it turned out; for through the selflessness of Aelred's prayer that brother ended his life clothed in the sacred habit, in Aelred's hands.

*   *   *

When Aelred went as abbot to Revesby, he seems to have taken this brother with him, so that he could continue to keep a fatherly eye on him.

*   *   *

22   During this period the brother I spoke of earlier, the one whose soul Aelred asked God to give him, consumed once more with the fire of his earlier restlessness, wanted to leave the monastery. He came to the abbot and addressed him thus: 'Lord, I am too light-minded for the burden of this Order. Everything goes against the grain with me, the daily chores and my whole surroundings irk me beyond bearing. The length of the night office is a torment to me, I often collapse under the manual labour, the food sticks in my mouth, more bitter than wormwood, and the coarse clothing bites through skin and flesh to the very bone. But over and above, my will is forever hankering after the world's delights, and sighs without ceasing for its loves, affections and pleasures.' Hearing this, that best of abbots replied: 'For my part I will provide you with more palatable food and softer clothing and allow you whatever indul-

gences a monk may have, if only you will persevere and bring yourself to live with me in the monastery.' 'I would not stay,' he said, 'if you gave me all the riches of this house.' 'And I in turn,' said Aelred, 'will taste no food until the Lord brings you back, whether you will or no.' What more? While the one runs to the gate to get away, the other enters his cell to pray. This kindest of fathers weeps over his son, bewails the fugitive with deep and heartfelt sighs, and refuses all comfort. When the assistant bursar, a kinsman of his, comes to him and says, 'What are you doing, crying your eyes out over that wretch? And have you really vowed to starve yourself to death if he doesn't come back?' Aelred replies, 'What is it to you? Do not, I beg of you, pile grief on grief. As it is I am in agony in these flames, and die I shall unless help comes to my son. What is it Lk. 16:24 to you?' The runaway, meanwhile, has arrived at the gate and would hurry through, but the empty air where the double doors stand open feels like an iron wall. Harder and harder he struggles to get out, and tries again and again to break through, but all his exertions are in vain and, willy-nilly, he advances not an inch. At last, in a fury of frustration, he seizes the hinges of the gate with both hands and, straightening his leg, stretches out one foot, but without managing to get it even as far as the middle of the road. At that, those present execrate the fellow's ingratitude to God and pay tribute to the love of their father Aelred, whose prayer made the air between the open gates into a barrier against him and prevented him from falling of his own volition into the pit of iniquity. He, meanwhile, contrite and in his right mind again, returns to his holy director, begs his forgiveness and pledges future constancy. 'Well done, my son,' replies the saint, 'welcome back. God who has brought you safely home has indeed been merciful to me'. Let all who have a special love for Aelred read this miracle over and over again.

*   *   *

Back at Rievaulx as abbot, Aelred still has the wayward monk in tow.

*   *   *

28   It was at this time that Aelred saw clearly in a dream what awaited that brother whose return to the world through the monastery gate he had impeded by his prayers. This monk had been sent

by the venerable Aelred along with Daniel my father and certain
others of our house to the abbey of Swineshead,[13] to enlighten it
with the Cistercian way of life, and was nearing Rievaulx on his
homeward journey. On the night before he was due to arrive at the
monastery gate, Abbot Aelred, whether dozing or sleeping, I do not
know – God knows – was lying on his bed, when suddenly a man
of venerable aspect stood beside him and said: 'Father abbot, tomorrow at the first hour that monk of yours will appear at the abbey
gate. See that he enters the enclosure, for within a few days he will
be struck down with a grave illness and will die in your hands.'
Having uttered this prophecy the soothsayer vanished, and the holy
man awoke from his dream. Night in due course gave way to day,
and at first light word came to the abbot that the subject of the
prophecy was at the abbey gates and begged the holy father to go
out to him. Gladly the saint got ready to go down to him, kissed
him affectionately when he saw him and, remembering his vision,
shed many a tender tear on his account. He bade the brother enter
and rejoice with spiritual joy, because 'Soon, very soon, you shall be
made perfect in glory.' Not taking his meaning, the other smiled
and murmured: 'What, am I to enter that unending death which is
the fate of the cloistered? No, no; at the very least, with your leave,
I shall go to visit my kindred for a month and enjoy with them for
that brief spell the good things of this world, and then indeed come
back to you again.' 'Not so, my son,' replied the father, 'come in
now, for I can no longer live without you, nor shall you die
without me.' And so with coaxing words he enticed the monk into
the monastery, and, when he was once inside, the abbot rejoiced
beyond belief and began to keep festival in the secret of his heart.
Some five or six days later his protégé fell ill. He lay prostrated,
bleeding continuously from the nose, and the community began to
despair of his life. The father meanwhile ran to and fro, comforting
his son and tending the invalid with sedulous care. A very few days
saw him oppressed with the pangs of death. The abbot was reciting
according to custom the solemn litany for the departing soul. But as
he prayed, forgetful of his vision, he neglected to take the dying
man in his arms; so it happened that he concluded the litany a first
and second time and was obliged to begin it yet again. At last,
recalling what he had seen, he took the man's head between his
hands and exclaimed, 'Saint Benedict, pray for him,' and, as soon as

2 Cor. 12:2

he touched the monk's head and uttered the name of the saint, the sick man breathed his last in Aelred's hands. But let us now move onward.

29   This man turned Rievaulx into a veritable stronghold for the comfort and support of the weak, the fostering of the strong and sound, an abode of peace and piety where God and neighbour might be loved in fullest measure. What man so crushed or scorned but found there a haven of quietness? Who ever came to Rievaulx crippled in spirit and did not find in Aelred a loving father, and all they needed of comfort in the brethren? When was anyone expelled from that house on account of physical or moral frailty, unless his wickedness was such as to offend the whole community or quench all hope of his own salvation? Hence it was that monks in want of brotherly understanding and compassion came flocking to Rievaulx from foreign countries and the farther ends of the earth; and truly they found peace there, and the holiness without which no one will see God. Certainly those rolling stones to whom no religious house   Heb. 12:14 would grant admittance came to Rievaulx, the mother of mercy, and, finding the gates open wide, passed freely through them giving thanks to the Lord. And if, in later days, someone presumed to take them loudly and angrily to task for unbecoming behaviour, Aelred would say to him: 'No, brother, no; do not kill the soul for which Christ died, nor drive away the glory from this house. Remember that we too are sojourners as were all our fathers, and the supreme   1 Chr. 29:15 and singular glory of Rievaulx is this: that it teaches us above all else forbearance with the weak and compassion for others in their necessities. And this is our conscientious conviction, that this house is holy inasmuch as it begets for its God sons who are peacemakers.' 'All,' he would add, 'weak and strong alike, should find in Rievaulx a place of peace, and there, like fish in the vastness of the sea, enjoy the blissful and limitless quietude of love, that it may be said of her: "Thither the tribes go up, the tribes of the Lord, a sign for Israel to give thanks to the name of the Lord." Now, there are tribes of the   Ps. 121:4 strong and tribes of the weak, and the house that has no patience with the weak is not to be regarded as a house of religion, for "your eyes beheld me, yet imperfect, and in your book shall all be written".'   Ps. 138:16

I must not omit to tell how Rievaulx, that blessed dwelling, grew under the holy father's rule. All that it contained he doubled:

monks, lay-brothers, hired men, farms, lands and chattels. As for
devotion and charity, these he increased threefold. On feast-days
you could see the swarms of brothers packed into the church like
bees into a hive; unable to move forward for very numbers, they
stood clustered together and compacted into what seemed a single
angelical body. So it was that, when he returned to Christ, our
father left behind him at Rievaulx a hundred and forty monks and
five hundred lay-brothers and servants.[14] His material legacy –
prudently managed – was sufficient to feed and clothe a larger
number yet and still leave a balance for those to come. When
receiving those who wished to enter the order, he would pretend to

Lk. 24:28 be going further, that he might be seen as giving way reluctantly to
the urgings of the brethren.[15] In consequence there were many
admitted of whom he had no personal knowledge, for he would
often leave it to the discretion and judgement of the others to accept
whom they pleased. Himself exceedingly diffident and indulgent
towards the weakness of others, he would never see anyone disappointed who appealed to him in the name of love.

31   During the last ten years of his life this most holy of men, on top
of his other ills, suffered almost continuously from the torments of
arthritis. So racked was he that I have seen him placed in a linen
sheet, its four corners in the grasp of as many men, and borne off
thus in mid-air to relieve himself or to a change of beds. He felt the
softest touch like a sword-thrust and would cry out from sheer
agony. It was this long torment that caused the General Chapter of
abbots at Cîteaux to make certain concessions in his regard: he was
to eat and sleep in the infirmary and make proper allowance for the
constraints of his illness – not that he was to hold his office as an
invalid, but rather that he might live the life and manage the affairs
of the community entirely as he wished. This applied to the singing
of mass in public or private, to his visiting the granges at his own
convenience, to the reciting of the hours wherever he chose in the
establishment, to his attendance in choir at times different from
those prescribed for other abbots, and to the general provision of his
church's needs. Accepting this liberal regime with diffidence, and
finding it in practice hard to bear with, he had a 'mausoleum' built
for himself next to the common infirmary, and there he took up his
quarters, surrendering the care of his illness to two brothers and
refusing with revulsion all dainties and superfluous fussing. The

building of this hut was a source of great consolation to the
brethren, who would gather there daily, twenty or thirty at a time,
and sit discussing the spiritual delights of the Scriptures and the
observance of the monastic life. There was no one to say to them,
'Get out; go away; don't touch the abbot's bed.' They walked and
lay about his bed, talking with him as a child will prattle to its
mother; and he would say to them: 'Sons, say what you like, as long
as you let no foul word pass your lips, no slighting of a brother or
blasphemy against God.' He was never prudish in his dealings with
them, after the fashion of certain foolish abbots who, if a monk
takes another's hand in his or says something that they take amiss,
demand his cowl, unfrock him and expel him. Not so, not so with   Lk. 22:26
Aelred. Seventeen years I lived there under his rule, and not one
monk in all that time did that most merciful of living men turn out
of the monastery. Four, however, left during that period without his
knowledge; but God brought them all back excepting one, in
conduct a true follower of Satan. Across one corner of this cell, so as
to form a sort of room within a room, he ordered a wooden
partition to be erected. Here he placed a cross and the relics of
certain saints, and set it apart as a place of prayer. And reflecting
how the guardian of Israel neither slumbers nor sleeps, he too, his   Ps. 120:4
vicar, slept little in his bed, but spent many hours at prayer in
that place. The slightest respite from his illness would find him there
on his knees, battering his heavenly Father with the prayers of a
contrite mind offered in the spirit of truth.

* * *

Letter to Maurice:[16]

* * *

Here the peace-loving Aelred, suffering from acute colic and tortured
by the stone, was one day miserably rubbing his painful limbs on an
old mat stretched beside the hearth. He looked like a leaf of
parchment as he sat by the fire, for his whole body was so contorted
that his head had quite disappeared between his knees. He was
plagued with a constant pain, which he fancied the warmth would
ease, and, as he rubbed his slight frame, you could almost have
believed that the tongues of flame were licking it. As he shifted this
way and that on his haunches, I, his son, was sitting alone with him

in dejected mood, for my soul was cast down and disquieted within me. In fact, however, the gnawing in my own mind, sharp as it was, troubled me less than the father's malaise. We two were sitting alone in the house when there burst in on us a monk in a perfect frenzy of rage. Bull-like of aspect and in the vilest of tempers, this man strode over to where Aelred was lying. Bellowing savagely and grinding his teeth, he grabbed with both hands one edge of the mat and, tossing mat and abbot with all his strength, he threw the father of at least a hundred monks and five hundred lay brothers into the fire among the cinders, shouting: 'Look, wretch! I'm going to kill you now, this minute, and it'll be a hard death I'll give you. What are you sprawled there for, you hypocrite, you fraud, you fool? There'll be no more telling lies for you, you're as good as dead!'

I flared up at the sight of this and, unable to stand by when the father was in danger, I rose in burning indignation against the bully and grabbed him by the beard, wishing to get even with him on the instant. The colossus followed up his assault on the father by hurling his vast bulk at me, but I, quick of mind and stout of heart, withstood him manfully and blocked his ill-intentioned efforts. Meanwhile some monks arrived to find the wolf standing over the sheep, or rather attacking the shepherd and, as it might be, tearing him with its teeth and devouring him with its savage jaws. Consumed with indignation at the sight, they would, in the heat of their zeal, have laid hands on that son of pestilence, but the abbot, heedless of his infirmity and mindful only of charity, forbade them, saying: 'No, no, my sons, I beg you, no, do not strip your father of his tunic of long-suffering. I am not hurt, nor am I shaken or upset, for it is my son who threw me into the fire, and by so doing has cleansed me, not destroyed me. He is my son, but he is sick. And I indeed, who am not sound of body, have by this sick man been made sound in soul; for blessed are the peacemakers: they shall be called the sons of God.' Then, taking his head in his hands, that most holy of men kissed him, blessed him and clasped him to his breast, and, just as though he himself felt no pain from his own illness nor distress from the injury done to him, he took pains to calm the fellow's ravings and soothe the groundless anger turned against him. Oh, the charity of the man, greater than many miracles! He did not order him to be expelled from the monastery, or beaten, nor did he have him bound or shackled as a madman, nor would he even suffer him to be accosted with a word of rebuke. 'Since it was against me,' he said, 'that he sinned, I, when I wish it, will avenge myself; and that will be never, for your father's charity must not be sapped, but on the contrary continuously perfected by such happenings until the end; and thus shall we be saved.'

* * *

48 During the whole twelvemonth that preceded our father's death his chest was racked with a dry cough, which, coming on top of his many and various ailments, so weakened, fagged and exhausted him that sometimes on returning from the church to his cell after solemn mass he would lie inert on his pallet for upwards of an hour, unable to speak or move. The cough was not brought on by catarrh descending, but by a general hoarseness caused by a dryness and constriction extending from the front of the throat down the whole length of the gullet. This obstructed the normal passage of his breath, an interference that, so to speak, almost prevented the flow and ebb of life to and from the heart, except for the slight transference of breath that took place along what might be termed the hidden bypaths of the nostrils. Moreover, a rigor stemming from the brain and spreading to the back of the eyes, the forehead and the whole head caused him such pain that he could not stand for an instant the weight of anything placed on him from the crown of his head to his toes. It was in fact my view that all this tightness of the chest and difficulty in breathing sprang from a rare distemper in the head, which brought on a fresh attack of fever. This in turn set up an irritation along with the rasping of the throat whenever the diaphragm was convulsed with coughing; for he felt a weight on his chest, his tongue was rough and the larynx ulcerated and constricted, while his throat burned with acute thirst.

He bore this discomfort for a whole year, as I have said, until at last on Christmas Eve not only did his physical torments greatly worsen and his illness begin to disrupt his daily living, but an intense and unconquerable longing seized his spirit to depart and be with Christ, which led him to say: 'Brothers, to be with Christ is by far the best. And how much longer, anyway, shall I be able to endure this excruciating affliction of the flesh? Therefore I wish and crave that God, if it please him, may swiftly free me from this prison and bring me to a place of ease, where I may dwell with him in the   Phil. 1:23
Ibid.

Ps. 65:12

Ps. 41:5 place of his wondrous tabernacle.' When the brethren heard these words – spoken, as they were, in chapter – there was sighing and weeping. And why? Because they saw without shadow of doubt that in their father body and spirit were now of one accord, and this brought home to his sons that he would be leaving them for good. That day, having edified them greatly by his witness to the word of God, he returned to his cell.

49 He came to vespers and again, in the night, to matins, and next morning in chapter he preached to us a sermon crowned with a proem of deep humility, which came from the heart and cost him dear in bodily fatigue. He was present too at mass and at vespers that day, sitting by the sanctuary steps. After vespers he was received back in his cell and laid on his bed by his attendants. There he lay for some two hours, apparently unconscious and half dead; whereupon I came in and saw our father sweating with anguish, his pale face flushed, eyes watering and nostrils twitching, his lips compressed between his teeth. 'Truly,' I said to one of the brothers, 'the lord abbot is in much pain now; for these bodily changes are signs of great suffering.' Then Aelred, gazing on me sweetly – he was the sweetest of men – said: 'Yes, my son, yes, yes, you are right, I am cruelly racked by this illness, but soon, the Lord Jesus willing, all these troubles will be at an end.' At that hour certain brothers were anxious to talk to him about the business of the house and were standing round the bed. He asked me to tell them that he had not breath enough to frame his words and was too tired to attend to anything, which I did, not without tears.

During the night he felt somewhat easier and the next day met my coming with a cheerful look and the words: 'Yesterday, my son, we were confused and could speak but little, which grieved us much – most of all because we had no adequate words to comfort the brothers as we did two days ago.' But the night that followed brought the father great suffering, and to us an even greater, for while his was a physical pain, with us it was our grief-stricken spirits that were racked on his behalf. From that night on, exceedingly frail in body but most valiant in spirit, he spun out his remnant of life, his physical strength ebbing slowly away but his mental powers untouched. As he lay in bed he talked constantly in gasps, and from day to day his body grew weaker, until on the third of January he ordered all the monks to be called before him and addressed them in these words: 'I have often asked leave of you, either when I had to cross the sea, or was obliged to hasten to far-flung parts, or had occasion to visit the king's court. Now with your leave and accompanied by your prayers I am going home from exile, out of darkness into light, from this evil world to God, for the time is now come when he who redeemed me of himself without me, and deigned of his grace to bind me yet more closely to him by the bonds of a better life lived here among you, will take me to himself. It is enough,' he added, 'to have lived this long, for we have a good Lord and my soul is happy now to come before his face. May he himself keep you ever holy and deliver you from all evil, and may he who does not forsake his saints be mindful of you always, our God who is blessed for ever more.' 'Amen,' we answered, and that kindest of fathers went on: 'I have lived among you with a good conscience, for as I lie here, at the point of death as you now see me, my soul calls God to witness that never since I took this habit has any man's malice or carping or quarrelling kindled feelings towards him in my inmost heart that proved strong enough to last out the day. Loving peace and having always at heart the salvation of the brethren and my inward quiet, I so ruled my spirit by the grace of Christ that no disturbance of my equanimity might endure beyond the setting of the sun.' These words had us all weeping, till we could scarcely see one another for tears; and most of all we wept when he, with tears in his own eyes, said to us: 'God who knows all things knows that I love all of you as myself, and, as a mother yearns after her sons, so do I yearn for you all with the affection of Christ Jesus.' Ps. 36:28 Heb. 13:5 Eph. 4:26 Phil. 1:8

51   He asked next for his glossed Psalter to be brought to him, along with the *Confessions* of Augustine, the text of St John's Gospel, the relics of certain saints and the little cross that had once belonged to Archbishop Henry of York[17] of good memory. 'See,' he said to us, 'I kept these by me in my little oratory and took the utmost delight in them when sitting there alone and at leisure. Silver and gold have I none, therefore I make no will, possessing nothing of my own; whatever I have and I myself are yours.' Regarding the election of his successor, he urged us all to be guided by the interests of God and not our own, and wished that the younger men might be led in this decision by the priors of the house and the older and wiser members. Then he gave us all his fatherly blessing and asked for that of God. Acts 3:6 Phil. 2:21

On the following day he was anointed with holy oil by Roger, the venerable abbot of Byland, and was fortified by the viaticum of the most sacred body and blood of Our Lord, which he received with tears, crying: 'Lord, I am not worthy that you should enter under my roof.' Afterwards his face seemed to have grown brighter and fuller, an appearance it kept throughout that day and the next until the second hour of the night. No solid food, however, passed his lips from the tenth day until his death.

Mt. 8:8

53   From the second hour of that second night after his anointing, his speech began to fail and he seemed detached from earthly things, as though he were already in heaven. He retained his five senses unimpaired to the end, though his words came brief and broken. All of us were as one in never doubting our father's passing to God, and in striving every one with pious zeal to do all we could to tend him in his weakness. Now twelve, now twenty, now again forty, now up to a hundred monks would be gathered round him, because we loved him so who so loved us. Blessed indeed is the abbot who deserves to be loved by his own as he was! And that he should be so loved he deemed his greatest blessing – he the beloved of God and men, whose memory is blessed for ever more.

54   As for me, I found it an awesome experience to wait by his bedside during those days, yet one which brought joys as well. Awesome inasmuch as angels talked with him, or so I fancy, though none but he heard them, and all the while, unless I am mistaken, he was replying to them; for over and again we heard him say 'Hasten, hasten', often gracing the words with the name of Christ, and in English too, for the word having only one syllable in that language it comes easier to the lips and is somewhat sweeter sounding to the ear. So he would say, to use his own words, '*Hasten, for Crist luve*'; that is, for the love of Christ, hasten. And when I said to him, 'What, lord?' he stretched out his hands as it were towards heaven and, raising his eyes like lighted torches to the cross that was held before his face, he said: 'Release me that I may go to him soon, him whom I see before me, the king of glory. Why so long? What are you doing? What are you waiting for? Hasten, for Christ's love, hasten.' To all who read these pages I say this: never in all my life was I so moved as by those words so often repeated, so awfully uttered, by such a man at such a time – a good man at the hour of his death. And these same words kept proceeding from his mouth for three whole days. Three days long did he drag out his life in

slow, gasping breaths, for so strong was the spirit housed in his frail body that, even when that body failed, he was scarcely able to yield himself to death.

55   During that time a member of our community, one indeed of the abbot's attendants, was sleeping flat out from exhaustion, when suddenly our father appeared to him, ill as he then was, and said: 'Brother, when do you think I shall depart?' To which the other replied: 'Lord, I do not know.' Then the father said again: 'On the day before the Ides of January, my soul, the handmaid of the Lord, will leave the earthly home it has dwelt in until now.' And it happened exactly as the abbot had foretold; for on the second day after the brother had heard this in his sleep from the father's lips, the father left the body.   Lk. 1:38

56   The day before he died, the abbot of Fountains and Roger, abbot of Byland were with him, together with nearly all the monks and several of the lay-brothers. One of the brothers was reading the story of Our Lord's Passion, while he listened, unable any longer to frame intelligible words. But whenever mention was made of Our Lord's humility, or the faithfulness of the disciples, being past speech he would eloquently express his delight in the reading with gestures of the hands, and now and then his lips would form the likeness of a truly spiritual smile. At other places, however, as where Peter denies Christ, or the Jews accuse him, or Pilate gives the nod, or the soldier crucifies him, he would weep and indicate with his fingers the cruelty of the act, and his face would grow long with grief. As this went on you could have seen the whole community at one in the expression of joy or sorrow, as laughter and tears, jubilation and sighs proceeded in perfect unison, with but one voice among us for the utterance of grief or gladness. For it was a kindness to rejoice with the father, and a kindness too to mourn with him, since it behoves a son to lament his father's death, and no less to rejoice with that same father when he enters into his joy.   Mt. 25:21, 23

57   I sat with him on that day and held his head in my hands, while the others were sitting a little farther off. I said to him in a low voice so that no one should remark us: 'Lord, look on the cross and let your eyes rest where your heart is.' And at once raising his eyelids and turning his pupils to the figure of truth depicted on the wood, he said to him who suffered death for us on the tree: 'You are my God and my Lord, my refuge and my saviour, you are my glory and

Lk. 28:46 my hope for ever more. Into your hands I commend my spirit.' He spoke these words as clearly as they are written, although it was two days since he had spoken so many at once, nor did he after speak three words together. Indeed the very next night his breath began to come more slowly, and he lay thus until close on the fourth watch. Then, when we realized he was at the point of death, he was laid, as is the monastic custom, on a haircloth strewn with ashes, and there, amid the great gathering of his sons, with the four abbots also present, he gave up his spotless spirit into the hands of his Father and fell asleep in Christ. He died about the fourth watch of the night before the Ides of January in the year of the Incarnation of Our Lord one thousand one hundred and sixty-six, which was the fifty-seventh year of his life.[18]

From On Spiritual Friendship

The treatise On Spiritual Friendship *is Aelred's most personal work, written, at least in the main, towards the end of his life. The work, which consists of three books and a prologue, is cast in the form of conversations between the abbot and three of his monks. The dialogue form, a literary genre like the letter and the sermon, is admirably suited to Aelred's purpose. It is a help in exposition ('But do tell us, Father, about such and such'), and the interlarding of the main bulk of the analysis with monastic backchat is a great enlivener.*

Aelred tells us that he wrote the treatise because of the importance that friendship had had for him since his school-days, when nothing had mattered to him so much as loving and being loved. Then he had found a mentor in Cicero, whose De amicitia *was on the 'essential book list' of the Middle Ages. Aelred digested it very thoroughly, and forty years on it still provided much of the background on which he embroidered a new and more rarefied design.*

The De spirituali amicitia *is personal because Aelred put so much of himself into it, not because the subject was in any way foreign to medieval man, let alone to medieval monk. Friendship between men is one of the great literary themes of the Middle Ages. The tree that was rooted in the pagan soil of antiquity burgeoned and blossomed in the new dispensation. By the eleventh and twelfth centuries the role of friendship in the world outside the cloister was hardly less important than within. From the sworn companionship of comrades-in-arms were slowly evolving the more complex bonds of chivalry. But Rievaulx seems little touched by cross-cultural echoes. Friendship for Aelred has its beginning and its end in God. His 'Christian Neoplatonism envisaged a continuous movement, from physical loves to those of the mind and heart and thence to the threshold of God. Even Augustine . . . separated decisively the love of one's fellow human beings from the love of God. Aelred saw no gap.'[1] It is not surprising that*

Aelred had come to find his beloved Cicero inadequate. And not only Cicero. There is a revealing exchange where Walter quotes a passage of St Augustine describing the commerce of friends in terms with which we could all identify and to which we might all aspire. Walter refers to Augustine as 'tuus Augustinus' and clearly expects to score a hit. Aelred dismisses friendship thus defined as 'adolescent': there can be no spiritual friendship between two people without Christ as a third on whom each of the other two is centred. As Gratian says with a hint of discouragement, such friendship is not of the common sort. It is a counsel of perfection offered to those who have set themselves to seek it.

*   *   *

PROLOGUE

When I was still a boy in the schools and being liked by my companions was my chief delight, among the tendencies and frailties which are the particular temptations of that age, the pursuit of love and affection occupied my entire mind. There was in my eyes no greater pleasure, no keener joy, nothing more beneficial than loving and being loved.[2] And as I see-sawed between various loves and friendships, my spirit was swept this way and that, and, knowing nothing of the law of true friendship, was often deceived by its simulacrum. At last there came into my hands the book that Cicero wrote on friendship, which charmed me doubly by the weight of its argument and the grace of its style. And although I did not see myself as fit for that kind of friendship, I was none the less thankful to have met with a certain rule on which I might pattern my wandering loves and affections. When it pleased my good Lord to bring back the wanderer, to raise the fallen and to cleanse the leper by his healing touch, I abandoned worldly aspirations and entered the cloister. At once I devoted myself to the study of the Scriptures, the mere surface of which had been more than my bleary eyes could previously encompass, used as they were to the murk in which I lived. As my taste for Scripture grew, and the scraps of knowledge that the world had given me staled in comparison, I found myself thinking of what I had read in Cicero's book and was amazed to find that it no longer held the same savour for me. By then nothing that was not imbued with the sweetness of Jesus, nothing that was not seasoned with the salt of Scripture could wholly capture my affection.[3] So as I turned Cicero's arguments over in my mind, I was looking to see if they might perhaps be supported by the authority of Scripture. I had read a lot about friendship too in the writings of the Fathers, and, finding myself incapable of loving spiritually as I wished, I resolved to write about spiritual friendship and prescribe for myself rules of chaste and holy love. I have therefore divided this little work into three books: in the first setting out the nature of friendship, its origin and cause; in the second putting forward its merits and the benefits to be derived from it; in the last elucidating as best I can how, and between whom, it may be preserved unbroken to the end. If anyone should profit by reading it, let him give thanks to God and entreat Christ's mercy for my sins; and, if he should judge it to be unnecessary or useless, may he have compassion on my plight, which has forced me to interrupt my thoughts on this subject with practical concerns.

*　　*　　*

A summary of Book I, the shortest:

While visiting Rievaulx's daughter house of Wardon, Aelred is approached by the shy Ivo,[4] who asks for his views on friendship and whether it can be brought into harmony with the pursuit of holiness. They start from Cicero's definition: friendship is agreement on things sacred and divine, accompanied by good will and love. Aelred insists on the eternal quality of true friendship, whatever injuries may be suffered. Ivo protests that such perfection is beyond him, but is reminded that no Christian should despair of acquiring virtue. There is a connection between love and friendship, but also a distinction between friendship, which is elective, and charity, which is universal. Friendship must be grounded in virtue and seek the other's good, else it is undeserving of the name.

Ivo asks about the origins of friendship. Aelred finds the desire for unity reflected in all creation. Man has a natural longing for friendship, but since the Fall friendship must be striven after by men of good will like the other virtues.

Aelred's panegyric leads Ivo to ask wonderingly if he is to say 'God is friendship.' Aelred answers that he would not hesitate to attribute to friendship anything that is predicated of love, as for example: 'He who abides in friendship abides in God and God in him.'

Books II and III have both been abridged.

*   *   *

BOOK II. THE BENEFITS OF FRIENDSHIP

AELRED: Come now, brother, draw nearer, and explain why it was that, while I was providing earthly food for worldly minded men, you were sitting alone and apart, now swivelling your eyes this way and that, now rubbing your forehead with your hand, now running your fingers through your hair, and looking by turns cross, querulous and recalcitrant.

WALTER: That is exactly how I felt. For who would sit patiently all day, letting those Pharaoh's agents have you all to themselves, when we, who have a special claim on you, so rarely enjoy your conversation?

AELRED: Ah, but those whose favours one hopes for and whose ill will one fears, they too must be humoured. And now that they are gone at last, the very irksomeness of the disturbance makes our present solitude the more delightful. Hunger is the best sauce for every dish. Neither honey nor spice gives wine the taste that a real thirst gives to water. And so perhaps our conversation now will serve you as a kind of spiritual food or drink and be the more welcome for the fever that preceded it. So go ahead and lose no time in airing what you were waiting to get off your chest.

WALTER: Very well, I will. For if I were to complain about the shortness of the time left to us, I should be making it shorter still. Tell me, then. Do you remember the conversation you had at one time with your friend Ivo on spiritual friendship, or have you forgotten it? Can you recall what you agreed on, the questions he put to you, and how much of all this you put down in writing?

AELRED: Ah yes, my beloved Ivo. His memory is so fresh, I hold him still so dear, that although he is loosed from this life's burdens – and he bore his share – he is not dead to me. I see his dear eyes smile at me, I hear his pleasant talk, till it seems to me either that I have accompanied him to a better place or that he is still living with me here below. But as for that little scroll on which I set down his questions on spiritual friendship and my answers to them, that, as you know, has been lost to us these many years.

WALTER: Yes, I know all about that. But that, to be honest, is the whole reason of my excitement and impatience. For I have been told by several people that the document was found three days ago and handed in to you. Do let me see it, father, please. I shall not rest until I have examined every aspect of the subject, including any overlooked in your debate. And every thought that comes to me and seems worthy of investigation I shall lay before your fatherly scrutiny for you to reject, accept or develop.

AELRED: Very well, do as you wish. But I want you to read what I have written when you are alone, lest it become public, for I might feel that cuts or additions were called for, not to mention corrections.

Walter returns after an interval, having studied Aelred's 'little scroll'.

WALTER: Here I am then, all ears. And if I hang so eagerly on your words, it is because what I read of friendship smacked so sweet. You gave so clear a definition of its nature that I would like you to tell me in detail the advantages it brings to those who practise it. Thanks to your cogent arguments I am in no doubt as to the importance of friendship, but a foreknowledge of the benefits increases the enthusiasm with which one presses to the goal.

AELRED: That is a great and weighty topic, which I am not qualified to treat as it deserves. On the human plane there is nothing striven after that is more holy, nothing sought that is more advantageous, nothing got that is harder of attainment, nothing experienced that is sweeter, nothing possessed that gives a greater return. Indeed, friendship yields a harvest both in this life and the next; its very pleasures give play to every virtue, its vital force roots out the faults and flaws, it tempers the ill wind and compounds success. In consequence there can be no true happiness for the man without a friend.[5] Those who have none to share in their good fortune or their grief, none on to whom they can unload their troubles, no one to whom they can communicate some sudden glorious illumination are like brute beasts. Woe unto him who is alone, for when he falls he has none to lift him up! The man without a friend is a man utterly alone. But what happiness, security and joy to have another self to talk with! One to whom you can confess a failure without fear and reveal unblushingly some progress that you may have made

1 Tim. 4:8

Ecc. 4:10

in the spiritual life; someone to whom you dare entrust all the secrets of your heart and in whose advice you can have confidence. But better still by far is the fact that friendship is at one remove from the perfection that is rooted in the knowledge and love of God; for our Saviour says in the Gospel, 'I do not call you servants, but friends', showing that human friendship leads to that of God.

Jn. 15:15

WALTER: Your words touch my heart and echo my own deepest desires. My longing for friendship is so intense that I don't see how I shall carry on living while I am deprived of a thing so good in itself and so prodigal of blessings. But it was your last proposition – that friendship is the highest step on the way to perfection – that virtually transported me to another sphere. Do please go into it more fully for me.

Oh, look, how opportune, here comes our Gratian,[6] a devotee of friendship if ever there was one, a man whose whole aim in life is to love and be loved – opportune for him, I mean, in case his very craving for friendship should lead to his being deceived by its counterfeit and he should end up taking the false for the true, the sham for the real, the sensual for the spiritual.

GRATIAN: I am grateful to you for your kindness, brother, in extending to a flagrant gatecrasher a belated welcome to this spiritual banquet; but had you been serious and not joking in calling me a disciple of friendship, I would have been summoned at the outset of the conversation, and not left to betray my eagerness so shamelessly. But carry on, father, with what you had begun, and set something on the board for me. If I am not to get my fill like Walter (who, after devouring I don't know how many dishes, has now condescendingly admitted me to his leftovers), let me at least refresh myself a little.

AELRED: Don't worry, my son, there is more than enough remaining to be said in praise of friendship. If you heard a man of wisdom carry on where we left off, you would think we had not even broached the subject. Listen, though, to a word or two on friendship as a stepping-stone to the love and knowledge of God.

In friendship there is nothing base, no hypocrisy and no pretence. In substance it is holy, spontaneous and true, and this too is the nature of love. But friendship has this surpassing privilege: when two are joined in friendship, they can count on happiness, tranquillity of mind and the delights of pleasant intercourse ensuing, while there are many whom charity teaches us to love who are a burden and a plague to us, and others for whom we have a genuine unfeigned regard, yet whom we none the less do not admit to intimacy. In friendship, on the other hand, integrity and pleasure, truth and happiness, desire and reality are one, and all have their beginning, their continuance and their end in Christ.

GRATIAN: Such friendship, I can see, is not of the common sort, nor such as we used to dream of. I don't know what Walter's views have been until now. Personally I thought that friendship was when two individuals had one will between them, to the extent that neither wanted anything the other did not want;⁷ indeed, so complete was their agreement on what was good and what was evil that nothing that belonged to either, were it breath, wealth, honour or anything whatever, would be denied the other, to use or misuse at his own discretion.

WALTER: What I remember learning from that earlier dialogue was very different. The definition of friendship given and developed there encouraged me strongly, and rightly, to look higher for its benefits. But having covered that point, what we now want is for you to fix for us the goal and the limits of friendship, chiefly of course for Gratian's benefit, in case, following the bent of his name, he should slide from graciousness to viciousness.

GRATIAN: I am so grateful to you for your concern, and might return the kindness promptly and with interest were I less keen on the discussion and didn't think we would both do better to listen to reverend father's answer to your question.

AELRED: Christ himself fixed the ideal to be attained in friendship when he said: 'Greater love has no man than this, that a man lay down his life for his friends.' That ought to be the extent of love Jn. 15:13 between friends: one should be ready to die for the other. Does that satisfy you?

GRATIAN: Since friendship could go no further, how could it not satisfy us?

WALTER: What if evil-doers engaged in crime and villainy love one another enough to die for each other? Are we to believe that they have attained to the heights of friendship?

AELRED: Certainly not! Friendship cannot exist between evil men.

GRATIAN: Explain to us, please, what kind of men it takes to initiate or to foster friendship.

AELRED: Briefly, the rule is this: good men will see its budding, better men its flowering, the perfect its perfecting.

GRATIAN: What hope of friendship for us then, who are not even good?

AELRED: I do not define goodness so strictly as some; they consider no man good unless he is already perfect. For me, a man who lives a sober, upright and godly life in this world, as best our mortal flesh will let him, who will neither solicit nor consent to a dishonourable act – he is a good man, and I have no doubt that friendship among such men can both arise and be brought to its perfecting.

WALTER: I am inclined to agree with those who say that friendship with its inevitable burden of worries, cares, fears and griefs is something to beware of. We each of us shoulder a big enough weight of private care, and it is a foolish man – so they say – who gets himself so involved with others as to multiply the anxieties and worries that afflict him.

AELRED: Cicero deals beautifully with this. Those men, he says, who ban friendship from their lives remove as it were the sun from the earth, for of all God's gifts to us it is the best and happiest.[8] What sort of wisdom is it that shrinks from friendship in order to be free of worry, care and fear? What a fool was Paul, then, for whom living was bearing others' burdens, and this with the understanding born of charity, for him the greatest of all virtues. He took on himself the weakness of the weak, he waxed indignant on behalf of the offended, he knew great sorrow and unceasing anguish in his heart for his own people. As for those who say one should live perfectly detached – uncomforted, unbothered, loving so little that one takes no pleasure in another's good, so little loved that one's bad behaviour leaves no scars behind – those I would call beasts, not men at all.

WALTER: Since it is certain that many are deceived by the semblance of friendship, I wish you would explain what sort of friendships we should avoid, and which we should seek, foster and conserve.

AELRED: Very well, I shall briefly list those we ought to shun. First, the adolescent friendship, the product of roving and undisciplined feelings, which stretch out their tentacles towards every passer-by; a friendship without reason, weight or measure, that takes no account of others' good or detriment. This kind of love affects

Titus 2:12

1 Cor. 9:22
2 Cor. 11:29
Rom. 9:2-3

one very powerfully for a time, it captivates and flatters. But affection devoid of rationality is an animal impulse leading to all that is unlawful; indeed it is incapable of distinguishing between what is and is not lawful. Although affection often precedes friendship, one should never give rein to it unless it is led by reason, tempered by integrity and ruled by righteousness. Therefore the friendship we referred to as adolescent – because in youth feelings predominate and relationships are always unstable, wavering in their loyalty and with an admixture of sensuality – such friendship is to be avoided at all costs by those who are drawn to the sweetness of spiritual friendship.

Then there is the bond that unites the wicked, like cleaving to like, and which I shall pass over since, as I said earlier, it is not deserving of the name of friendship. Besides these, there is the friendship inspired by considerations of advantage, which many think should be sought after, cherished and conserved for that very reason. But such a criterion would debar a multitude of those most fitted for friendship, those from whose empty hands no one can hope to derive temporal benefit. Of course, if you place counsel in times of doubt, comfort in times of trouble and suchlike things among advantages, these indeed are to be expected from a friend, but should follow friendship, not precede it. For friendship is its own reward, and the man who looks for any other has not yet understood its true nature; and it is when friendship is wholly transmuted in God, and sinks in his contemplation those whom it unites, that this reward is fully reaped by those who cultivate it.

As for what should be yielded up in friendship and what endured, and in what measure, and as to the circumspection needed, there is no time to look into this today.

GRATIAN: I must admit that I owe a great deal to Walter, since it was his questioning that inspired you to discuss these matters and sum them up for us in a way that fixes them vividly and distinctly in the mind. Do please carry on and tell us something about the obligations of friendship, particularly what limits should be drawn and what precautions taken.

AELRED: Yes, there is more to be said on these and other matters too, but this is not the moment, for others are waiting now, as you can see, with pressing business.

WALTER: I am sorry to go and will certainly return tomorrow at the appointed time. Gratian had better make sure he is here early, or he will be taxing us with not bothering about him, while we accuse him of being late.

BOOK III. THE CONDITIONS NECESSARY FOR FRIENDSHIP TO CONTINUE UNDISTURBED

AELRED: And what brings you today?

GRATIAN: Surely you remember?

AELRED: No Walter, then?

GRATIAN: That's his affair. He certainly can't accuse us of being late this time.

AELRED: What subjects would you like to discuss then, Gratian?

GRATIAN: I feel sure that Walter will turn up. I admit I need his presence here; he is quicker to understand, more articulate in questioning and has a more retentive memory than I.

Walter comes in.

AELRED: Did you hear that, Walter? You have a better friend in Gratian than you thought.

WALTER: Since he is everybody's friend, he can't avoid being mine. But since we are both here, with your promise in mind, let us not waste this moment of leisure.

AELRED: The fountainhead of friendship is love; for love can exist without friendship, but friendship without love, never. Love can be inspired by instinct, by a sense of obligation, by reason alone, by feeling alone, and sometimes by the two combined. By instinct, as in mother love. By a sense of obligation, as when a benefit conferred and received unites both parties with a special affection. By reason alone, since we love our enemies not from any spontaneous inclination but urged by precept. By feeling alone, as when someone inspires affection in others solely by reason of such outward graces as beauty, strength and eloquence. By reason and feeling jointly, when he whom reason bids us love for his virtue wins our hearts with the sweetness of his ways and the charm of a life that merits only praise. Here reason and affection meet to give us a love that reason renders chaste and liking sweet. Which of these loves seems to you most fitted for friendship?

WALTER: Clearly the last, inspired by virtue and graced by sweetness of manner. But I should like to know whether all whom we love in this way are to be admitted to the very heart of friendship?

AELRED: First we must set this spiritual love on a firm foundation in which its beginnings must be anchored, and the greatest care must be exercised, when soaring to the heights of friendship, to keep within the established limits. This foundation is the love of God, to which all things should be referred – whatever love or affection may suggest, whatever one's inner promptings or a friend may recommend. And you must be very aware that any further building needs the closest scrutiny to see that it is adapted to the footings, and, should there be any excrescence, it is to be brought back within the norm and conformed to it. Not all those whom we love, however, are to be received into friendship, for not all will be found fit for it, since friendship is a twinning of minds and spirits where two become as one. Your friend is a second self from whom you withhold nothing, hide nothing, fear nothing. The first essential, therefore, is to choose someone whom you judge suitable, then to try him, and finally to admit him to your friendship. For friendship should be stable, unfaltering in affection, holding a mirror to eternity. That is why friends are not to be changed by childish whim according as we blow hot or cold. Since there is none viler than the man who violates friendship, nor mental anguish worse than being forsaken or attacked by a friend, a potential friend must be picked with the utmost care and tested with all circumspection. But once he is admitted to intimacy, you must bear with him, follow him, draw him after you, so that, as long as he does not withdraw irrevocably from the given basis, you hold all things in common, both material and spiritual, and are thus one in mind and heart and will and purpose. So you can distinguish four stages by which one ascends to the perfection of friendship: the first is choosing, the second testing, the third accepting, the fourth the achieving, through charity and good will, of total unanimity in matters human and divine.

WALTER: I remember your giving your approval to that definition in your first debate with Ivo. But since then you have discussed various kinds of friendship, and I should like to know whether it comprehends them all.

AELRED: Since true friendship can only exist between good men, men who are incapable of willing or doing anything contrary to faith or morals, obviously this definition does not embrace any friendship you like to think of, but only that which is true.

GRATIAN: What of the concept of friendship dearest to my heart until yesterday's debate: namely, an identity of likes and dislikes. Why does that not rate the same approval?

AELRED: In my view there is nothing wrong with that, provided the friends are men of faultless morals, regular life and ordered affections.

WALTER: Perhaps Gratian had better make sure that these prerequisites exist both in his own case and his friend's, and that their common tastes and wants are of such a sort that he could be neither tempted to solicit nor asked to concede anything wrong, improper or dishonourable. But about the four stages you mentioned: we are waiting for you to inform our judgement.

AELRED: First, then, let us talk about choice. There are certain character faults that, if marked in a man, would prevent his observing for long the laws and customs of friendship. Such men as these should not be lightly chosen – I speak of the irascible, the unstable, the suspicious and the over-talkative. None the less, if the rest of their lives and behaviour is pleasing, you should give them all possible help to overcome their faults and fit themselves for friendship.

WALTER: Yet, if I am not mistaken, we have seen you sedulously cultivating the friendship of the most short-tempered of men; and, although he hurt you often enough, we never heard you speak an unkind word to him as long as he lived.

AELRED: Some men who are choleric by disposition are yet so punctilious in their self-control that they never transgress the five
Sir. 22:27   grounds that Scripture gives for breaking off a friendship, although they may sometimes offend their friend by a thoughtless word or act, or by undiscerning zeal. Should we happen to make friends with such men, we ought to bear with them patiently; and, since we are assured of their affection, some intemperance in word or deed should be forgiven, or brought to their attention pleasantly, with care to spare their feelings.

GRATIAN: A monk who many of us fancy is your closest friend in the community, apparently moved by anger, both said and did something the other day which he must have known would be displeasing to you. Yet from what we see, he stands just as high in your favour as before. This left us somewhat dumbfounded, since you, as we were saying among ourselves, never fail to gratify his slightest wish, yet he will not put up with the least inconvenience for you.

WALTER: Gratian is a bolder man than I. I too was aware of all this, but knowing how you felt towards him I did not presume to bring the matter up.

AELRED: The man is certainly very dear to me, and, having once accepted him as a friend, I cannot withhold my love from him. And since in that respect I happened to be the stronger, it was easier for me to subdue my will than for him to master his. Since there was no impropriety involved, since faith suffered no injury nor virtue any loss, it was right that I should yield to my friend, both in bearing with his excesses and, where his peace of mind was threatened, in putting his will before mine.

Yet it is not only the highly irascible you should avoid choosing as friends, but also the unstable and the suspicious. One of the great boons of friendship is the confidence with which you entrust yourself to a friend, yet how can there be any security in the love of one who is blown about by every wind and assents to every proposition, whose feelings are like soft clay that can be moulded all day long into different and contrasting shapes? As for the suspicious man, he lacks the first essential to be sought in friendship: the peace and tranquillity of heart that each can give the other. You should therefore choose for your friend a man who is free from anger's fretting, who knows his own mind, is not eaten up with suspicion and does not cast gravity to the winds with idle chatter, and above all one whose character and conduct are compatible with yours.

WALTER: And where is one to find this man who is neither hot-tempered, unstable nor suspicious? The talkative of course are obvious enough.

AELRED: I grant you one is hard put to it to find a man who is not naturally subject to these failings. But there are many who have risen above them: who curb their irritability with patience, who cultivate seriousness as a check upon their levity, and banish distrust by fixing their minds on love. And the best-trained for friendship, I would say, are precisely those who have fought and overcome. The harder they have struggled against their weaknesses, the more dependable they are as friends.

WALTER: If one should incautiously rush into friendship with those whom you just told us to avoid, or if some of the types you recommended should either fall into the vices described or others still worse, what loyalty and favour would still be due to them?

AELRED: These situations are best guarded against at the time of choosing or in the probationary period, lest undue haste lead us to love the least deserving. Those who are worthy of friendship are loved for qualities inherent in them. Nevertheless, it does quite often happen that vices surface in those who have been tried and found worthy. Such friends should be carefully nursed back to health. Should this prove impossible, I think the friendship should be not so much broken off or sundered as, to use another's elegant turn of phrase, gradually picked apart.[9] There is nothing worse than open hostilities waged against someone with whom you have been living on close terms. Yet you may well have to suffer such attacks as these on the part of someone you once admitted to friendship, for there are men who render themselves unworthy of being loved by their own behaviour and yet, if something goes amiss with them, lay the blame for it on their friend. The relationship is damaged, they say, and therefore any counsel given them must be suspect. If they are exposed and their offences made public, having no other course open to them, they redouble their hatred and abuse of the erstwhile friend, conducting a whispering campaign, exalting themselves and accusing others with equal mendacity. So if you should be subject to such attacks after the breakup of a friendship, endure them as long as you possibly can, for friendship is eternal, as we read: 'A friend loves at all times.' If he whom you love wounds you, love him regardless. Even if his conduct forces you to withdraw your friendship from him, never withdraw your love. Work for his salvation in so far as you are able, have a care for his good name and never betray his confidences, even though he may have betrayed yours.

Prov. 17:17

And now, if you have heard enough about choice, let us proceed to the testing of friendships.

WALTER: A good idea; for my eye is always on the door in case someone should burst in and either put an end to our delights or introduce a disagreeable note or add some fatuity of his own.

GRATIAN: The bursar is there now and if you let him in you will not be able to carry on any longer. But I will guard the door and you, father, keep going and hold to your course.

AELRED: There are four things to be tested in a friend: loyalty, intent, discretion and patience. Loyalty means being able to entrust yourself to him in all security. Intent, that you expect nothing from the relationship excepting God and the benefits naturally inherent. Discretion means observing the fitness of way, time and place when giving or requesting, and when dispensing sympathy, praise or reproof. Patience indeed is needed neither to resent correction nor dislike or despise the man who administers it, but to put up gladly with some adversity for friendship's sake. But the most important quality of all is loyalty, which is friendship's nurse and guardian. In good or ill fortune, in joy or sorrow, in happy times and bitter, loyalty shows itself steadfast and unchanging.

GRATIAN: If no adversity comes to cloud our days, how shall we test our friend's loyalty?

AELRED: Although ill fortune provides the best test of loyalty, there are many other ways of testing it. 'He who is faithful in small things will be faithful in great' is a gospel truth on the basis of which Lk. 16:10 we confide certain secrets to friends of whom we believe some further trial is necessary – not all secrets, and not the most intimate; in the first instance some ones of slight or middling importance, whose concealment or disclosure is of no great moment. Yet the same precautions must be taken as if their leaking would be enormously damaging and their keeping of the greatest advantage. And if your friend be found faithful in this, do not hesitate to try him with greater things.

Again, we said that intent needed testing, and this is absolutely necessary. For there are many who value nothing, on the human plane, that does not bring in a temporal return. They love their friends as they might their oxen – for what they hope to get out of them – and are quite lacking in true and spiritual friendship, which is to be sought for God and for itself. This is how intent should be tested: if you see your friend more interested in what you have than in what you are, and always on the watch for what your efforts can confer on him in the way of honour, glory, riches, rights, then on the day you bestow these on a worthier man, or find yourself unable to gratify his wishes, you will soon discover why he stuck so close to you.

Let us take a look now at discretion. Some men perversely, not to say impudently, want their friends to be what they are incapable of being themselves. They are the sort who are intolerant of the slightest faults in their friends, criticize them fiercely and, with a sad want of discretion, neglect important things while making an issue of details; they make a mishmash of everything, never knowing what should be revealed to, or kept from, whom, or when, or where. This is why you should test the discretion of the friend of your choice, in case you associate yourself with someone improvident or imprudent and bring on yourself daily disputes and quarrels. It is easy enough to see that this virtue is essential in friendship, for whoever lacks it is like a rudderless ship, drifting erratically as the wind blows.

Certainly one should beware the sudden rush of enthusiasm which pre-empts sound judgement and deprives one of the possibility of testing. It is the part of a prudent man to hold back, to restrain this impulse, setting a limit to cordiality and proceeding step by step in affection until he can entrust himself entirely to the proven friend.

WALTER: I must confess that I am still impressed by the opinion of those who think that life would be simpler without such friends.

AELRED: You surprise me. No life could possibly be happy without friends, and the perfecting and extending of true friendship is the great and wondrous happiness that we look for in the life to come. God himself is at work pouring out between himself and the creature he has raised up, between the various hierarchies of his creation, and between each and every one of his elect such reciprocal friendship and charity that each loves the other as himself. Each, in consequence, rejoices in his neighbour's happiness as in his own, so that the bliss of each is shared by all, and the sum total of that bliss is everyone's. There no thoughts will be hidden and no feelings veiled. This is the true and everlasting friendship, which has its beginnings here and its consummation hereafter. And if such reciprocity is hard to come by in this world (since it is laid up for us beyond), should not our happiness grow according as we find it?

The day before yesterday, walking round the cloisters where the brethren were sitting, as it were a very garland of love, I was gazing on them as one might admire in paradise the leaves and flowers and fruit of every individual tree; and finding none there whom I did not love and by whom I did not believe myself loved, I was filled with a joy that soared above all the pleasures of this world. I felt my spirit pass out into all and their affection flow back into me, until I found myself saying with the Psalmist: 'Behold, how good and how pleasant it is when brothers dwell together in unity.'   Ps. 132:1

GRATIAN: Surely we are not to suppose that you have taken all the brethren who love and are loved by you into your friendship?

AELRED: There are many whom we embrace with all the warmth of our affection and yet do not admit to intimate friendship, which consists chiefly in baring our hearts and minds and purposes. Does not Our Lord say in the Gospel:'No longer do I call you servants, but friends'? And explaining the reason why they were worthy of   Jn. 15:15 the name of friend, he goes on: 'For all that I have heard from my Father I have made known to you.' And again: 'You are my friends   Ibid. if you do what I command you.' With these words, as St Ambrose   Jn. 15:14 says, 'he gave us the pattern to follow in friendship: to do our friend's will, to open our hearts to him and unbosom ourselves, and he in turn will make us privy to his secrets. So if you have a friend, bare your whole heart to him and he will do the same to you, for a friend keeps nothing back. If he is a true friend he pours out his soul as the Lord Jesus poured out the secrets of the Father.'[10] So says Ambrose. But think how many we love to whom it would hardly be safe to bare our inmost souls in this manner – all those who have neither years, understanding nor discretion enough to take the strain.

WALTER: Friendship such as that is so sublime and perfect that I don't dare aspire to it. The kind of friendship described by your favourite Augustine is good enough for me and Gratian here: 'to talk and laugh and to do each other kindnesses; to read and discuss books together; to pass from lightest jesting to talk of the deepest things and back again; to differ without rancour, as a man might differ with himself, and when, most rarely, dissension arose, to find our normal agreement all the sweeter for it; to teach each other and to learn from each other; to be impatient for the return of the absent and to welcome them with joy on their homecoming; these and suchlike things, proceeding from our hearts as we gave affection and received it back, and shown by face, voice, eyes and by a thousand other pleasing ways, kindled a flame which fused our souls together, and made, of many, one.'[11] This is our idea of friendship, and our conscience would prick us if we did not love where we are loved again, or return the love of those who love us.

AELRED: Such friendship is not of the spirit; it is characteristic of young men, young as were once Augustine and the friend of whom he was speaking there. However, provided no element of impropriety creeps in, we may tolerate it (idle talk and lies excepted) in the hope of richer grace, since it may form the basis of a more holy friendship. From such foundations, as devotion grows hand in hand with a zeal for spiritual studies, as age brings gravity, as the spiritual faculties are enlightened and the heart purged of dross, a man may take the next, close step to higher things, just as we said yesterday that it was easier to pass, on account of a certain analogy between the two, from human friendship to that of God himself.

But it is time that we looked at how friendship is to be fostered. The mainstay of stability and constancy in friendship is loyalty. There is no stability where there is bad faith. Friends must be open, direct and affable with one another, like-minded, moved by the same things – all qualities conducive to loyalty. A complicated and over-subtle person cannot be loyal. Nor can those who do not share the same feelings or opinions be steadfast in friendship or in loyalty. Beware above all of suspicion, the bane of friendship. Never think ill of a friend, never believe or agree with anyone speaking ill of him.

On top of that, we must see that our speech is agreeable, our expression cheerful, our manners gentle, our look serene, for in these lies friendship's far from negligible relish. A long face and an austere expression have a certain fine gravity about them, but friendship should be at times more easygoing, freer, sweeter, smoothing the way for affability and ease without levity or licence.

Giving to a friend should be done without reproaches or any thought of reward, without frowning, averting the face or looking down one's nose. Show him instead a serene face and a cheerful countenance, and intercept his request with a pleasant word; meet him warm-heartedly halfway, so that you may seem to give what he seeks without being asked. A delicate mind finds nothing more embarrassing than asking favours. And since you should be one with your friend in heart and soul, it would be totally wrong not to share one purse.

WALTER: What of us religious who can neither receive nor give, what grace can we derive from spiritual friendship?

AELRED: Seneca says that men would lead the happiest of lives if the words *mine* and *yours* were removed from their midst.[12] Holy poverty – holy because voluntary – gives in fact great strength to spiritual friendship. Since greed is the great destroyer of friendship, a newborn friendship has the best chance of survival where minds are freest of this poison.

But spiritual friendship offers other benefits by which friends can help and succour one another. First, there should be a mutual caring: friends should pray for each other, blush and rejoice for one another, each should weep over the other's lapse as though it were his own, and look on his friend's progress as his own. In whatever ways he can, he should encourage the timid, support the weak, console the sorrowful and restrain the hot-tempered. Moreover, he must respect the eyes and ears of his friend, and never presume to wound them with an unseemly act or an unfitting word. A becoming reserve is friendship's best companion: take reserve away from friendship and you deprive it of its greatest ornament. How often has a sign from my friend damped down or quenched the smouldering fire of anger, already on the point of flaring out! How many times have his graver features checked the undignified remark already on the tip of my tongue! How often when I have heedlessly dissolved into laughter, or fallen into idle chatter, has his arrival restored me to a proper gravity! Besides, if there is something that needs saying, it comes better from a friend and leaves a deeper mark. A recommendation must carry real weight when the giver is known to be loyal and yet not given to flattery. Therefore between friends sound advice should be given confidently, candidly and freely. Mutual admonishment is an integral part of friendship; it should be kindly and not roughly given, and patiently, not resentfully, received. For believe me, there is no scourge of friendships like flattery and complaisance, the characteristic vices of the light-minded and smooth-tongued, those who say what's sure to please and never what is true. So let there be no hesitation between friends, none of the pretence that is so utterly incompatible with friendship. One owes a friend the truth; without it the word friendship has no meaning.

This brings to mind two friends of mine who, although they have now passed from us, are still for me a living presence and always will be. As regards the first,[13] I was a young man still, newly embarked on the religious life, when I was drawn to him, so like were we in character and intellectual leanings. The other,[14] but a youth when I picked him out, was tested in many ways and raised to the heights of friendship when my own hair was already turning grey. The former was the companion chosen to share in the pleasures of the cloistered life and the spiritual sweets into which I was then being initiated, long before I was burdened with any pastoral cares or preoccupied with day-to-day concerns. I asked nothing of him, I gave nothing to him apart from affection and such proof of that affection as charity dictated. The latter, admitted already as a youth to a share in my cares, became a true helpmeet in my labours. Distinguishing between these two friendships with the benefit of hindsight, I see the first resting chiefly on affection, the second chiefly on reason. Then, too, the first friend was torn from me in the early stages of our intimacy, so that, although I chose him, I was never able to test him as we recommended. The second, who was mine in heart and loved by me from youth to middle age, passed with me through all the degrees of friendship, as far as our mutual imperfections allowed. It was the quiet observation of his virtues that endeared him to me first; for it was I who, having originally brought him from the south to this northern waste, gave him his first instruction in our rule of life. From then on he was the master of his body, and his endurance of toil and hunger made him an example to many and excited wonder. As for me, I gloried and delighted in him. It was then that I decided that he should be formed in the principles of friendship, since I saw that nobody found him hard to get on with; on the contrary, he was universally liked. He came and went at the beck and call of the older men, gentle, austere in manner and sparing of words, incapable of anger, a stranger to grumbling, rancour and detraction. All these things implanted him in my heart in a wonderful way and persuaded me to make of an inferior a companion, of the companion a friend, and finally my dearest friend of all. Between us there was no pretence, nothing counterfeit and nothing fulsome, no undue harshness either, no detours, nooks or crannies, but everything bared to view. I felt my heart to be in some sort his, and he felt the same of mine. For us, climbing undeviatingly towards the heights of friendship, reproof gave rise to no resentment and agreement was untainted by complaisance.

A friend to me in every way, he did his utmost to ensure my peace and quiet. He would expose himself to dangers and meet any difficulties halfway. Sometimes – for he was already ill – I wanted to make his life a little easier, but he forbade it, saying we must beware lest such indulgences be seen as the measure of our love, and it be ascribed to my human affection rather than to his need, and my authority be thus diminished. Thus he was as it were my hand, my eyes, the staff of my old age. He was the couch on which my Tob. 5:23 spirit rested, easing itself of all its pains. When toil had wearied me, I took refuge in the bosom of his love, and it was his advice restored me when I was plunged in grief or gloom. He pacified me when I was upset, he smoothed me down when I was angry. Anything unpleasant that cropped up I took to him, sharing the burdens that I could not bear alone. Well? Was it not a measure of bliss so to love and to be loved, to give and to receive help, to have that sweet brotherly love as a footing from which to soar up to the divine, climbing love's stairway even to the embrace of Christ himself, and then to descend again and take one's sweet repose in love of neighbour? If in this our friendship, inserted here to serve as an example, you see anything worthy of imitation, take it and use it to your own advantage.

But the sun is fast sinking, and I must bring our intercourse to a close. Let the last word be this: friendship proceeds from love. Who can love another who does not first love himself? For the love of neighbour must be patterned on the love of self. Now a man who asks or forces himself to perform a base or shameful action does not love himself. The first thing therefore is to purify oneself, tolerating nothing immoral, preserving whatever serves God's purpose. This is to love oneself, and one should love one's neighbour after the same fashion. But this kind of love embraces a great throng, from which one must select the man one will admit to the fullness of one's affection, to whom one will lay oneself open, baring one's heart and the very marrow of one's bones, one's inmost thoughts and purposes.

That choice should not be determined by fancy or feeling, but by a clear-sighted assessment of compatibility and the virtues to be admired in him. Then, in open-hearted enjoyment – but keeping levity at bay – one may devote oneself to one's friend, rendering him all those services that kindliness and charity suggest. Then comes the time to try his loyalty, his probity, his patience. A deepening exchange of confidence will gradually follow, a concentration on the same spheres of interest, and finally a similarity of facial expression. The affinity between friends should be so close that as soon as one sees the other his features take on his friend's expression, be it the droop of depression or the smooth contours of happiness. How right and proper it then becomes to grieve for one another, to toil for one another, to bear each other's burdens, when each finds his pleasure in neglecting himself in favour of his friend, in preferring the other's will to his own, in putting his friend's needs first, in setting himself in the way of whatever threatens. How delightful it is meanwhile to talk together, to confide one's aspirations, to try and ponder and weigh, and arrive at the same conclusions! And on top of all this, reciprocal prayer, which gains in efficacy with the depth of the affection that inspires it, accompanied by the tears precipitated by anxiety, released by emotion or called forth by grief. And while one is entreating Christ in one's friend's favour and seeking to be heard, one is stretching out towards Christ himself in love and longing, and comes the moment when suddenly one's affection passes from one object to another without one's being aware; and as though one were experiencing at close quarters the sweetness of Christ in person, one begins to taste for oneself the

Ps. 33:9, 99:5 delights of his presence. So it is that we ascend from that love, already holy, with which we embrace our friend, to the love with which we embrace Christ, thus savouring joyfully and freely the fruit of spiritual friendship; whose plenitude we look for in the future, when the mutual anxieties that beset us will have been wiped out, and the difficulties that we now must bear for one another's sake have been dispelled, when death's sting is no more and death

1 Cor. 15:55 itself destroyed – that sting whose wearisome pricks compel us so frequently to weep for one another – when security at last is ours. Then shall we enjoy that sovereign good for all eternity, then will the friendship to which here we can admit but few be poured out upon all, and thence back into God who shall be all in all.

From *The Mirror of Charity*

The Mirror of Charity *was written at St Bernard's particular request. Aelred pleaded his inadequacy, but Bernard would have none of it. The two men had met in 1142, when a delegation of which Aelred was a member broke the return journey from Rome to report to the Abbot of Clairvaux. Perhaps it was then that Bernard first asked the English monk to write 'some little thing to answer the complaints of those who are trying to follow the narrow way after a life of self-indulgence'. Some months later, after entreating, charging and commanding him to no effect, in the letter that stands as a preface to the* Mirror *Bernard ordered Aelred in the name of Jesus Christ to set down his thoughts on charity – its excellence, its fruits and its proper ordering.*

From the work that resulted, the first and perhaps the best-loved of Aelred's treatises, but one that does not lend itself easily to abridgement, I have taken the short chapter on liturgical music. It has been included partly for its content – it treats of an aspect of the monastic life passed over in Bernard's Apologia, *a work with which Aelred was certainly familiar and in sympathy – and partly as a nice example of rhetorical overstatement. Aelred, who never consciously indulged in 'fine' writing, allows his abhorrence of the latest musical trends to prove him by no means deaf to the music of words.*

*　　*　　*

OF THE IDLE GRATIFICATION OF THE EARS

II, 23　　Since we thought it best to exclude from our deliberations those openly given to evil ways, let us turn our attention now to the sort of people who pursue enjoyment under the cover of religion and make use, for their own self-flattery, of practices that served in ancient times to foreshadow the truth to be revealed. What need has the Church, I should like to know, now that types and figures have been superseded, of thundering organs, clashing cymbals and the monstrous heaving of the bellows? As for the voice, so naturally pleasant, why do we hear it now strangled and muted, now cracked, now at full throttle, now subjected to the constraints of elaborate three-part singing? Sometimes, I am ashamed to say, one hears it forced into a nasal whinny, or raised from its manly register to a shrill, womanish falsetto, or again, drawn out in a protracted, mannered warbling. I have seen monks with mouths agape, the sound cut off in mid-breath, as it were threatening the world with silence, and looking as though they were either at the point of death or lost in ecstasy, rather than singing. This ridiculous performance is accompanied by all manner of theatrical gestures: lips grimace, arms saw the air and fingers flex to greet each note. And this effeminate clowning goes under the name of religion. Furthermore, it is where the practice is most prevalent that God is held to be most honourably served. Simple people, certainly, are impressed by the swoosh of the bellows, the clash of the cymbals, the sweet sound of the pipes and the tremendous thunder of it all; but as for the wanton gestures of the singers and the lewd modulations of their voices, these are met with jeering and laughter, as being more suited to the stage than to the choir. There is no awe of God's dread majesty among those standing in his presence, no reverence for that mystical crib they serve,[1] where Christ, in hidden manner, lies wound in linen bands, where his sacred blood is poured out in the chalice, where the heavens are opened, earth and heaven meet, and men consort with angels.

Thus the practice instituted by the Fathers as a devotional aid, a help to human weakness, has been made into an instrument of pleasure-seeking. For sound is not to be preferred to sense, yet sense and sound together are, as a rule, an acceptable means of stimulating fervour. But the sound must be restrained and low-pitched enough not to draw the attention to itself, but to leave it largely free to concentrate on the meaning. Does not blessed Augustine say that hymns will move the mind to devotion, yet if the singer takes more pleasure in the sound than in the sense he is not above reproach? And again he writes of himself: 'When I find the singing more moving than the words, I confess that I have sinned grievously, and would rather not hear the singers.'[2]

Take a man, then, who has turned his back on such pernicious histrionics and embraced the moderation of the Fathers. If his ears begin to itch whenever he recalls those ludicrous performances, and the dignity of plainsong inspires him with an immeasurable loathing; if he gets to the point where he feels nothing but contempt for what we might call the Fathers' holy homespun, that style of singing instituted by the Holy Spirit through those who were his mouth-pieces, namely Augustine, Ambrose and, chief among them, Gregory, preferring instead what are known as the Spanish tunes, or God knows what fanciful inventions of latter-day schoolmen; if he yearns and pines and goes through agonies of longing for what he once jettisoned in disgust: what, I ask you, weighs him down like that – love's yoke, or the lure of the world oppressing him?

cf. Mt. 11:29
cf. 1 Jn. 2:16

THE CONSOLATIONS OF SCRIPTURE[1]

Brothers, however cast down we may be by harassment or heartache, the consolations of Scripture will lift us up again, for all the things that were written in former days were written for our instruction so that we, through steadfastness and the encouragement the Scriptures give us, might have hope. I tell you, brothers, no misfortune can touch us, no situation so galling or distressing can arise that does not, as soon as Holy Writ seizes hold of us, either fade into nothingness or become bearable. This is the field where Isaac walked in the evening meditating, and where Rebecca came hurrying towards him and soothed with her gentle charm the grief that had befallen him. How often, good Jesus, does day incline to evening, how often does the daylight of some slight consolation fade before the black night of an intolerable grief? Everything turns to ashes in my mouth; wherever I look, I see a load of cares. If someone speaks to me, I barely hear; if someone knocks, I scarcely notice; my heart is turned to stone, my tongue sticks fast, my tear-ducts are dry. What then? Into the field I go to meditate. I reread the holy book; I set down my thoughts; and suddenly Rebecca comes running towards me and with her light, which is your grace, good Jesus, dispels the gloom, puts melancholy to flight, disintegrates my hardness. Soon sighs give way to tears, accompanied in their turn by heavenly joy. Unhappy are those who, when oppressed in spirit, do not walk into this field and find that joy.

Rom. 15:4

Gen. 24:63-7

Pastoral Prayer

Aelred's Pastoral Prayer shows us an abbot reflecting on his charge and praying for the strength and wisdom to live up to his spiritual responsibilities and discharge them to the benefit of those in his care. It adds light and shade but no new features to the portrait drawn by Walter and the less detailed sketches left by Gilbert of Hoyland and Jocelyn of Furness. Aelred was not a man of surprises and his depths were not hidden, yet though his voice is much less varied, it is as unmistakable as St Bernard's. The Prayer, like the still more personal Meditations of William of St Thierry, was probably shown only to a few close friends. It too is preserved in a single manuscript, emanating from Rievaulx itself and written in the thirteenth century. The translation gives a slightly shortened version.

* * *

Jn. 10:11, 14 **I** O Jesus, O good shepherd, another shepherd calls on you, a wretched, unfit bungler of a shepherd; one who, for all his failings, is yet some kind of shepherd of your sheep. He calls, this bad shepherd, on you, the good, anxious on his own behalf and anxious for your sheep.

* * *

Aelred looks back over his past life and reflects on his unworthiness.

* * *

3 I confess to you, Jesus my saviour, my hope and consolation, I confess to you, my God, that, regarding the past, I am not even as contrite nor as fearful as I should be, nor in respect of the present as careful as I ought. And you, sweet Lord, have set up such a one as

Mt. 24:45
Ps. 73:1 me over your household, over the sheep of your pasture, bidding me who am so careless of myself to care for them, me, who cannot

even pray for my own sins, to intercede for them, and me, who have taught myself little enough, to be their teacher. Wretch that I am, what have I done, presumed, agreed to? Or rather, what have you, dear Lord, agreed to with regard to the wretch I am? I pray you, is this not your household, dearest Lord, your very own people, whom you have led out of Egypt for the second time, whom you have created and redeemed, and finally assembled from the four quarters to make them live a common life under the same roof? Why, therefore, O fount of mercy, did you commend those so dear to you to one, like me, beyond the pale?

4   Whatever your reason for placing me, or allowing me to be placed, unworthy and sinful, in this office, you bid me, for as long as I am permitted to occupy it, to watch over them and pray for them punctiliously. O Lord, it is not on the ground of my righteousness that I lay my prayers before you, but on the ground of your great mercy; and where desert is silent, the office speaks. So let your eyes be upon me, your ears open to my prayers. But because, according to the divine law, it is the office of the priest to offer the sacrifice first for himself and then for the people, first for my own sins I offer to your majesty this sacrifice of prayer, such as it is.

Dan. 9:18

Ps. 33:16

Lev. 9:7
Heb. 5:3

5   Behold, Lord, the wounds of my soul. Nothing escapes your gaze, which is living and active, piercing to the division of soul and spirit. You see, my Lord, without a doubt you see in my soul both the scars of past sins and the risk of sins present, as well as the causes and occasions of sins to be committed. All these you see, Lord, and I would have it so. Indeed you know, you who scrutinize my heart, that there is nothing in my soul that I want to hide from your eyes, even if I could avoid their gaze. Alas for those whose will is set on concealment: they will escape neither your gaze nor your punishment, but merely your healing touch. Look well at me, sweet Lord, look well. I place my hope in your compassion, God of mercy, for you will look at me either like a caring physician bent on healing, or as a kind teacher anxious to correct, or again like the fondest of fathers, to excuse and overlook ... May your good Spirit, Lord, come down into my heart and prepare for himself a dwelling there, cleansing it from every defilement of body and spirit and granting it an increase of faith, hope and charity, together with sorrow for sins and feelings of affection and kindness towards others. May the dew of his blessing quench the heat of every appetite, his power bring to

Heb. 4:12

Prov. 24:12

cf. Isa. 29:15

2 Cor. 7:1

heel all passions and affections that are of the flesh. May he grant me to work, watch and fast with fervour and discretion, to love and praise you, pray and meditate with effectual zeal, ever to act and think according to your will, and so to persevere to my life's end.

6 These things, O Lord my hope, I have need of on my own account. Others of which I stand in want touch not only myself but those whom you bid me care for rather than command.[1] One of the ancients once asked for wisdom to be given him that he might 2 Chr. 1:10 know how to rule your people. He was a king and his words were pleasing to you and you listened to his prayer; yet you had not as yet died on the Cross nor revealed to your people that wondrous love. Here, sweet Lord, stand in your sight your very own special people, who have your Cross before their eyes and bear in themselves the signs of your Passion. To rule over them you have appointed this your sinful servant. My God, you know my folly and my Ps. 68:6 weakness is not hidden from you; which is why, dear Lord, I do not ask for gold or silver or precious stones, but for wisdom that I may rule over your people. Send her forth, O fount of wisdom, from the Wisd. 9:10 throne of your glory, that she may be with me and toil in all I do and say; that she may order my thoughts and words and all my deeds and counsels according to your pleasure, to the honour of your name, to their benefit and my salvation.

7 You who know my heart, Lord, know it is my wish that whatever you have given your servant should be wholly and utterly employed and expended for them. And I myself, over and above, will gladly 2 Cor. 12:15 be expended for them. So be it, my Lord, indeed. My understanding and speaking, my leisure, my activity, my doing and thinking, my good and ill fortune, life and death, health and sickness – let absolutely all that I am, experience, feel and understand be employed and expended for them, for whom you yourself did not scorn to expend your very life. And so I pray you teach your servant, Lord, teach me by your Holy Spirit how I may spend my substance for them. Grant, Lord, by your grace, that I may bear patiently with their frailty, sympathize kindly and support with tact. Let your Spirit teach me to console the sad, strengthen the faint-hearted, raise 2 Cor. 11:29 the fallen; to be weak with the weak, indignant with the scandalized 1 Cor. 9:22 and to become all things to all men, that I may win them all. Put into my mouth true words and well-chosen, which will build them up in faith, hope and love, in chastity and humility, in patience and obedience – men fervent in spirit and devout of mind. And since you, Lord, have given them a blind man to lead them, an ignorant to teach them and an incapable to govern them, then, for their sakes if not for mine, teach the teacher, guide the leader and govern the man you have appointed to rule others. Teach me accordingly, sweet Lord, how to chide the restless, comfort the timorous, sustain the weak and adapt myself to the demands of each man's temperament, character, feelings and degree of understanding or simplicity, in whatever circumstances you provide . . .

8   O merciful God, my office obliges me to pray to you for them, love makes me want to and thinking on your kindness gives me courage. Hear my prayer on their behalf. You know, sweet Lord, how much I love them, how my heart goes out to them and melts for them. You know I do not rule them with rigour or dominate by force of personality. You know how I choose rather to serve with love than govern from authority, to yield humbly to their wishes and so to share their feelings as to be one of them. Hear me therefore, O Lord my God, when I ask that your eyes should be ever on them, day and night. Spread out your wings and shelter them, stretch out your right hand and bless them, pour your Holy Spirit into their hearts that he may keep them in unity of spirit and the bond of peace, chaste in body and humble of mind. May he Eph. 4:3 himself be with them when they pray and inspire the prayers it pleases you to grant. May the same Spirit abide in those who meditate, so that, enlightened by him, they come to know you and fix in their memory the God whom they invoke in their distress and look to in time of doubt. May that kind comforter be swift to succour those who struggle with temptation and sustain them in the trials and tribulations of this life. And may they, dearest Lord, always by the operation of your Spirit be at peace in themselves, with one another and with me; unassuming too, and kind, and among themselves compliant, helpful and forbearing. May they be Col. 3:13 fervent in spirit, rejoicing in hope, enduring poverty, absti- Rom.12:11– nence, toil, vigils, silence and monastic quiet with never-failing 12 patience. Drive from them, Lord, the spirit of pride and vainglory, of envy and melancholy, listlessness and apathy, despair and mistrust, fornication and impurity, presumption and discord. Stay in their midst according to your faithful promise, and, since you know the Mt. 8:20 needs of each, strengthen, I pray you, what is weak in them, spare Ez. 34:4

ISAAC OF STELLA

What little is known of Isaac of Stella has been gleaned from his own writings and can be set down in a few lines discreetly padded with conjecture. Born around 1100, he was of English birth, a fact that he came to regret when Aquitaine went with Queen Eleanor to the English crown, exposing the 'exile' to local resentment. Isaac had been drawn to France as a young man by the reputation of the Schools and may, like Geoffrey of Auxerre, have been a pupil of Abelard. It is likely, too, that he spent time at Chartres, along with Thomas Becket, whom he knew well and later championed. Whether he was professed at Pontigny or at the Savigniac foundation of Stella – l'Étoile – near Poitiers, which was affiliated to Pontigny in 1145, is uncertain, but he was undoubtedly abbot of Stella in 1147. He knew St Bernard and wrote of him with fine appreciation. At some time during the next twenty years he took himself off with a group of monks to the Ile de Ré in search of greater austerity and solitude. All the circumstances surrounding this episode are exceedingly obscure, and it is not even known whether he died there or returned to Stella. For an abbot to leave his monastery, whatever the reason, was very rare, but Isaac's many references to the venture in sermons preached or written on the island are proof of its having happened, and it is further confirmed by an undated charter of donation. He died between 1167 and 1169, leaving fifty-five sermons and two treatises in letter form.

If Isaac of Stella's life has shrunk to a couple of dates and a few hypotheses, his personality is quite sharply focused, thanks to his sermons. Like William of St Thierry, he was a man with a thirst for God that drove him ever deeper into the wilderness. For Isaac poverty was more than a means; it almost became an end. And yet to each the stark spiritual landscape that had beckoned as the gateway to the Promised Land appeared at times both flat and forbidding. William found his peace at Signy, in so far as peace is of this world; Isaac's itinerary is less well charted, but the first of the two sermons given here, so resonant with wind and sea, gives an idea of the course he steered.

Despite his years in the Schools, Isaac's theology is fundamentally monastic. Symbolic, figurative and rooted in Scripture, it has as its end and focus the sanctification of the individual. Yet speculation remained a pleasure to him, not an activity fraught with danger and tainted with presumption. He had an agile mind and enjoyed using it, seeking out different and sometimes surprising metaphors through which to explore the mysteries of faith. He would surely have approved St Bernard's dictum that the Bride of the Word has no business to be foolish.

Two Sermons

SECOND SERMON FOR THE FOURTH SUNDAY
AFTER EPIPHANY

'And while he was asleep there arose a great storm.' And what did
the Lord do here, dearly beloved, other than bring about, by
sleeping, the thing that would arouse the disciples from their spiritual
sleep? For it was while he slept that his power took effect, bringing
forth winds from his storehouses, and in the absolute silence of sleep
that the Word spoke, bringing home to the disciples the danger of
letting the master lie silent, inert and asleep. It is in times of quiet
that we learn wisdom, but not in idleness. Indeed there is nothing
busier than that repose, nothing more industrious than that leisure,
where we drink in wisdom and put our questions to the Word of
God. Martha toiled, Mary was at leisure, but not inactive or listless;
it was Lazarus who was listless and rapidly passing from inertia to
death, from death to corruption. How many are there today who,
freed from the benefits of manual work, inwardly lazy and listless,
with all their needs met, give their time to fantasies and musings and
have lost Martha's diligence without acquiring Mary's devotion? And
so it is that in Bethany itself – the house of obedience[1] – they fall into
listlessness and sloth. Poor wretches! Weak when strength is at hand,
foolish where wisdom abounds, blind in the light and dumb before the
Word, famished they waste away with the bread of life and understanding on the table. Of such as these is it written: their soul found
all food repugnant and they were brought to the very gates of
death. And just as the Lord allowed Lazarus to die so that he might
be raised from the dead, so too with the apostles in their apparent
torpor (or symbolizing people in that state) he chose to sleep, so that
their jeopardy, if nothing else, might move them to rouse him.

Mt. 8:24

Ps. 134:7

Lk. 10:39–40
Jn. 11:1

Sir. 15:3

Ps. 106:18
Jn. 11:11–15

He therefore fell asleep in body, they being withdrawn from him in spiritual sleep, and showed them in his outward being their inner state. But proving insensitive to this gentle and discreet instruction, they were given an outward and more brutal warning: the wave Ps. 92:4 arose majestic to reflect the majesty of God on high. Asleep, he gives in the storm a lesson to the complacent; aroused, he teaches in the ensuing calm those who have profited from the shock. Believe me, brothers, both storm and calm, his sleeping and his waking, are utterances of that holy Word. As he lies asleep, he thunders in the voice of the storm against sloth, sloth that results in thoughts in turmoil, a tempest sweeping irresistibly through the mind; awake and watchful, he commends with a calming word vigilance of mind and fervour of spirit.

We ought therefore, my brothers, to keep the keenest watch, our vigilance sharpened by the fact that we have chosen a yet remoter solitude, lest in the coracle of our inner man, to which the outer man is as the sea, the Word of God should sleep, who in himself neither Ps. 120:4 slumbers nor sleeps. If Christ is inactive, he cannot keep watch for us, and it is, in brief, his wish that we should be forever questioning him or entreating him, or at least giving our full attention when he speaks. For, brothers, if you start to fall asleep while he is speaking, he at once ceases to be awake to you. But woe to you if he sleeps where you are concerned! The wind is awake and watching, the sea is awake, the storm is awake, and the gale in your mind and the suck and surge of a thousand temptations, all will be watching for you if he alone should sleep. So pray to him in the words of the Prophet, Ps. 12:4 saying: 'Lighten, O Lord, my eyes, lest I sleep the sleep of death.' And indeed, unless you have already begun to fall asleep, he will keep a tireless watch for you. It was because Peter could not watch for an hour with Christ that he was able three times to deny him; for he had indeed been asleep when the Lord said to him: 'Watch and Mt. 26:41 pray, lest you enter into temptation.' Where are those who crumple over their books in the cloister, snore during the readings in church or sleep in chapter through the living words of the sermon? In each of these instances the Word of God speaks and is neglected. He who Jn. 13:13 is Teacher and Lord speaks, and man, the disciple, sleeps.

There are three essentials: reading, meditation and prayer. In a reading or sermon, which is a kind of reading, God speaks to you, Mt. 11:15 which is why he says: 'He who has ears to hear, let him hear.' In meditation you question him; you entreat him in prayer. Hence the saying: 'Ask and you will receive, knock and it will be opened to you.' It is prayer that asks, while meditation knocks at the door. Mt. 7:7 Those who have their faculties trained by the practice of spiritual discipline know what I mean. The natural man,[2] even if he leads an Heb. 5:14 outwardly spiritual life, has no apprehension of such things. I have told you repeatedly and want you to remember that, just as some live an outwardly spiritual life but remain inwardly in the natural state, others who live a carnal life have a spiritual understanding; others again are carnal both in their mode of life and their mentality; others are wholly spiritual. Now in these three exercises – reading, meditation and prayer – consists the entire formation of a spiritual understanding, together with a capacity for dwelling in spirit on a certain celestial plane where, like Moses on the mountain, we speak and listen to and converse with God as we might with a neighbour, Ex. 33:11 but in spirit only. Our form of life affords its own separate approach to God, for, 'draw near to me and I will draw near to you', says the Jas. 4:8 Lord. So it is that some, as I was saying, are close to God in their understanding and far away through the life they lead; with others it is the reverse; some are far from God in both respects and others in both respects close.

So let us keep watch, brothers, especially for the bane of listlessness, so often the product of a premature sense of security. The more advanced, easy in conscience, lie back as though the vices were already routed and there was no further cause for fear. The less perfect relax in the material security of a life where all their needs are met by others without effort on their part. That is why, dearly beloved, the holy Fathers, whose footprints on the steep and narrow track we men laden and gross, not to say fat and sleek, have made Dt. 32:15 bold to follow, made poverty the cornerstone in either wall of their spiritual building, discerning it as twofold and distributing it accordingly: on the one hand material poverty, on the other, poverty of spirit, so that, if any sees himself as deficient in one or other, he can give his attention to both and take care to neglect neither.

And this, dearly beloved, is why I have led you to this remote, sere and inhospitable wasteland. It was a shrewd move, for you can be humble here but never rich. And in this ultimate solitude, which, surrounded as it is by sea, has almost nothing in common with the world, you, deprived of all worldly and almost every human solace, may live without any echoes of the world, for apart from this little isle, this farthest speck of land, the world for you has ceased to be.

O Lord, my going was a flight, and in my flight I went so far that you alone know – for I do not[3] – where I might find a farther spot to flee to. Filled with a great desire to flee and thirsting after solitude, I finally fetched up one day in this remote and empty waste, where some of my – if I may term them so – confederates in this venture left me and very few held fast, and even these have a dread of the very horror of solitude, a dread that I confess I feel at times myself. Solitude was heaped on solitude, O Lord, and silence upon silence. For in order to be more fluent and at ease with you alone, we forced and forced ourselves again to keep silence with each other. But the main thing, dearly beloved, is for us to fix our minds in thanksgiving and praise on the mercy, passing all our hopes, that God has showered on us in deigning to arrange for us this place of exile, which sets us free to pray and meditate and read, yet compels us to work so that we do not lack the wherewithal to give to those in need, in this instance our still physical bodies. For it is indeed in the sweat of our own brows, rather than that of servants or oxen that we have to eat our bread.

And so, brothers, companions of my captivity and flight, as the Prophet says: 'You who keep the Lord in remembrance, do not be mute nor keep silence with him.' Be alert to him, so as not to find him sleeping. As for me, Lord, I will always cry to you. Do not you, my God, keep silence with me, lest, if you stay silent, I become like those in peril at sea. When I knock in meditation, open; when I question, answer; when I entreat you, hear my prayer. That you will surely do, liberally and most kindly, unless I should have shut my ears to you when you were speaking. When we listen, you give ear; when we heed you, you pay heed; but whoever refuses to listen to your law, his very prayer is an abomination. Speak therefore, Lord, for your servant is listening, and answer him when he speaks. While we are both on the high seas, may neither of us sleep. For if you sleep in regard to me, your servant, the sea does not and nor does my memory of the world. Nor, if you sleep, is there any abating of the swell and surge of my thoughts. And so, O Lord, my refuge at the last, you who could have been the force to stop me fleeing you at first, roused now by the inarticulate cries of my heart and by my very need, which is never silent, awake, awake! Arise,

Dt. 32:10

Eph. 4:28

Gen. 3:19

Isa. 62:6

Ps. 27:1

Prov. 28:9

I Sam. 3:10

rebuke the winds and the sea, save me from faintheartedness and the | Mt. 8:26
tempest, so that within and without there may be a great calm, and | Ps. 54:9
Mt. 8:26
men and angels, to whom we have become a spectacle, may marvel, | 1 Cor. 4:9
saying: 'What kind of man is this, that even the winds and sea obey
him?' And this without a doubt, brothers, is what will happen to me | Mt. 8:27
and you if we obey him who lives and reigns. Amen.

THIRD SERMON FOR THE FEAST OF PENTECOST

'The love of God has been diffused in our hearts by the Holy Spirit
which has been given to us.' The gift of God's Son, dearly beloved, | Rom. 5:5
confirmed by the words of Scripture – 'unto us a child is born, unto
us a son is given' – would not be enough had the Holy Spirit not | Isa. 9:6
been given to us too. Might it be that the Father himself will be
given to us one day, so that we who are nothing may receive all, we
who have lost all that made us human may be endowed out of the
fullness of the Godhead? Who ever heard the like? We were blind, | Isa. 66:8
and a light dawned in the darkness, a light to enlighten us. And this | Jn. 1:5, 9
is the birth of Christ for us – for us, one of us, born in us. For the
birth that he underwent for us he also gave us to be ours, which is
his baptism for us – as it were another birth by which we are born
in him, who was born one of us. And just as he in us, so we in him:
he by the Holy Spirit born, Son of man, of the Virgin Mary; we by
the same Spirit made sons of the virgin Church. When we were
under the power of sin, we were bad servants. He served well on
our behalf, obedient to the Father in righteousness, his obedience | Phil. 2:8
Rom. 6:16
paying what was due from ours. This was the life Christ lived for
us. Death, through sin, had a part in us, for the wages of sin is death; | Rom. 6:23
but he, in dying for us, purged the guilt of our offence. This is the
death of Christ for us.

Consider, dearly beloved: for you, whose birth was blighted,
whose life runs awry and for whom death is perilous, everything,
through the grace of Christ, is changed for the better. Birth is now
holy, since we read 'the holy thing which will be born of you'. Life | Lk. 1:35
is righteous, for does not Paul say 'my righteous one shall live by
faith'? And death is victory, thanks be to God, who gives us the | Heb. 10:38
victory through Our Lord Jesus Christ. Why then, I ask, if these | 1 Cor. 15:57
lofty mysteries have won for us such an accumulation of graces, is

there a need for the further favour of today's feast? In those who have been perfectly reconciled, what possible lack needs making good? He who gave us the Son, has he not given us all things with him? Are not all things ours, whether it be Paul, or Apollos, or Cephas, if we are Christ's? I note that this visible world with all its elements, and these elements in their wealth and beauty, are there to serve us, for are not all the angels ministering spirits sent to serve, for the sake of those who are to inherit salvation? This is a trifle. God, the Son of God, and himself the Son of man did not come to be served by us but to serve us and to lay down his beloved life, which he gave as a ransom for many. Who ever saw the like of that? Wherever we turn, Our Lord is our servant. For us he was born, for us he lived and died and rose again, for us he ascended, having said: 'I go to prepare a place for you.' He prepares a place in heaven for those whose place he takes away on earth, and for us he will come again from heaven and take us to himself. Truly, he who made us has done everything for us. Why should we not do the same for him?

And so I ask again: where is the need for this solemnity? What more will the Paraclete perform? We offended against God, but, to put it crudely, we did right by him, we settled the chief cause of complaint and gave, so to speak, a recognizance for the offence: we took a man from him and gave him back a better one, we abducted a servant and released the Son. What more? We were summoned, heard the charge, were convicted and, in accord with the judgement, made total restitution. Surely that is enough? Enough indeed to pay our ransom, but not to buy our master's favour; enough to satisfy justice, but not to win his friendship. Look at man now – justified as regards the past; but what about the future, given that he stumbles seven times a day? He has had a crooked bent from youth, so who will keep him straight? Or pick him up if he falls? Pity the man who is alone: if he falls, there is none to lift him up. I make bold to say that without the Spirit a man is alone, for he who has only Christ without the Spirit is alone.

It was with good reason that the Spirit was sent after Christ: 'It is to your advantage that I go away, for otherwise the Paraclete will not come.' Let us put it simply, especially for the benefit of the simple and uneducated brothers who only understand plain speaking: a great man draws up an account with his servant, accuses the fellow

Rom. 8:32
I Cor. 3:22-3

Heb. 1:14

Mt. 20:28

Jn. 14:2

Prov. 24:16
Gen. 8:21

Ecc. 4:10

Jn. 16:7

of having done him an injury, finds him guilty, holds him fast, censures him, squeezes him until he has repaid the last farthing, and imposes a punishment for the offence. What then? He sends him away, saying: 'Go, and do not sin again lest something worse befall you. You are free, but should you fall into my hands again you will not escape like this; it is a dreadful thing to fall into the hands of the living God.' But what servant could guard himself from everything his lord might spring on him? How could he survive if his master insisted on watching all his doings, pardoning nothing and holding everything against him? It is a wretched servant to whom his lord imputes every fault, and a wise one, therefore, who, after making full restitution to his master, goes on to seek his favour, and his love beside, together with the assurance of good relations in the future, lest the master be on the watch for any slip, or turn a ready ear to anyone with a complaint against him. And over and above, he must ensure that he receives his master's kiss, the sign and seal of charity and peace.

Mt. 5:26

Jn. 5:14

Heb. 10:31

This, dearly beloved, is the grace of today's feast. We stood convicted of robbery, and what we were unable to repay Christ paid for us. We were made free men, but not yet friends. We had escaped from the past, but were without security for the future, and who could face his justice a second time if love remitted nothing? Who could hide from him if love afforded no shelter? What we have said at such length, dear brothers, David renders in a few words: 'Who', he asks, 'can withstand his cold', that is, the unyielding rigour of his justice which sees and imputes each thought and act? 'He will send forth', he adds, 'his word' – which is Christ – 'and melt' (that is, free) them', for all things are loosed by Christ, who came to undo the work of the devil. 'He will make his wind blow', says David – just like today, when there came a sound from heaven like a rush of mighty wind. And the frozen waters melted by the Word will flow on unhindered to eternal life. And so through the Holy Spirit are given kindness and mercy to follow justice, and the servant who was sent away a free man by the Son is today made into a friend by the Spirit. Today, with justice done and reparation for the wrong accepted, the Lord embraces his servant; indeed, friend kisses friend with a kiss of his mouth. For if the Son is rightly understood to be the Father's mouth, the Spirit is properly said to be that kiss, sealing the promise of love and charity, for charity is

Ps. 147:17

Ps. 147:18
1 Jn. 3:8
Ps. 147:18

Acts 2:2

S. of S. 1:2

Rom. 5:5 diffused in our hearts by the Holy Spirit which has been given us. Charity covers all, imputes no blame, bears all, excuses all and
cf. 1 Cor. 13:7 pardons all. Seven times a day he whom Christ has justified falls through his own fault, and seven times daily he is raised again by the Spirit.

And so today God gives us through Christ who intercedes for us his charity and love, so that as God, in Christ, reconciled the world
2 Cor. 5:19 to himself, not holding its past faults against it, so too through the Spirit, which also is God, he united the reconciled world to himself, absolving it of blame for future faults; and blessed indeed is the man
Ps. 31:2 to whom the Lord imputes no guilt! Through Christ all things are remitted; through the Spirit none are imputed, though it may be that he does not wholly clear of future blame all whom he has wholly pardoned. So Christ is as it were our mediator in the way of justice, the Spirit in that of friendship. Through Christ we attain to truth, through the Spirit to charity; through Christ to forgiveness, through the Spirit to safety; through Christ to remission, through the Spirit to perseverance; through Christ we are loosed, through the Spirit reassembled. Yet there is no division between Christ and the Spirit in all that they do; for Father, Son and Holy Spirit, who are one yet differentiated, do everything at the same time and in the same way. The Son, however, has as it were his own particular embassy from the Father and is sent by him alone; and the Spirit also has his embassy from both. The Son appeases, so to speak, the Father's anger and loosens enmities, the Spirit tempers and after a fashion palliates his justice and joins in amity. Between the guilt of the offender and the equity of the judge the Son intercedes as reconciler and advocate; between the weakness of him who has been reconciled and the majesty of the one appeased the Spirit intervenes to soothe and strengthen. For as the air is like a balm or bath for all things living, tempering to all below through its mild and pleasant nature the unbearable heat of the upper firmament, just so does the Holy Spirit
Gen. 1:2 move over the spiritual waters, a kind of mediator between the sluggishness below and the steel of heaven's justice, protecting and cherishing them, and quickening them with his love and grace, lest they be utterly consumed and the earth crack open with drought.

It was this prospect that inspired the Prophet to say: 'My soul
Ps. 142:6 thirsts for you like a parched land without water' – you, that is, who
Heb. 12:29 consume with the fire of heaven. Make haste to answer me, Lord,

and send your Spirit, for my spirit fails. Because the Spirit is likened   Ps. 142:7
to air, we say that love is diffused by the Spirit. It is the property of
earth to lie below, of fire to be kindled above, of water to slip away   Prov. 25:3
and air to be diffused. They say that the heavens, which appear to be
standing still, are whirling in fact from east to west and round to the
east again with such an irresistible thrust that all below would be
destroyed in a trice, had their course not been slowed by the
providence of him who made the seven stars known as the planets
and set them in counter-motion; so that, just as the atmosphere
protects from the sun's heat, so the planets serve as a defence and
safeguard for all below against the furious impetus of the firmament
(a statement which accords well with our topic, and ever since the
creation of the world we have been able, through our understanding
of created things, to descry spiritual realities). Likewise the sevenfold   Rom. 1:20
grace with which the Holy Spirit counsels and strengthens us serves
as a counter-force to mitigate the lightning rush of God's justice,
which at the same time subjects all things to its clear and steady
scrutiny. This grace acts as a brake lest the Father should forthwith
enter into judgement with his servants, who cannot answer him once   Ps. 142:2
in a thousand times, for no man is found guiltless at his tribunal, nor   Job 9:3
  Ps 142:2
is heaven itself pure in his sight, for he found depravity even in his   Job 15:15
angels. It is only this kindness of God, moving in a sevenfold manner   Job 4:18
over us, that tempers his severity, inclines his majesty towards us and
holds back his chastising arm. And during the time that he, who is as
good as he is great, as kind as he is mighty, is thus at odds, so to
speak, with himself, the sinner finds a space for repentance, as Paul
saw when he said: 'Do you not know that God's kindness is meant to
lead you to repentance?' David, reflecting on this combination of   Rom. 2:4
kindness and might, says: 'Great is the Lord and greatly to be praised
in the city of our God' – as praiseworthy and lovable for his kindness   Ps. 47:2
as he is terrible in his greatness and severity. Pondering on his
severity while overlooking his kindness leads to despair, while
contemplating his kindness and forgetting his severity gives rise to
presumption. The Apostle recommends us to note 'the kindness and
the severity of God, severity towards those who fell, but kindness to
you as long as you persevere in it; otherwise you too will be cut off.'   Rom. 11:22

    We leave it to you, brothers, who have to make a lot out of little
and derive much weighty matter from these elliptic notes, to work
out the reference between the graces of the different spirits and the   cf. Isa 11:2–3

GILBERT OF HOYLAND

Gilbert of Hoyland, otherwise of Swineshead, drew his appellation from the fenland known as Hollandia bordering on the Wash, where he spent a large part of his life as abbot of the monastery that furnished his second style. Swineshead started its existence in the Savigniac fold. It may be that Gilbert did likewise, entering before the Savigniac abbeys were received into the embrace of Clairvaux in 1147, or he may have been a Cistercian from the outset, one of the group that Aelred sent from Rievaulx to help the monks of Swineshead adjust to their new Cistercian identity. Whether a native son or an import, he was elected abbot around 1150 and ruled over the community for the next twenty years.

When St Bernard died in 1153, leaving his commentary on the Song of Songs unfinished, it speaks highly for Gilbert's reputation that it was he whom the General Chapter asked to continue the master's work. He added some fifty sermons of his own before death took him in turn. Like Aelred and many another, Gilbert fretted under the abbatial yoke. He longed to have more time for prayer and writing, and spoke of laying down the burden. Because he died in 1172 at the abbey of Larrivour, near Troyes, it has been suggested that he executed his threat, but it is at least as likely that death caught up with him on his annual pilgrimage to the General Chapter. Besides his Sermons on the Song of Songs, which enjoyed a wide circulation, Gilbert left seven short treatises and four letters.

To continue in Bernard's footprints was a daunting task, and Gilbert modestly insists that he will confine himself to the moral sense and not attempt to scale the mystical heights. In fact he deals in much the same way as Bernard with the relations between the Word and the soul. He addresses, as was customary, his monks, but also a wider audience, often apostrophized as 'fidelis' or 'felix anima'.

Certain sermons are addressed to nuns, possibly the Gilbertines close by at Sempringham. His spirituality is markedly Christocentric, with emphasis on the humanity of Christ, the one and only pattern for our own. The sermons are rich and lively with Gilbert's own humanity, drawing readily for their imagery on rural life and land-scape.

Friendship, as attested by his letters, was important to him. He was close both to Aelred, of whom he wrote a moving obituary (see p. 221), and to Roger of Byland. The two letters included here both leave us with unanswered questions. We would dearly like to know whether Adam heeded the call and how the proposed visit of Richard, clearly inclined to take himself too seriously, passed off. If Gilbert did, in the event, find him a burden, he doubtless bore it with a tolerant smile.

Two Sermons

SERMON II ON THE SONG OF SONGS

1   'I held him and would not let him go until I had brought him into my mother's house, and into the chamber of her who conceived me.' Love is the most delicate of affections, and the slightest thing [S. of S. 3:4] can mar spiritual bliss. Love is impatient of outside occupations, having enough to do with minding its own affairs. It delights in leisure and prospers in quiet, wishing to have time free for its intimate pleasures. Is it not just this you feel that the Bride is hinting to you, in drawing her beloved towards her private chamber? She knew that secure and total possession of the beloved was impossible outside its walls. It is hard for the lover to divide himself equally between Christ and the world, hard indeed to have outside cares invade the purlieus of love and the world's turmoil disturb the converse of heaven. 'I think of God and I am ravished; I am exercised and my spirit faints.' If delight in thinking on God [Ps. 76:4] exercises the Prophet and exhausts his spirit, how could he possibly embrace other and outside occupations in addition? So it is with perfect justice that the Bride seeks out a chamber with her beloved, where she may devote her untrammelled attention to him and where, present to him in spirit, she may enjoy him fully and, in quietness of heart, embrace him without reserve. It is clear that she is led by charity and speaks with a bride's affection in seeking an opportunity for the interchange of love.

2   As for us, if we so much as·brush the fringe of what is Christ's – his wisdom, his sweetness, or the taste of contemplation – how do we not struggle to break free! Not content with grace nor considering our capacity, we spurn the chamber and flee the proffered rest. And what a rest is that! 'In peace I will both lie down and sleep.' [Ps. 4:9]

Lk. 10:39   Mary, sitting at the Lord's feet, preserved that rest, while Martha
Lk. 10:41   was troubled about many things. From a multiplicity of things
Lk. 10:42   comes trouble, but only one thing is needful – even, indeed,
pleasant, for how good and pleasant in fact it is for lovers to dwell
Ps. 182:1   together in unity. And there is no dwelling together in unity unless
it be in love – love which brings those with a common way of life
Ps. 67:7   under the same roof. What is it to have a common way of life but
to be conformed by the bond of love? Love inclines and unites the
human spirit to God. 'When he appears,' says John, 'we shall be like
1 Jn. 3:2   him.' Like God? How so? Because the inestimable beauty of the
divine majesty entrusts itself unveiled to pure minds. The affection
of the beholder is ravished by it and fixed upon it to the exclusion of
all else, and through this very concentration of the attention the
spirit is conformed to the object of its contemplation. It is the
S. of S. 1:3   fragrance that draws us, but the vision that transforms. How beneficial, then, is the practice of contemplation, which effects a unity of
mode and form between the human spirit and the supreme majesty.
Here is our rightful home; there is nothing beyond for us to wish
for, nor should we wish for less. Who gives me this to be my resting
Ps. 131:14   place for ever? Happy the man who can say from his heart: 'Here
Ibid.   will I dwell, in this my chosen home.' Mary chose the better part,
Lk. 10:42   which shall not be taken from her. Knowledge will be swept away,
1 Cor. 13:8   prophecies made void, and tongues will fall silent. Contemplation
alone will not fail in the future. So choose for yourself here and now
the portion that will never be taken away, that your soul may say:
'The Lord is my portion, therefore will I contemplate him.' The
Lam. 3:24   Prophet says: 'therefore will I hope in him.' Rightly so. He hopes
for the fullness of that good which he already possesses in part.
Whoever enjoys the benefits of contemplation here can hope for an
increase in the same, but not for something different.

Lk. 12:19 **3**   These good things are laid up for us, enough for many years, nay,
for all time. Therefore, happy soul, you who enjoy all this, be
Ibid.   merry, eat your fill, for the portion set before you will not be
required of you again; on the contrary it will be poured out and
renewed more freely still. This repose will be yours for ever more.
2 Kgs. 19:15   Here will I dwell, in this my chosen home; dwell here and you will
Ps. 98:1   dwell with him who has his seat above the cherubim, the plenitude
Isa. 37:16 etc.
1 Tim. 6:16   of knowledge, and dwells in unapproachable light. So take your
place where you can look on the light. This place is that of your

218

mother the Church, her own place, her home. All the activities and
duties devolving from temporal necessity look to this end. That
which pertains to action is transient, to contemplation, permanent. It
is good for you to be here: pitch here your tent. Not one for Mt. 17:4
yourself and one for your beloved, but one for the two of you. Lead Mk. 9:4
your beloved into this chamber, enter into your rest, that you may Heb. 4:11
rest from your labours just as God did from his. On the seventh day Heb. 4:10
he rested from the work of creation, and on a seventh day he rested Heb. 4:4
again from that of restoration: initially, after the institution of the
world, latterly, when he constituted himself anew within the tomb;
first, after setting the world on course, secondly, after redirecting
the course of humankind.

If you have sought and found and thrown your arms round your
beloved, then hold him fast: hold him, cleave to him, press yourself S. of S. 3:1
against him, that his likeness may be printed afresh on the wax of
your soul, till you bear the stamp of that seal. This is what will cf. Rom. 8:29
happen if you cleave to him, for he who cleaves to God will become
one spirit with him. It may be that, like hard matter, you do not 1 Cor. 6:17
take the impression easily at first; but if the process of imprinting is
arduous, the cleaving is sweet. The six days' labour to remould
yourself is wearisome, but the sabbath with its sweet repose comes
after.

4 Let us bury ourselves with Christ, therefore, through his sabbath Rom. 6:4
death, for 'blessed are the dead who die in the Lord; henceforth, says
the Spirit, they are to rest from their labours.' The Spirit it is who Rev. 14:13
says this, speaking to us through the repose we already enjoy and the
operation of grace whereby he himself bears witness with our spirit. Rom. 8:16
The Spirit says this because it is he who brings it about. He is the
speaker because he is the giver too. 'Henceforth,' says the Spirit,
'they are to rest from their labours.' He says from their labours, not
from their works, 'for their works follow them'. Works follow the Rev. 14:13
Spirit as heat follows fire or light the sun, as the shadow follows the
substance and the effect the cause. He who takes his sabbath rest in
the Spirit will have no need to follow his works, for they will
follow him. Their works: what are the works of those at rest, of
those who have died in Christ and are buried together with him, the
works of those enjoying their sabbath rest? They consist in keeping
joyful holiday. Make haste to enter into this rest, this sabbath Heb. 4:11
holiday. But notice that sabbath joy is reserved to those who have

been buried with Christ; it is withheld until after the sixth day, that
Rom. 6:6 day which is seen as marking either the crucifixion of the old self or
the perfecting of the new. For it is with respect to the former that it
is said that those who have died with Christ rest from their labours,
while with reference to the latter we read that God, having created
Gen. 2:2 the new man on the sixth day, rested from his work on the seventh.

You too should prepare a sabbath rest for yourself by making the
Eph. 5:16 most of your time and staking your claim to hours that are free
from outside occupation. Take care, however, lest your enemies make
Lam. 1:7 a mockery of your sabbaths, lest your leisure serve their purposes
and you devote your time to them instead of to God. 'Be still,' it is
Ps. 45:11 written, 'and know that I am God.' Leisure is good, but let it be
wisdom you write in the hours of your leisure. Write it across the
whole breadth of your heart; a heart not pinched by cares is broad
enough. Engrave on your innermost heart letters that will not be
effaced, and inscribe the tablets of the Spirit with symbols of
wisdom, that you may be able to say: 'The light of your countenance
Ps. 4:7 is a seal set upon us, O Lord. You have given me joy in my heart.'
Rejoice and keep holiday with your beloved, and make merry, as
you are bidden, at the entrance to glory such as this. The sabbath,
Isa. 58:13 according to Isaiah, is delightful, and holy, and glorious. Delightful,
he says, and holy. Every person at leisure has desires, but not all
desires are holy; there are, for instance, those who want to grow rich
1 Tim. 6:9 and thereby fall into many senseless and harmful desires. You note
how the Apostle considers that the multiplicity of desires is in itself
bad. What if these desires should also be shameful? There are many,
unable to indulge their base desires, who think and speak about such
things in private, affording themselves in this way some minor
gratification. Isaiah, to make the distinction plain, was not content
to say that the sabbath was delightful: he added 'and holy and
glorious to the Lord', that there might be no confusion between that
glory and your own vainglory. If you are at leisure, you keep
sabbath. If you use that leisure to look on and to contemplate the
Lord's delights, then your sabbath is delightful, and holy, and one
Isa. 66:23 that is glorious to the Lord. From sabbath to sabbath, that is from
leisure to leisure: the first kind of leisure is good, provided you are
not attentive to the world; the second, where you cease concentrating
on yourself and consider how you can please God, is better; best of
all is the third, when, yourself forgotten, your whole attention is for

God alone, to ponder on the Lord's delights and the ways in which he pleases you.

Your sabbath should not be an occasion for sloth, but for doing the works of God. The work of God is your believing in him. It is with faith that you see. We see now in a mirror, so apply your leisure to looking in it. This looking is a wholly delightful work – the looking on God, above all. For the rest, there is no need for you to strive after faith: just delight in it. It has already been rescued from the objections and perversions of persecutor and heretic. Place it in the forefront of your mind, that you may think thoughts that are time-honoured, faithful and sure. Amen.

Jn. 6:29
1 Cor. 13:12

Isa. 25:1

IN REMEMBRANCE OF ABBOT AELRED[1]

'I came to my garden, my sister, my bride; I gathered my myrrh with my spice; I ate my honeycomb with my honey; I drank my wine with my milk.' What a huge, what a copious honeycomb was taken up a few days since to the heavenly banquet. I mean the Abbot of Rievaulx, whose death was announced to me while I was working on this passage. Our garden, it seems to me, has been left bare by his removal and a great bundle of myrrh has been returned to the gardener, God. There is no such honeycomb left in our hives. In him are exemplified both the honeycomb and the bundle of myrrh. For whose life was purer than his, whose doctrine more prudent? Who was more sickly in body yet more vital in spirit? His speech, like the wax of the comb, dropped a mellifluous knowledge. In body he languished, yet how much more again did he languish inwardly in spirit after the things of heaven! From the myrrh of his bodily suffering and the fragrance of his mind he offered up in one long holocaust the sweet-smelling incense of an unfailing love. His flesh might be withered and sere, his soul was feasted as though with marrow and fat, and the praise of the Lord was ever on his joyful lips, lips which distilled nectar. And as the man spoke, so was he, bodying forth in his unassuming countenance and the tranquillity of his bearing the serene affections of his soul. His mind was quick, but he was not hasty of speech. He would question quietly and reply with diffidence, bearing with the importunate, himself importunate to none. His understanding was keen, his reporting scrupulous, his

S. of S. 5:1

S. of S. 1:12

Ps. 62:6
S. of S. 4:11

temper at all times even. I remember him when, as often happened, someone sitting near rudely interrupted him in mid-flow, how he would break off while the other opened the sluice-gates of his spirit. And when the tumultuous flood of speech had ebbed away, with the same composure with which he had borne the interruption, he would take up the thread of his argument, speaking and silent by turns, and each in season.

me with such friendly savagery that I feel myself being rubbed all over with the salt without which it is not lawful to offer sacrifices to the Lord. You have flown at me like one of the seraphim, a living flame, and with the burning coal taken from the altar you have purged the fault from my lips. The graver my fault, the more acceptable the rebuke. Truly, I find you other than I had supposed. Now at last you have given me a certain taste of your sagacity, for it is by his patience that one knows a wise man. I admire and honour your patience. You overlook injuries, restore the aggressor to favour, placate the tormentor and reward the undeserving, nay, ill-deserving. Your gifts please me greatly: my pleasure is in the giver and in the gift. They make you present to me and show me to myself as well. A wise man's gifts cannot be mute. What are you hinting to me in the staff, if not that ʃ ʃhould be upright and strong, and not pliant and flimsy and reed-like, like Egypt which the Prophet called 'that broken reed of a staff that will pierce the hand of any who leans upon it'? Such a one you found me, and your hands might have been bloodied on the shards of my fracture, but for being tougher, so that they blunt any hostile points. Blessed hands, unable to break the bruised reed – strengthening it rather – or quench the smouldering flax. 'The flax-workers, the combers and weavers of subtleties, will be confounded', says the Prophet. In which case I, who underwove the wool of your simplicity with the flax of my dissembling, am covered in confusion. Perhaps you sent me the cup to match the affront of that insincerity;[6] for 'varying weights and measures are an abomination', and 'woe to the man who gives his friend to drink, pouring out his gall and making him drunk, so that he can see his nakedness. He will be filled with disgrace instead of glory!'

Where is all this leading, brother, except to my commending your good nature and condemning my unfairness? But because it would take a long time to run through it chapter by chapter, I will give you a compressed and final version: I spoke foolishly, like some silly woman. I plead guilty: do you now pardon. Having been asked, you will not refuse the forgiveness already freely offered. I might advance excuses, attenuate the enormity of the offence, lay the burden of my sin on someone else and brandish my sword over the head of the man who struck and wounded me, but I refrain, turning rather to prayer and entreaties. I do not want, while patching a rent, to effect a fresh tear, nor to protect my own flank

Lev. 2:13

Isa. 6:6–7

Prov. 19:11

2 Kgs. 18:21
Isa. 36:6

Isa. 42:3
Isa. 19:9

Prov. 20:23

Hab. 2:15–16

Rom. 9:28
Isa. 10:22–3
Job 2:10

by wounding another's. This much, however, I will say: your house is not weather-tight. Its covering shingles are not close-set and it is exceedingly easy for a breeze, not of peace but dissension, to find its way between. To the rest – namely, that I deferred the day, that I   Job 41:6–7 resisted at length, that I am still dragging my heels, that I said you would be a burden to me – I will reply briefly. We advance many things in conversation, seeking to explore the other's mind rather than pressing our own desires. But to speak plainly now and in all sincerity: I chose to have your company and that is still my wish, but I postponed your coming in the interests of convenience, and, because we seem not unalike in character and intellectual interests, I fully expect that you will be more of a comfort to me than a burden. I only wish that you were coming as a permanent and not a transient guest, to stay for good and never to go home. Farewell.

LETTER II. TO A CERTAIN ADAM[7]

If you could only know for yourself, my dear Adam, how much I yearn for you in the heart of Christ Jesus, for I haven't words   Phil. 1:8 enough to express it to you! To have your company has been a long-standing wish, but an element of despair has always tempered it. But now the desire has grown hugely and intensified, blazed out in fact in a longing for your conversion. A slender – very slender – hope was engendered by your own words, but I have hesitated to write and my hand has dragged on the page[8] for I was afraid (if you'll forgive me for saying so) that the words merely slipped out of you, the fruit of a fleeting impulse. But however they were spoken, whether they escaped from a sudden surge of feeling or were the product of mature deliberation, given your family example I can certainly expect nothing but good of you. Would that *our* examples might incite you, put you indeed in mind of certain truths! Would that you might, after a late start and thanks to some fortunate short cut, outfly me and, taking the wings of a dove, fly away and be at rest! How wide a window you would be throwing open for   Ps. 54:7 emulation, you who would soon be an example to others; a great door, indeed – to use a familiar expression – leading to the path of   1 Cor. 16:9 virtue! To cap it all, I seem to hear that verse of the Canticle being

chanted about you: 'Draw us after you; let us hasten in the fragrance
of your perfumes.'

Happy indeed and twice happy if you were to make your
conversion into an occasion of salvation for others; if you were to
draw towards life and truth those who are currently running in your
wake – after vanity, I wanted to say, but feared to pain an affection
newly conceived in Christ and tender still. Not that I personally
disparage the study of the arts,[9] the ready recall of teaching and a
keen understanding, which together form the basis of sound learning.
A knowledge of the liberal arts is an excellent thing, provided it is
rightly used, that is as a step, a foothold on which one does not
loiter but presses down[10] as one ascends to higher and holier things
– the deeper mysteries of wisdom, whose delights lie hidden and
sequestered and in that unapproachable light in which God dwells.
This of all knowledge is the pearl,[11] the law and form and norm
and ground, the universal paradigm, uniform and unchangeable.
We cannot pass beyond it, but should equally not be satisfied with
less. Compared with this, all other wisdom, of whatever nature and
extent, is not only vain if it falls short of this but positively hurtful if
it does not tend towards it. If we succumb to the temptation to
study such wisdom for its own sake, the mind, entrapped and
beguiled, its energies expended within these limits, falls idle, having
been prevented from advancing to more hidden lore, and fed on
emptiness and make-believe in order that it may never hunger and
never taste the sweetness of the Lord. For what is truly sweet but the
Lord? You take delight in the little and dubious knowledge of
elements and laws to which one attains with difficulty by long and
roundabout ways; it captivated your mind and stole your heart.
What then of creative wisdom itself, which gave to all these things
their being and made them accessible to our knowledge? Surely the
acquiring of this wisdom will tempt you more persuasively and
instil its pleasures more soothingly into your quietened senses, as it
awakes with novel feelings an insatiable yearning for itself? Indeed,
Wisdom herself says: 'Whoever eats me will hunger for more, for
my spirit is sweeter than honey.'

You, dear friend, have ample containers for that honey: a sharp
and well-trained intellect and a wide knowledge of matters of great
complexity. But these, in my opinion, are like the cells of a
honeycomb: capacious but still empty. Draw near, therefore, and

Marginal references:
S. of S. 1:3
I Tim. 6:16
Ps. 33:9
Sir. 24:29
Sir. 24:27

receive an inpouring; let your containers be filled! Their spate will come brimming over and pour itself out again on us, who will rightly praise you in the words of the Canticle: 'Your lips distil nectar.' Ah! to hear you one day holding forth in the Lord's house, expounding the veiled and mystic meanings, attaining to and distilling for us with fine discernment something of the essence of God's majesty, of his eternity, immensity, simplicity – simplicity in which is nothing small, immensity that is not manifold, an essence wholly infinite, but not by being dragged out in time nor by extension of its mass in space, but of its own intrinsic energy and power. This essence is in its entirety both everywhere and in itself contained, there being nothing in which the whole of its might, truth or will is expended or expressed. There may be degrees we can discuss or distinctions that we name, but it itself is one and indivisible. All things are to be wondered at, worthy of reverence, delightful to explore. But at the last, as Scripture says, our eyes are not satisfied with seeing, nor our ears with hearing. S. of S. 4:11

Ecc. 1:8

Gladly will I listen to you prophesying in this manner. And when, in your diligent search for truth, you have plunged into the vast depths of this sea, I shall watch you sprinkle with the refreshing dew of life-giving wisdom those inapt for a more generous wetting. When you have truly turned your attention to God's benefactions, then I shall listen to you developing more fully your understanding of his pardon, grace and glory, of what the Lord has given, restored or added to us, and of all that he has endured for us and bestowed on us. You will talk to us of present sufferings in Christ and of the glories to follow, about patience in time of trial, the anticipation of reward, the elements of faith and laws of morality, running through all the stages of renewal and progress. You have a rich subject-matter here and all you could wish for in an occupation, for there is no field in which an ardent and instructed natural talent can exercise its skills more fruitfully or reap a richer harvest. 1 Pet. 1:11

4   I have said all this in case you should excuse yourself on the grounds of your futile literary studies, chasing after a shadow and depriving yourself of light; or lest, your thinking warped by Aristotelian arguments, you were to make a pretext of our silence and simplicity. For these latter are indeed the principal means whereby, gazing on the glory of the Lord with unveiled face, we are changed into his likeness from one degree of glory to another, as it were by

2 Cor. 3:18 the spirit of the Lord. Does our silence strike you as meaningless and
dead — the silence in which this inner activity is taking place, in
which one learns and practises the art of progressing towards God in
an undeviating line by changing and transmuting oneself into a new
man, the new Adam, and of reaching up right to the mind of
Col. 2:3 Christ, in whom are hidden all the treasures of God's wisdom?
Never failing are the gleaming veins of precious metal here, and
wellnigh visible, should anyone choose to mine their depths rather
than stand begging at the door.

I am not going to rehearse for you here the benefactions and
graces conferred on you by God, and your ingratitude, or rather the
poor requital made for the best of gifts; nor the destructive pleasures
of the world into which we hurl ourselves with such enthusiasm that
we turn our backs to the Lord instead of our faces. I am playing
things down as much as I can. Neither am I setting forth the
medicinal effect of present hardship, nor threatening future punishment and holding out the hope of glory, projecting your fear and
expectation into the distance. It is only of a present pledge[12] that I
am talking, not of a reward to come; of first-fruits, not of plenitude.
I have not the ability to pursue the matter in words, and it is not
fitting that so sublime a subject should be compressed by the
poverty of my verbal skills. If only you will try it out, you will
learn that the statutes of the Lord are worthy to be sung even in this
Ps. 118:54 place of pilgrimage, and that the crops to be garnered at the end of
cf. Ps. 125:6 time are sown long before in joy. Don't defer these delights for
another year, and don't resist grace which pours itself freely out
upon you. Alas for me if you shut out that grace which I have
found in you! Follow with a quick and eager step where it first
beckons you enticingly. You bade me send to you: if only you were
to be found there where I left you, yes, in the very gates and
virtually on the threshold, your back already half turned on the
world! If I can do you any service as a friend, I am wholly at your
disposition, being all yours. I await your presence rather than a
letter. Farewell.

JOHN OF FORD: THE LIFE OF WULFRIC
OF HASELBURY

Nothing is known of John of Ford's life before he entered the Devon monastery of which he would one day bear the name.[1] Working backwards, one may presume him born around 1150, perhaps a little earlier, one of a generation who never knew the founding fathers of the Order or the harsh poverty of its beginnings. It is likely that he received his schooling in Exeter and entered the monastery shortly before, or perhaps on the coat-tails of, the more famous Baldwin – of Ford, Worcester and ultimately Canterbury – who, the higher he mounted, the worse he did.[2] Baldwin was a learned man, a theologian and a canonist, and it was during his ten years at Ford, the last six as abbot, that he gave his full intellectual measure in the form of tractates and sermons. John, who became his prior, must have found encouragement for his own literary leanings in such a mentor. In the mid 1180s Ford lost both abbot and prior, Baldwin to the see of Worcester, John to the abbot's stall at Bindon. His tenure of it was brief: in 1191, the abbacy of Ford falling vacant, he was elected and recalled to the mother house. He continued in this office for twenty-five years, travelling regularly to Cîteaux to attend meetings of the General Chapter, which frequently deputed him to investigate, correct abuses and settle disputes in the English monasteries.

The reign of King John was to bring great trouble on the English Cistercian houses. Initially the king appeared to favour the Order. John himself was for three years the king's confessor before – with relief – relinquishing the post to the Abbot of Bindon. But the king's need for money was great and always growing. Intransigence on both sides resulted in 1210 in the imposition of huge fines on the abbeys, which led in some cases to their ruin and closure. Nor was that all. Since 1208 England had lain under the interdict imposed by

Innocent III. In the monasteries mass was celebrated once a week, but nationwide the people were deprived of the sacraments, and John sorrowed and fretted on their behalf. So if, at the outset of his abbacy, he knew relative calm, his life grew ever more strenuous, and the last years were clouded with worries and sadness. John of Ford died in 1214, before the effective lifting of the interdict, and was buried in the abbey church, without pomp, as he had lived.

A considerable body of work survives him, but a proportion has been lost. His letters too, like Aelred's, are missing. There remain a sermon for Palm Sunday, the Life of St Wulfric and, in a single manuscript, the hundred and twenty sermons that he wrote completing the commentary on the Song of Songs begun by St Bernard and continued by Gilbert of Hoyland.[3] John's continuation attracted little notice – by 1200 monastic theology had been relegated to a backwater by the sweeping tide of scholasticism – and remained until recently unedited. These sermons, composed during the last and most troubled years of his life, admirably reflect the serenity of spirit of a man whom one might otherwise see as bowed down by money worries and rumours of wars.

John was still prior of Ford when he embarked on the Life of Wulfric, the recluse of Haselbury, one of the many solitaries who lived on the margins, yet close to the spiritual heart, of medieval society. Recluses fell into two classes: the hermits and the anchorites. The former lived in isolation but retained a certain freedom of movement, enabling them to provide for most of their own needs. Such a one was Godric of Finchale, holed up for sixty years on the bank of the Wear, where Aelred used to visit him. The anchorite in contrast lived in a cell – often in a city – where he buried himself with Christ. This entombment could be literal, for it was usual when the inmate died to bury him or her in the cell. Wulfric was such an anchorite: he spent nearly thirty years in voluntary incarceration, yet his mission was to the world and the world queued up at his window. During his lifetime his fame spread countrywide, but circumstances depriving him of a marked grave led to his being quickly forgotten, and John, writing thirty years after his death, laments that it was 'almost as though he had never been'. Almost, but not quite, for it was tales told in the cloister by monks who had known the anchorite or hailed from villages where his memory was kept burnished that set John on his trail. Distressed by the 'odious silence' that had closed over the saint's unhonoured head, John spoke to his abbot, who in turn approached Bartholomew, Bishop of Exeter. The latter appointed a committee of three bishops to supervise the projected Life: himself, Baldwin, ex-abbot of Ford, and Reginald of Bath.[4] This was after Baldwin's translation to Worcester in 1181, but we know that John had been gathering material, squirrel-like, over a number of years, for some of his chief informants were dead by the time of his writing.[5]

John has no interest in the physical context of Wulfric's life, except as it reflects his holiness. However, by careful collation it is possible to build up a coherent picture. Haselbury Plucknett is a Somerset village a few miles from Ford and nearer still to the Cluniac priory of Montacute, which furnished Wulfric with his daily bread. The church has been almost entirely rebuilt since Wulfric's day, but his cell is known to have abutted on to the north wall of the chancel.[6] A door from the cell into the chancel was used by the recluse, who regularly said the night office before the altar of St Michael. Against the east wall of the cell he had his own altar, while high in the north wall was a window giving light. There was a latrine, probably on the western side, where the ante-room was also situated. Here his servant prepared his food, his scribe, when he employed one, worked, and his visitors sat and spoke with him at a window with an opening shutter. The ante-room had a door to which his servant kept the key. He often gave hospitality of a frugal kind to those who came to see him. Most visitors will have eaten in the ante-room or out of doors, but intimates, like Brother William of Ford, were admitted to the inner cell to share the anchorite's own meal.

For the rest, the Life is self-explanatory and contains all that is known to us of Wulfric of Haselbury, whose influence in his day was great and whose body still lies, or is presumed to lie, in an unmarked spot in the west end of the church, where Osbern the priest secretly reburied it. As for John, he must have been gratified by the success of his work. Of the four extant manuscripts, three were written during his lifetime, a sure indication of popularity, but what will have mattered more to him was the renewal of interest in his saint: the church at Haselbury, described by him as desolate, became a place of pilgrimage and so remained until the Reformation.

John of Ford had a deep love for his subject. The affection as well as the veneration he felt for the man he calls 'Wulfricus noster' is evident on every page. This does not prevent him sieving the evidence as scrupulously as he knows how. He uses only informants he can vouch for personally and once sent three monks on separate occasions to check a story.[7] As a biographer he had the gift – uncommon in his day and very rare among hagiographers – of making his characters live, and it is our good fortune that he has given us in his Life of Wulfric so much more than he intended. He wanted to hallow the memory of a neglected saint for the benefit of the local and universal Church; he has in fact resurrected a whole community and fixed it on the pages of, as it might be, a Book of Hours. But as well as Wulfric, the village and the visitors, there is another, hidden participant in the Life, and this is John himself. The writer who, in his simplicity and directness, has acted as a window on to a peopled landscape has exposed himself also to the reader's gaze. He is not putting himself forward – he is always the servant of his material – but in his attempts to commend it to his readers, to reassure them as to its accuracy, to interpret Providence in its more baffling manifestations and Wulfric in his less edifying moments, he reveals a lot about himself, about the monk that he was and the abbot he was shortly to become.

John's Life of Wulfric is singular and thereby precious among Cistercian writings in that it takes us outside the cloister and offers glimpses, as through a squint, into unrecorded lives. Unusual too is the absence of monastic trumpet-blowing: there is no disparagement of secular society or the lay state. Yet, untypical in some ways, the work remains profoundly Cistercian in its spirituality. Like St Bernard, John of Ford writes with his pen dipped in the ink of Scripture. There are meditative passages where there is scarcely a phrase that is his own, and yet the meaning is entirely his. The emphasis on contemplation and the place given to the imagery of the Song of Songs are the hallmarks of Cistercian writing in the twelfth century. Archbishop Baldwin, sometime abbot of Ford, author of theological treatises, can have felt no call to censor the work of Brother John.

From *The Life of Wulfric of Haselbury*

CHAPTER I. HIS CALLING AND CONVERSION

Blessed Wulfric, a man of English stock and common extraction, was born and reared in Compton Martin, a village eight miles from Bristol. There he lived and there for some years he also served as priest. He was ordained unusually young, and it is thought that his motives for entering the priesthood were more frivolous than spiritual, as might be the case with a youth who did not yet know God and in whom the flesh spoke louder than the spirit. His priesthood, for instance, did not prevent him from hunting and hawking, and until his calling he spent his days among men in thrall to worldly vanities, though it was not long before he was freed from this bondage by the inspiration of God's grace. For while he was engaged one day in this lunatic activity, which he pursued with no lack of zeal, he was suddenly met by a man – and a poor man too to judge by appearance and clothing – who begged him humbly for a new coin. There had been a new minting in England then, in the days of King Henry I, and, being so new, the coins were still hard to come by. But when Wulfric replied that he did not know if he had a new coin to hand, the other said: 'Look in your purse and you will find tuppence halfpenny.' Wulfric looked in astonishment, found the coins, and devoutly offered what had been asked.

This was the beginning of graces dispensed to Wulfric, his beloved, by God who went before him with the blessings of his sweetness, having first singled him out like another Nathaniel under the figtree. For there is good reason to believe that the stranger was a Jn. 1:48 messenger of the Lord, using the request for new currency as a pointer to the need for spiritual renewal.[8] Wulfric himself, recount-

235

ing the story in later years, used to say: 'He was no man, for all he seemed one.' And indeed, after taking the coin the other disclosed what it was that was being asked for and accorded: 'He for whose love you did this will repay you,' he said, 'and I in his name announce to you that you will soon leave this place for another, and soon enough you will move to another again; there you will find rest at last, and in a narrower dwelling-place you will persevere with God to the end; and thus at the last you will be called to join the company of the saints.'

These things took place in a village called Deverill, where Wulfric first had charge of souls. From that time on he could truly be termed God's saint, whereas before it had merely been his predestined end; for God who was calling him breathed into his nostrils the breath of life and, in ways known only to himself, formed in Wulfric a new creature fired with a hatred of iniquity, a contempt for vanities and a love of truth and the highest good. Not long after, he was invited by the venerable William fitzWalter, the lord of Compton, to take up his priestly duties in his birthplace, and he joined his patron's household and ate at his table. Such members of that household as are still alive testify even now to the energy, the fortitude, the wholehearted commitment with which he seized on the virtue of abstinence. Indeed, he gave up meat entirely, saving the occasions when respect for the company obliged him to observe the general custom.

Thus it was that a light kindled in darkness gleamed bright in that very darkness, and shining tokens of sanctity gave promise already of the plenitude in Christ that was to come. For the man of God, who aspired now with all his heart after solitude and purity of life, made them his own here and now in hall and banquet, and with greater merit in those harder circumstances. On the point of leaving Egypt, he girded up his loins in readiness and ate the Passover of holiness and innocence, and this while in Egypt still. He worried constantly, meanwhile, as to how and where he should give birth to the purposes he had earlier conceived by the Holy Spirit and carried now within him, and he did what so often holds back those who are striving after higher things: he hesitated as to which form of religious life would best nurture his new-formed aspirations. But here too the Lord showed him the way. Counselled and assisted by the lord William, and guided by the Holy Spirit, he moved to

Gen. 2:7
2 Cor. 5:17
Ps. 118:163

Ex. 12:11

another of his patron's villages, namely Haselbury, some thirty miles east of Exeter. There was a cell next to the church, which had been empty for some time, and there, without being inducted, as is usual, by the bishop, without any solemn blessing, with no authority except that given in private by the Holy Spirit, he buried himself with Christ; to be shortly transformed with him as it were in the glory of the Resurrection, in newness of life, in cheerfulness of spirit, in the power of signs, in the grace of prophecy. But all these were attained at the cost of much toil and sweat, of great affliction of body and spirit, and with God's grace going before.

Rom. 6:4
Rom. 15:19

CHAPTER 2. THE GRACE OF THE INNER MAN

Once Wulfric was walled in stone away from God's countenance and the glory of his majesty, he began to build himself an inner solitude, and reaching out into its further purlieus he began to explore the hiddenness of God's face, and to call on the Holy Spirit with a fervour that sucked the very marrow of his bones. Besides, to condemn the body alone to close confinement while the soul is at loose without, as sometimes happens; is a deplorable folly. That is no true solitude; it is but a shadow, like the Law. Such was not blessed Wulfric's way, indeed not; he, on the contrary, felt he had found all space itself within those narrow confines. In the freedom seclusion gave him, he began to bring forth all that he had conceived, longing for what was heavenly, striving for what was spiritual, and meditating day and night on the law of God. Nor was the true manna from heaven lacking to this true solitary, for God in his kindness and bounty rained it abundantly on his needy servant. He sought the Lord in truth and thereby deserved to find him faithful, as the truth is in Jesus, and he learned by experience the nature of what is promised an hundredfold, and of the water that wells up to eternal life, for the Holy Spirit taught him and bore witness to the truth. And God gave his beloved Wulfric the choice gift of faith with which to quench all the flaming darts of the evil one, because he had shown a trusting spirit, looking to God in confidence and relying on him in all his needs, and in the intimate exchange of love he called the Lord God his lord in his native tongue. There was in

Eph. 4:21
Mt. 19:29
Jn. 4:14
Jn. 5:33
Eph. 6:16

Isa. 50:10

him a true simplicity that further refined his faith and overlaid it with pure gold. It was inborn, but by the sanctifying power of the Holy Spirit the gift of nature had become a gift of grace. And so the Lord formed him in holiness through these two qualities, that his humble simplicity might temper the grandeur of his faith, and that, as growth in grace continued, the first might be strengthened by the second, the second hidden and safeguarded in the first. I have touched on, rather than exhausted, what is personal and inward, and that only in so far as an outsider may properly look into the holy of holies; the rest I leave to him from whom nothing is hidden, not even the innermost depths, and for whom not a hair can fall from the beloved's head without receiving its due meed of praise. Accordingly, my part in rendering homage to the man, provided I am found worthy of the role, is to loose the thong of his sandals; more, to show how beautiful were the steps in sandals of the prince's daughter: that is, to give a faithful account of all that was admirable in his outward being and doing, both initially and as he progressed.

Lk. 21:18
Acts 27:34

Jn. 1:27
S. of S. 7:1

* * *

Wulfric's austerities, which John of Ford here details, were of a kind to impress even a Cistercian. He lived on oatmeal bread and porridge, and not much of either according to one of the lads who served him. No strong drink passed his lips, save at great festivals when he might be persuaded to taste a little wine in honour of the feast. Maurice Bell surmises his usual drink to have been 'something of the nature of barley water'.[9]

He took no regular sleep, catnapping during the night with his head propped against the wall, or resting on his elbow facing the altar step. When he needed to rest from time to time during the day, he snatched a short sleep on his bed, though the bed itself afforded more of torment than of rest, being a hurdle woven of branches. However, with approaching age he did mitigate that racking at the express order of Robert, Bishop of Bath, who also obliged him to use a bolster made of twists of hay. His plain outer clothing covered a hair shirt, worn next to the skin; but he soon grew used to its roughness and began to aspire to a hauberk, or shirt of mail.

* * *

CHAPTER 5. OF ROUGH CLOTHING AND COLD BATHS

The lord William, made aware of this desire, paid a reverent and hurried visit, pressing his anxious hope that he might share in the warrior's triumph by furnishing the arms. He handed over his own hauberk, as though to a mightier knight than he, and dedicated this piece of military equipment to the use of God's recruit. And so the soldier newly harnessed advanced to the spiritual battle, striking terror into the foe by turning the arms of the world into weapons of righteousness. Thus did he equip himself for daylight warfare. At night he plunged himself naked in a tub of cold water, and there Christ's little lad would offer his master all the psalms of David, singing to him with drum and psaltery. Thus after each new *Ps. 149:3* baptism he bloomed afresh in the splendour of innocence and, like a flock of shorn ewes that have come up from the washing, emerged *Jg. 4:2* from the water whiter than milk. Putting back on his shirts of hair and mail (noble both, but the second emphatically nobler), he spent what remained of the night office in hymns and prayers, punctuated with frequent genuflections.

CHAPTER 7. THE GRACE AND FREEDOM OF HIS ADDRESS

But I must not forget to describe the man as he appeared to men. When called on to converse he showed himself gracious in the extreme, and, like the bridegroom leaving his chamber, and drawing as it were on the riches of a full cellar, he proffered spiritual counsel filled with authority and grace. Having made little formal study of the Scriptures, it was out of his own heart – that sanctuary of God – that he drew the living precepts that he earnestly imparted on every matter put to him. His words, like loaves fresh from the oven, being potent with his grace and power, gave off to those who heard them a delicious scent of purity and simplicity of heart. In conversation he was no respecter of persons: eschewing, whether by intent or artlessness, all use of styles and titles, he contented himself with plain John or Joan, however grand the visitor. This lover of simplicity and truth reserved his worship for God alone and either could not or would not worship men. In fact, robbing the greatest princes and even kings who came to see him of the glory of a spurious appellation, he was tacitly telling them that they were men like all their fellows. It furnished him with a good opportunity for instructing those who bore an excessive weight of worldly success, plaudits and adulation: for an hour at least they found their true selves in the mirror of his truth. He would criticize any persons in authority with a freedom comparable to the severity he had shown King Stephen at his coming, when he had censured him for seeming to wield the sword without just cause – the king fearing that, if he were milder and more easygoing, he would be unable to do judgement and establish justice in the land.

CHAPTER 3. HIS GREAT LOVE OF SILENCE

With all this he was a man of few words, well able to check any inclination to talk, and to keep a hold on his tongue, to the point where even religious people were given short shrift. Having dealt succinctly with the business in question, as soon as he felt his interlocutor sliding to other matters he would shut the window and retire to the inner cell. So just as one thought one held him fast, that lover of solitude would slip from one's grasp and, like some angelic vision, vanish as suddenly as he had come. Perhaps this might seem churlish to the worldly minded, but anyone gifted with spiritual understanding will excuse him wholly, knowing the inward fra-
cf. S. of S. 1:3 grance that recalled him, the sacred and secret rapture that dragged him irresistibly – and yet how happy – back. Least of all will it surprise those who have merited to be brought into the king's
S. of S. 1:3 chambers and who have heard the zealous concern, the pressing
S. of S. 2:7 entreaties of the Bridegroom for the quiet of the Bride. May all who have committed themselves to the spiritual life be aroused to greater fervour by such depths of loving affection in the Word of God, such heights of virtue in the man of God, and learn besides that the face on which Christ has looked so ardently is not easily exposed for long to the human gaze. I have no regrets at having introduced this

topic: it may remind certain members of our Order not to go out so often, and, when they do, to conduct themselves with greater discretion and reverence.

CHAPTER 9. THE CUTTING OF THE HAUBERK

A manifestation of the power of the Spirit marked the beginnings of Wulfric's fame in the world. Known hitherto to God alone, he broke like a new and saving day on the consciousness of men. This is how it happened:

The mail shirt with which he had armed himself to do battle in God's cause flapped heavily against his knees and got in the way of his repeated genuflections. He therefore sent for the knight who was his confidant and henchman in that combat, and discussed with him the excessive length of the garment. 'Have it sent to London,' said the knight, 'and it will be cut back to the size that you yourself mark out.' 'Far too much fuss and delay involved in what you are saying,' replied Wulfric. 'Besides, one couldn't avoid the danger of ostentation.' 'Well, look,' said the knight again, 'Exeter is near; you can get it taken there.' 'There is no need; just take the shears yourself and get on with the job right away, in the sight of God.' The lord William, flabbergasted, was looking at Wulfric as though he were raving, when an inspired thought entered his mind. Wulfric cannot be deceived, he said to himself, nor yet want to deceive me. Wulfric meanwhile strengthened the faith of the hesitant knight out of his own superabundance, and handed him the shears as soon as they had been fetched from the latter's house. He then ran a thread through the rings of the hauberk to mark the limit of the resection, and laid it in the window in front of him. To the knight, still awkwardly rooted to the spot and muttering about the outlandishness of the task (and indeed it was both hard and strange), Wulfric said: 'Stand firm, and see that you keep calm. As for me, I am going to pray to my Lord about this matter. You, meanwhile, apply yourself to the job in faith.'

So the two soldiers set to, the one to prayer, the other to cutting, and the work prospered in their hands. It seemed to the knight that he was cutting cloth, not mail, such was the ease with which the shears ran through the steel. But at length, Wulfric having left his prayers, William too had to leave off cutting. The shears had been driven by the power of prayer, and they sensed its loss at once and refused to respond to the knight's pressure. As he squeezed still harder, the iron fractured in his hand, but without breaking in two. At that moment the holy man returned and asked him how it had gone. 'Very well up to now. But just as you came in the shears broke and seized up.' 'Don't let that trouble you,' said Wulfric, 'just carry on and finish what you began in the power of faith.' So the knight, his faith in the saint's word re-established, completed his task with the same ease as before. This was the first of blessed Wulfric's signs, when the hand of another man served to commend the power of God and the saint's faith.

CHAPTER 10. THE PARTING OF THE LINKS

The working of this miracle was celebrated with all due honour in the neighbourhood and brought him many visitors, to whom he distributed piecemeal for the curing of their ills that mail shirt worn for the love of God and cut with the power of faith. Without recourse to shears this time, but with no less faith and simplicity, he parted the rings one from the other, the Holy Spirit giving such skill to his fingers that there was no trace of a scratch on any link. And the ease and speed with which they were parted were as miraculous as their undamaged state. The matter was serious, yet he gave the impression of someone playing, or even performing conjuring tricks, as he innocently pilfered ring from ring in a kind of spiritual thieving. And truly in Wulfric's fingers God's

Prov. 8:30–31 wisdom was graciously at play in her father's presence, bantering gently with the simplicity of her faithful, teaching them, as regards the mysteries of faith, to be content with faith alone and pure. He grew at length so used to detaching the rings that he appeared to have the miracle 'at his fingertips', and what with the frequent repetition he was almost able to dispel the admiration it excited. Nor was there anything that malice or incredulity could possibly misrepresent, since he operated openly and the eyes had no choice but to believe what they saw. Moreover, the daily re-enactment refreshed the truth and added to the power. Throughout the district pious people still conserve these rings, seeing them as a great gift and a sacred deposit bearing witness to Wulfric's holiness and ensuring their own good health.

So much I had from Brother William, the guest-master of Ford, and Dom Walter, monk of Glastonbury, not to mention others whom it would take too long to name. Some give varying accounts of the cutting of the hauberk and other details, but the differences are merely circumstantial. I think, however, that I have learned the truth after long scrutiny and by relying on what I believe to be the more dependable testimony of proven honesty and age.[10]

CHAPTER 14. A DUMB MAN CURED AND A QUARREL WITH BRICHTRIC

Brother William, the assistant guest-master of Ford, was one of Wulfric's closest friends. A man of the highest repute, yet deserving in our opinion of even greater esteem for spurning in the flower of his youth the pomp of the king's court, he still reigns happily to this day in the poverty of Christ. Having knit Brother William to him with a strong affection, as fervently returned, there was nothing of all his store that Wulfric would not share with his friend, clearly judging him worthy to be brought into his treasure-house and apprised of his innermost secrets. He would talk with him of the kingdom of God and of the blessed hope of the saints, of God's mercy, how courteously it had come to him and how favourably followed, always speaking of spiritual things, matching the subject to the man.

One day Brother William called on him as was his habit and asked him how he was. 'Well,' said Wulfric, 'except that our priest Brichtric has exasperated me with his reproaches, and has wasted the whole day up to now with quarrelling.' 'Whatever has provoked so mild a man to anger, especially with you?' 'They brought a dumb man to me,' said Wulfric, 'and I prayed to my Lord for him and laid my hand upon him, whereupon the man spoke plainly and without impediment, and not only in English but in French as well. This so upset the priest that he couldn't contain himself for indignation and upbraided me fiercely, saying: "Look, I've served you all these years, and today I have proved plainly enough that it's been for nothing up to date. Here is this stranger who merely needed his tongue loosing so that he could speak, and you in your piety have provided him with a double function for it. You haven't given me the use of French, and when I come before the bishop and the archdeacon I have to stand as mum as any mute."' Brother William laughed as he listened, and with his humorous directness Wulfric reduced what was a miracle to a delightful story.

CHAPTER 16. IN PRAISE OF BRICHTRIC

I fear I should be doing that good man Brichtric an injustice if I contented myself with laying bare his imperfections without ever a mention of his qualities, which were many and great. He much resembled blessed Wulfric, being a simple man and humble, and like him devoted himself day and night to prayer and the recitation of the Psalms. Indeed, in so far as his ministry allowed, he kept a perpetual watch in the church, and in order to gain extra moments of untroubled solitude he would ride home at midday so as to have his horse to hand to take him back to the church as soon as the meal was over. The close intimacy between those blessed and kindred spirits was marked by a continual friendly rivalry in self-abasement and humility. Brichtric assisted the anchorite as though he were his master, humbly calling him such, while blessed Wulfric, forever belittling himself in comparison with Brichtric, used to say that the priest was the true anchorite of the place, while he, who was always available for consultation, ought really to be called the parish priest. So each angelically maintained that he was inferior to the other, his superior in Christ, who was in turn most surely in their midst, the life and joy of both. It was Gen. 1:26 as though Brichtric had been made in the image and likeness of his friend, to be for blessed Wulfric a comfort furnished by God Gen. 2:18 and a helpmeet like himself; but enough of this for the time being.

* * *

Wulfric sang vigils nightly in the church, standing before the altar, and there, on one occasion at least, he is said to have been caught up to heaven and shown the glory of God and the hope of the saints. John was less surprised by this than by the quality of the anchorite's devotions.

* * *

CHAPTER 19. HIS TOTAL ABSORPTION WHEN RECITING THE PSALMS

That a good man and a friend of God who habitually sang the Psalter right through with unwavering attention should be granted an hour's ecstasy will astound no one. For my part it is the concentration of that exceptional soul that I truly admire and venerate, I who have rarely managed to fix my mind with unbroken attention for the duration of one or even half a psalm. I sinned a sin against God and therefore I became unstable, and myself forsook my God, and so my own heart forsook me too. Because God has driven me from his presence, there is no longer any place for me; none makes me welcome and I am become a burden even to myself. In psalms and prayers I seek to be reconciled to my God so that all things may be reconciled to me; but I am thrust out, excluded, rejected with upbraiding as of someone saying to me and my like: 'Dogs outside.' I admit that at the last I derive some comfort in the face of God's judgement and my own incapacity by repeating to myself: Who has gathered the wind in his hands? Only the father of spirits can do that, he who commands the winds and waves and they obey him. Thereupon I flee from the wrath of God, a wanderer and a fugitive in a foreign land, until the days of my repentance and my exile are accomplished; and so the spirit returns to him who gave it, in whom alone is lasting happiness and the peaceful rest of the spirits of the blessed.

Lam. 1:8
Ps. 39:13
Gen. 4:14
Job 7:20

cf. Col. 1:20

Rev. 22:14

Prov. 30:4
Heb. 12:9
Lk. 8:25
Gen. 4:12
Ex. 2:22
Ecc. 12:7

But my being as I am gives me no grounds for disbelieving that such a man as Wulfric can attain to what is beyond me. My weakness – common indeed – can in no way prejudge that special freedom of the saints that anyone may receive from the hand of Christ in the measuring of his gifts. Moreover, any who might find it hard to credit should remember both that no guile was found in his mouth and that he said to one of our monks who went to him to deplore his own weakness in this respect: 'I feel I carry through with total attention from "Blessed is the man" to "Let everything that breathes praise the Lord."'

Isa. 53:9

Ps. 1:1
Ps. 150:6

I knew a man – and he is still alive – who refused to believe what was said of Wulfric, maintaining energetically that a simple man had fewer powers of concentration, and that Wulfric, lacking a wide-ranging intellect, had not meditated deeply enough on anything, which was why he had made such claims. Not long after, a divine judgement overtook the speaker – yet what a merciful one it was! For coming to the night office he had a new and never-repeated experience: he received of the Spirit so abundantly that he concentrated, he said, on every verse with consummate ease and pleasure, singing in spirit and in mind as well. His opinions on the subject were less aggressive thereafter, and he understood the danger of holding out against the truth.

CHAPTER 28. THE SCRIBE'S LAPSE OF MEMORY AND WULFRIC'S PROPHETIC INSIGHT

The man of God applied himself to copying books either for his own use or for the church his cell adjoined. He once told his scribe to leave something out of a transcript because he had it elsewhere. The young man forgot all about it, but, when he got to the place, something prevented him from carrying on. The power of Wulfric's command stood in the way of the pen and brought its advance to a sudden halt. But the scribe, unaware, and blaming it all on the pen, sharpened it over and over again until, having reduced it by degrees to a stump, he threw it away in anger and disgust. Wulfric, meanwhile, knowing all this in spirit, returned from prayer and made a pretence of scolding the scribe: 'Now, now, Richard,' he said, 'why did you want to disobey your instructions in this way?' Recollecting too late, the scribe began to smile at his accuser and, not without cause or subsequent profit, enjoyed the joke at his own expense. I had this from Richard himself.

CHAPTER 29. A MONK CURED OF INSOMNIA

Richard the scribe later entered the monastery of Ford, where he served first as choir monk and finally as cantor. He had a son who followed him into the religious life and exercises his father's office at Ford to the present day. This monk as a youth suffered dreadfully from insomnia – and just how punishing an affliction that is to those of our profession his fellow-sufferers know. His father appealed to the holy man on his behalf. 'Let each monk recite the Lord's Prayer for him three times,' said Wulfric, 'and he will be cured.' 'But why, sir, are you reluctant to pray for him yourself?' The reply came back magnificent in its simplicity: 'I could obtain this from my Lord on my own; how much more all of you.' Richard's son was cured in the same hour and boasts to this day that the grace then won still keeps him sleeping like a log. The power manifested in the cure is far from insignificant, but for me it is outshone by the simplicity of Wulfric's answer, and it is to illustrate this purity of spirit that I have set down the story, which I had from Richard.

CHAPTER 30. THE MOUSE THAT DIED FROM A THOUGHTLESS CURSE

I will give another example of Wulfric's faith, or, if you prefer, simplicity. The holy man was sitting one day in his cell, alone with God and himself, when his glance fell on a cape recently sent him by a prior who held him in regard, and he noticed that it had been nibbled by a mouse. He took the mishap somewhat hardly. 'Perish the mouse,' he exclaimed, 'that has damaged my cape!' At this the mouse shot out of the wall, scurried across and fell dead at his feet. Such was the force contained in a passing word let fall without any real intent, that the mouse, as though accused of a crime, came running to submit to the death sentence, and by dying gave glory to God and peace to his saint. It was a trifling matter, yet it gave signal proof of the love of Christ, who caught the word thrown out so lightly and, lest it fall to the ground, gave it the power of a decree. 1 Kgs. 8:56 But that most simple of men was more humbled than otherwise by this sign. Brooding over the matter and muttering to himself about what he had done, he sent for Brichtric the priest, who during his lifetime bore witness to all these things, and humbly confessed that he had killed a mouse by an unthinking curse. 'If you would only be good enough to dispatch all the local mice in the same way!' said Brichtric. 'God preserve me,' replied the holy man. 'Once, with one mouse, was a very grave fault. And,' he added, 'if I didn't think it would displease my Lord, I would pray to him to bring this mouse to life again.' Such was the man: a marvellous combination of greatness and simplicity, each quality pleasing in itself, yet how much more so in conjunction!

CHAPTER 31. KEEPING VIGIL

S. of S. 3:3,
5:7

Blessed Wulfric was like one of the watchmen who go about the city. His nights, as I said earlier, were spent in watching and waking, and the watch he kept was that of love. As Jerusalem slept, vulnerable in the darkness, he stood through the long night keeping guard over her. At daybreak he went out to his work and to his labour until the evening, and there, sharing freely and ungrudgingly what he had freely received, he disbursed the riches of salvation with an open hand. People came to him from every quarter, as it might be to an ensign lifted up on high, to a horn of salvation raised in the house of David, and he was the humble dispenser of this great treasure, its faithful steward. In the evening, after he had dismissed the crowds, he went up his own mountain by himself to pray. And taking again the wings of the morning (his morning), he would fly away like a dove to his window and be at rest. And truly as the night grew bright with the reflection of the true light, it shone resplendently on his delights. It was during the night that he worked out his own salvation, for by day he was working the salvation of others in the midst of the earth. But even at night he was concerned for those others, for with joy he was drawing water from the wells of salvation, which he would pour out again the next day for those who came to him and had nothing to draw their own water with, for the well is deep. Blessed is the servant whom the Lord finds awake in whatever watch of the night – better still, at whatever hour of the night he comes. And do you think he would have come empty-handed to that waiting servant – he who is full of grace and truth, and never more so than when returning from the wedding feast? Surely that was the time, when blessed Wulfric was released from the cares of men and Christ himself was at leisure, after a fashion, since all the world was fast asleep or nodding off, the time when in the joy of his love he would speak to Wulfric's holy soul, saying: 'My beloved is mine and I am his.'

Ps. 103:23
Mt. 10:8
Isa. 33:6
Mk. 1:45
Isa. 62:10
Lk. 1:69
Lk. 12:42
Mt. 14:23
Ps. 138:9
Ps. 54:7

Ps. 138:11
Phil. 2:12
Ps. 78:12

Isa. 12:3

Jn. 4:11
Lk. 12:37

Jn. 1:14

S. of S. 2:16

CHAPTER 35. THE LIGHT ABOVE THE ALTAR

In case someone should object that I give more space to my own opinions than to the facts, what follows is an eyewitness account. One Sunday when Master Brichtric was blessing the water in the church, it was found that the aspersorium was missing. His son had accidentally taken it home, and now the worried boy did not know what to do. Suddenly, by what is believed to have been divine inspiration, it occurred to him that he might this once use the aspersorium of the man of God. On opening the door of the cell he saw a light of dazzling brightness over the centre of the altar. The saint was standing motionless before the step, gazing at the light. The boy, lost in wonder, handed the aspersorium to someone else to give to the priest and returned to what he had seen. Having silently closed the door till he could just peep through with one eye, he watched the light move gradually towards the left-hand corner of the altar and thence, crossing a chest that stood beside it, go out through the north window. When Osbern asked what the beautiful bright light was that he had seen above the altar, the holy man said: 'Did you see it, then, boy?' 'I saw it, master.' 'Ah! if you were here around midnight, you might often see the like and, what's more, have your nostrils filled with so sweet a fragrance that all the world's delights would count for little in comparison.'

CHAPTER 41. THE LOAF MIRACULOUSLY MULTIPLIED

There came to the man of God a woman of high position – Bence she is called to this day – bringing her son Alfred of Lincoln and a retinue of the sort and size that befitted so noble a lady. The man of God called to his servant and said: 'Look, here is Bence. She must eat with us. Have you something you can set before her?' 'We have nothing, master, except one loaf.' 'That will do,' said Wulfric, 'put it on the table.' So the woman sat down with all her company and the loaf was set before them, a sight to whet the appetite rather than hold out any prospect of refreshment, especially to people used to more refined and richer fare. But because such great faith must needs display its resources when put to the test, heaven's blessing came to the aid of holy poverty, and after the guests had had their fill there was half a loaf left over. Later, when these had left, another group presented itself, wanting to see and speak with the man of God and receive his blessing – a matter of no small importance in those days. With his usual gracious hospitality the man of God invited them to eat, and the half loaf left from the earlier meal was set before them. When the blessing had been given to those who were cutting and eating it, instead of growing smaller it kept its original size. In case the reader's faith should falter under the weight of such a sign, let me add that Brother William, the guest-master, claims to this day to have heard it from Wulfric himself, who also related to Henry, the venerable abbot of Waverley, that he had fed forty men from one loaf; but whether these were the same we have just spoken of, or possibly others, I would not make bold to say.

CHAPTER 45. THE TERRIBLE DEATH OF THE MONK WHO WAS A THORN IN HIS SIDE

Wulfric's natural mildness was once severely tested; and woe to that man through whom temptation came! There was an agreement with the monks of Montacute, whose house was not far off, that they would provide him with food, but after a while, thanks to a certain bursar of theirs, their devotion towards him cooled and they broke the covenant. When Wulfric's servant went to ask for his master's portion, this bursar showered him with insults which disparaged not only the lad but his master too, and either served him, grumbling, with short measure, or more often sent him empty-handed home. The same bursar, passing one day through Haselbury, called for some unknown reason on the man of God. Since he appeared friendly, Wulfric received him, had the table laid according to the requirements of hospitality and served him generously with what he had to hand. After the meal, as the other was about to continue on his way, the man of God, who up to this point had maintained a pregnant silence, now began to speak. 'Thus far,' he said, 'you have walked contrary to me and have made my spirit bitter: now may God judge between you and me.' The bursar,

Mt. 18:7

Jos. 7:11

Lev. 26:21, 40
Ps. 105:33
Gen. 16:5

judged, went out condemned and bearing his judgement with him, but paid scant heed either to his own temerity or to the sentence pronounced by heaven. In consequence, having added obstinacy to the original injustice, he grew hugely inflated and, taking pride in transgressing, came to sin beyond measure through contempt, so that when Wulfric's servant returned to him again he heaped him with invective and sent him back to his master carrying nothing but blasphemies and curses. Hearing what had happened, Wulfric blazed out and loosed a lethal word: 'May God this day,' he said, 'take that man's food away who has taken mine from me!' Whereupon, as the bursar was covering the day's stage towards death, he was suddenly carried away by a flood and, meeting a fearful end, fell into the hands of God.　　　　　　　　　　　　　　　　　　　　　Heb. 10:31

We are on slippery ground now, where I personally watch my feet, and I would advise you to do the same in case you stumble in our present darkness. I say this to prevent any passing of premature judgement – whether to predict the man's everlasting death or the　I Cor. 4:5 salvation of his soul when and if God should so decide – and arriving at an over-hasty verdict about a death that consists at present in the destruction of the body. It is the height of blind presumption and a temptation passing human strength to seek to define what lies beyond our mortal day – matters reserved to a higher court and to be judged by God alone.

When God's servant heard what had happened, he was seized with a consuming bitterness, fancying that the breath of his lips had killed the bursar. Deafening God and his friends with his lamenta-　Isa. 11:4 tions, he sought by additional penance to atone for his guilt in the bursar's death. When his friends reproached him in private, asking　cf. Ez. 3:18 him why he had said so harsh a thing, he replied: 'It was what I had to do, and what I needs must say.'

These things are for those to understand who can; others must trust at least in the Gospel truth: that it was expedient for this man to hasten to his destruction and be drowned in the sea of this death with a weight of judgement fastened on him. In that way he　Mt. 18:6 deterred the carnally minded like himself from following his example　I Cor. 2:14 and, it might be, causing one of the little ones to sin – the carnally　Mt. 18:6 minded who have no understanding unless it come through a heavy　Ps. 31:9 punishment, which exalts their judge, as exemplified in the sign of the millstone. Perhaps there was no better way for him of healing　Mt. 18:6

the soul of the holy man he had so grievously wounded than by teaching him, who was weeping already over his own lapse, to lament his enemy's death as well, at the same time arming him with the virtue of charity against any similar occasion in the future. All this I had from Brother William, and he from Wulfric, but there are other very reliable witnesses, including a well-respected and religious woman named Muriel of Beauchamp.

CHAPTER 46. BLASPHEMY REPENTED: A JUDGE-MENT AND A CURE

It is true that in consequence of this incident Wulfric grew gentler and better at loving his enemies, yet the Lord continued jealous on his behalf, and proved it even in the king's court and in respect of the king's good friend. The name of this friend was Drogo de Munci. Originally from overseas, he was a great man in the household of King Henry. When he heard Wulfric's name extolled at court and his doings reverently recounted by members of the household, the wretch began to curse and scoff: 'The king would do well,' he sneered, 'to send to the cell of this charlatan and confiscate his money. It's impossible that a man whom so many go to see has not laid up plenty for himself.' The blasphemous words were still in his mouth when Satan, to whom he had been delivered so that he might learn not to blaspheme, threw him to the ground, and there he lay contorting himself and foaming at the mouth, a mouth that was now twisted round to his ear. There was instant uproar as people crowded round, crying: 'Ah!' and 'Woe!' and 'Alas, most noble lord!'; for this was not any ordinary member of the household, and his illustrious name gave an awful solemnity to the judgement. And all the witnesses stored up the memory of what they had seen and heard, declaring that blessed Wulfric was truly a saint of God, and that the hand of the Lord would come down on all who touched him.

Those present at once reported the matter to the queen, who reported in turn to the king and begged him – growing daily more insistent – to be sure to approach so great a friend of God, whose prayers and merits could so profit himself and his kingdom. When reasons arose for his travelling to Wessex, the king was glad to seize the opportunity offered and bent his way to the man of God. Casting aside the mantle of pomp and circumstance, he spent some time in humble converse and commended himself earnestly to Wulfric's prayers. Finally, at the suggestion of the queen, he put in a plea for the stricken knight, telling Wulfric both of his folly and its ensuing punishment. Having heard him out, the holy man replied meekly: 'As for me, I do not hold this sin against him.' There were those who insisted that he should lay his hand on him – for the king had brought the man, gravely ill and fearful to look at, along with him. To them the man of God replied: 'I am ready to do whatever I ought.' So one of the bystanders took his hand and placed it on the sick man's face, whereupon his mouth reverted to its proper position and the man recovered his senses and spoke clearly, magnifying God and magnifying, too, the saving graces of his servant. Meanwhile, in all who were witnesses to these events the lesson of his example lives on, expressed in the words: Touch not God's anointed ones and do his prophets no harm. The king and his followers, looking on, I Chr. 16:22 marvelled at this sign and went away strengthened by Wulfric's blessing and highly delighted with his appearance. I had this story from Brother William and from Muriel of Beauchamp, to whom the holy man had told it on a different occasion.

*   *   *

John of Ford confirms that Wulfric did receive many gifts in coin and no doubt in kind, adding that it would not have been proper for the rich to present themselves empty-handed. But the anchorite continued to live in the same simplicity and poverty, using the money to succour the poor and endow the parish church. The monks of Ford were frequent recipients of his generosity, and for them he had a special love and veneration.

CHAPTER 48. HIS PRAISE OF THE CISTERCIANS, AND A CRITICISM TOO

Nor was it only the monks of Ford: he clasped all Cistercians in a close embrace, like sons of his own body, or rather of Christ Jesus. He lauded the Order to the skies and never hesitated to direct to it those who came to consult him about reforming their lives. There was only one matter, according to this friend and champion of our

Order, in which the Cistercians displeased God: when it came to lands made over to them, they exercised their rights too freely and, more intent on law than on justice, seemed insufficiently mindful of their duty to those men committed to their lordship.[11] In all else he said that they were like angels of God: in their renunciation of food and clothing, in discipline, in charity – in the practice of every kind of holiness to please him whose approbation they desired.

CHAPTER 50. THE CONVERSION OF ABBOT HENRY OF WAVERLEY, FORETOLD BY WULFRIC

I should like to recount at this point the story of Henry, of gracious memory, who followed the Lord Abbot Gilbert as the humble servant of the saints at Waverley.[12] I am familiar with every detail of the story, for I heard it myself from his own lips, as though God had chosen me in advance as a witness fit and able to transmit it all to you. I shall tell the tale in his own words to give it a livelier pace, so prepare yourselves to listen and believe.

Acts 10:41

'In the time of King Stephen,' he said, 'men took advantage of a providential period of peace, affronting God who had given it with their growing lawlessness, whereupon there was sent, as you know, a sword into the kingdom of England, which banished peace from the land, severed alliances, created conspiracies and eventually wreaked general havoc. Like beasts of the forest leaving their lairs at nightfall, the men of war sallied out of their hiding holes and dispersed to rob and pillage throughout the land, and the thoughts of many hearts were revealed. The enemies of peace prospered in their ways, and wickedness believed it had seized the opportune moment, and was active all night long in works of darkness.

Lk. 2:35
Ps. 36:7
2 Macc. 4:32
Rom. 13:12

'I at that time (and it helps to remind me of the greatness of God's grace) was among the henchmen of those who hated peace, and strove to ply my soldier's trade as circumstance allowed and with more success than many of my kind. Such as I was, however, I bethought myself from time to time of God, and, just as in the temptations that we suffer now, I knew instinctively what was right, but for a long time lacked the will to do it. Something arose to take me into Wessex, and it occurred to me to go to greet the holy man of Haselbury of whom so many marvels were related, that I might obtain his blessing. So I set out on my journey, but, getting to Haselbury too late in the day to see the man of God, I had to resign myself to waiting until the morning. As soon as day broke I attended his mass, and, on hearing him say a special collect for a friend, I said to myself: "Lucky fellow to be so honoured as to have the holy man say a collect for him." When the mass was over, Brichtric, the priest of the church, came up to me, saying: "Come to my master, he is asking for you." Filled with a high hope by that summons, I followed Brichtric to the man of God. With a merry look he greeted me at once, as though he already knew me, while I returned his greeting most respectfully. Afterwards, when I had sat down, he began: "I said a collect for you during my mass." This was glad news indeed. With gestures of joy I started to pour out my thanks. Meanwhile, giving me a long look – and his gaze was intensely bright and penetrating – he burst into tears, saying: "Happy would be the man to whom it was given to do what you are to do one day!" Exulting in wonderment at the suddenness of this promised salvation, I replied: "Master, I am a sinful man, steeped in sin   Lk. 5:8 and living in sin to this day." "So I was aware," he said, "but I am no less aware of what you will become." Whereupon he unrolled my past life for me, and gave me a detailed account of the future, laying them before me as it were in an unbroken chain. "That church," he said, "which you seized by force: you must restore it." He spoke to me also in detail about the success of my journey, and, regarding events that were to take place before my arrival in the parts that I was going to, he foretold them accurately and in the order in which they were later proved to have happened. To be brief, having heard him out and derived much hope and edification from the gracious words that proceeded from his mouth, I finally   Lk. 4:22 took my leave and went on my way rejoicing, with the promise of salvation folded in my heart.

'Some time later, having successfully dealt with the reasons for my journey and the events that had occurred while I was on the road and that had been foretold me, I returned as promised to the messenger of my peace. For a while, like a suckling child, I was permitted to drink in the milk of his words – better by far than that wine he found me drunk on. And when he had watered his seedbed, I carried away the fruit of a second blessing.

'But alas! poor wretch that I was, with precipitate haste, before

Gal. 4:19   Christ was formed in me, I allowed myself to be torn away from him. How heavy the yoke of wickedness, and how wretched the state of my servitude! In no time at all I succeeded in wiping all that had happened from my mind. Yet just as a prisoner escaped by stealth is recaptured and held in stricter custody thereafter, and forced to pay the penalty for his flitting, so I too, fleeing from the face of the Lord and of his saint, was caught in deeper darkness yet. And as in the days of old when, after the coming of Moses to the people of Israel, Pharaoh's hand weighed heavier upon them, at the last I too, like them, began to

Ex. 15:24   murmur to myself against my Moses and give utterance to my just
2 Sam. 19:28   complaint. "Where are my prophet's fine words now?" I muttered. "Where is the promise God made me through his mouth?" Neverthe-

Tobit 14:6   less, because the word of the Lord could not fail, in the fullness of time, as he had preordained it, God bethought himself of his mercy and truth towards me and, arousing me to repentance, quickened his servant's word in me. My weaknesses being greatly increased, I fled hotfoot to make my profession with the humble, that I might hide in the shadow of this Order from the face of God and the glory of his majesty. He himself since then has known of my progress, and his eyes have seen

Ps. 138:16   my imperfection; but this is the track my feet have left and this the
Job 13:27   order of God's mercies on his servant, which continue to this day.

'I understand no better by what order of God's judgements I was called to be abbot of Tintern when the novice I was had only just become a monk, unless it be that God will not suffer me to rest but has me going to and fro on the earth and walking up and down on

Job 1:7; 2:2   it after the pattern of my former ways. So it is that I groan and labour under servile burdens still.

'But certainly, now that all was well with me, I did not forget the man who had made it possible. On the contrary, I was constantly comparing what he had said with its outcome in my life, until I said to myself: "I will go and see the man of God and congratulate him on his accuracy in my regard, and tell him that not one out of all his

1 Kgs. 8:56   words has failed of its promise. And indeed, if he promised me so many good things when I was an enemy still and a traitor, what will he not announce to me now that I am reconciled? And should there be miracles – who knows? – for me to work, he would certainly not keep it to himself." So it was that I secretly opened my heart to the poison of pride, for which God, without my knowledge, had already secretly prepared a salutary antidote. On a readily found pretext

I undertook the journey, and greeted the man of God on arrival with the words: "Master, I am that man to whom you once foretold things that now, by God's grace, are fulfilled in me. Here before you, you see the fruits of your prophecy. I have therefore come back to you to enable you to give thanks for me to God, who has had mercy on me and proved you truthful as well." Back came this medicinal word: "Quite so, my son; keep the rule of your Order and you will be able to save your soul."

'The let-down, I confess, was instant. My inflated ideas fell away, and the wound inflicted by my pride was bound up. Suitably chastened by this reply, I turned for home, and added this last to the Lord's mercies as I repeated: "It is good for me that I was humbled, that I might learn your statutes."'   Ps. 118:71

Such was the tale that venerable man related in genial style to the Lord Abbot of Ford[13] and myself on our way to the Cistercian chapter – a tale that made the journey seem a short one and that, by its familiar example, made us who heard it give praise to God for his predestinating grace, and strengthened our faith in all that touches our Wulfric. As for the teller, all his acquaintance knew him for a man exceptional in his humility, and so long-suffering as to be almost insensible of injury. Regarding the careful, unremitting toil he never mentioned, his works speak for him: in particular the monastery,[14] depleted and dilapidated almost past recall, which he rebuilt – simply and modestly as is our way – and established on a sound footing, leaving behind a memory crowned with praise. The continuing and exhausting burden of work that this man discharged thereafter on behalf of his community left him in spirit unconquered, however much he neglected his body, and could never prevent him singing the Psalter through each day and night, emulating in this his blessed master and prophet. But we leave to others the telling of these and additional matters; ours to bring the story of our Wulfric to its close.

CHAPTER 52. ABBOT HENRY'S VENERATION FOR THE MAN OF GOD

The same reverend father related another story well worth remembering, and one he could vouch for personally since it concerned a matter arising between those two men of surpassing virtue, blessed Wulfric and blessed Bernard, in which he had been the intermediary.

Father Henry had been conceived in Christ by Wulfric's gift of prophecy, and he in turn had for the other man a son's love and reverence. An enthusiastic hearer of all his doings, he recounted them even more enthusiastically, particularly to those who, by virtue of their own holiness, had a special veneration for holiness in others. Wherever he went, he had Wulfric's praises in his mouth and carried his name around with him as a lutanist does his lute, Mt. 27:9 purchasing for his Wulfric as it were at a set price the friendship of holy men. When at last he obtained an audience with the Pope, he duly produced his Wulfric, and, although he spoke passionately and at length, he could not say enough for the pontiff, who proved a no less passionate listener. During this time there were great men waiting outside, pillars of the Church anxious to gain access but unable, and matters of vast importance and the business of all the lands of Christendom requiring the Pope's attention were left in suspense.

The Lord Pope, meanwhile, and Father Henry were within, fore-gathered in Wulfric's name. Wholly occupied with the mystery of holiness, they were eating their honeycomb with their honey and S. of S. 5:1 drinking their wine with their milk. And Father Henry, as he told us later, was secretly glorying in the fact that he had all to himself the attention of the man whom the whole world waited on, and was seen to enjoy not only the right of access to such greatness but even a certain intimacy and fellowship. Later, visiting blessed Bernard of Clairvaux, he unrolled the famous story yet again and preached the faith and splendour of Wulfric's angel-like simplicity to that holiest and wisest of men. Rejoicing mightily in the glory of God and in his saint, the abbot also humbly confessed to Father Henry an intemperance of his own, and commissioned him to ask blessed Wulfric if he would solicit God's mercy towards him in respect of it.

54 It had happened that during the schism,[15] when it was still uncertain to which side God would grant the victory, and the people of Rome were still wavering between the two parties, blessed Bernard opened his mouth in the midst of the church and harangued the populace. Speaking at length and with eloquence, he said in so many words that it was the will of heaven that the Church should turn to Innocent. Now the Abbot of Clairvaux, being spiritual, scrutinized his every action, lest the merest spot should

discolour that face so fair in the eyes of the heavenly Bridegroom. In
consequence, when he caught a whiff of presumption in that discourse, he withdrew the words and tore his heart from them as from
a blasphemy. He then, zealot that he was, dealt with himself with
the same unrestraint that he habitually used towards kings, princes
and magnates, as one established by God over peoples and kingdoms;
one who, through the authority of the Holy Spirit, which shone in
him with a rare brightness, was to those princes as awesome and
terrible as an army with banners. And as in the house of the just man
there were not diverse weights, it was with as harsh a judgement and
as fierce a zeal that he took himself to task and, not feeling adequate
on his own to reconcile God to himself, sent an embassy to our
Wulfric, asking for prayers to be offered for his sin. So it was that
Father Henry came to his father in God, greeted him in blessed
Bernard's name and, explaining the case, said: 'Blessed Bernard sent
me to ask you to pray to the Lord for a sin that he fears has
endangered his soul.' But that was all he ever got out, for Wulfric
interrupted him there, saying: 'Why did he try to usurp the knowledge of God?' Then he added: 'If he did say that he believed it to be
the will of heaven, what he said was entirely right. All the same,
God has accepted his penance, and to have spoken thus will not be
held against him as a sin.' As for Father Henry, he was left quaking
before the sage's insight and reckoned he had told him quite enough.

cf. S. of S.
1:4–5

S. of S. 6:3
Prov. 15:6 etc.

CHAPTER 72. THE MONK WHOSE WORDS MET WITH A JOCULAR RIPOSTE

Brother William, the assistant guest-master, was required one day to
go to Waverley, and one of our monks, named Robert of St Albans,
was sent with him. When William turned aside, or more accurately
made a beeline for the man of God (for he would have thought it an
imprudence to pass by without greeting him), his travelling companion said to him: 'I have often visited the man of God, and I am
surprised that he has never once invited me to eat with him.'
Brother William smiled: 'I shall be surprised too,' he replied, 'if
what you have just said doesn't rebound in your face today.'

Both men were given a joyous welcome on arrival and after a
short stay, got ready to go, bidding the man of God farewell. 'Hold

on,' he said, 'and you will eat with me.' And giving Brother William the benefit of a jubilant smile, he added: 'This monk has never eaten a meal with me, so today I must make up for what my courtesy has lacked in that respect.' The monk, flushing a deeper red than if he had been caught pilfering, stood tongue-tied. Whereupon the man of God took pity and wiped away the glow of shame with the serenest of looks and the words: 'If I have not invited you to a meal before, it was not out of meanness or arrogance: it was more a fit of negligence and forgetfulness.'

Armed with the holy man's blessing, the two pursued their interrupted journey, urged on by necessity or their own wish, and whiled away the miles with long and happy conversations about blessed Wulfric. When they got to Waverley and had dispatched the business that had taken them there, Robert of St Albans stayed at the abbey, while Brother William returned home, taking with him a monk of Waverley who was himself eager to see the man of God. Brother William having led this monk to his desired and plainly desirable goal, the holy man came out to them, his mind alight with religious zeal and his face with pleasure as he greeted his guests with formal courtesy. While they were talking together, Brother William began to commend his colleague to the holy man's friendship, and ventured to ask if he would give him one of the rings of his hauberk as a token of brotherly love. So, putting his hand to that part of the hauberk that covered his chest, he detached a ring with the greatest of ease and put it in the hand of the monk, who sat there open-mouthed in wonderment at seeing the things he had heard a short while back now taking place before his eyes. Brother William, meanwhile, intent on strengthening the man's faith by a repetition of the prodigy, said: 'Would you please give me one, too?' At which Wulfric returned to his treasure store and, the same gesture producing the same result, reached out a second ring to Brother William, from whom I had the story.

CHAPTER 74. MASS HELD BACK FOR A LATE ARRIVAL

The following story was related by Osbern, the parish priest of Haselbury, who succeeded his good father Brichtric in that charge. He said that he used, as a lad, to go in to Wulfric's cell to serve his mass. One day, when the man of God, having vested as usual, was about to begin the celebration, and the boy took a taper to light the candle, it happened that Wulfric bade him stay his hand. The boy stood about for a little while, albeit grumbling and put out, for his pursuits were still those of a child, and even there, at that moment, his heart was wholly in them. 'Wait,' said the man of God, 'because someone is hurrying to this mass and we must wait until he comes.' And so Osbern waited a little longer, though less than satisfied with the prophecy, until after a bit the holy man said to him: 'Run along now, quickly! Here comes the man we were waiting for; you will run into him.' Out went Osbern, and, just as he was leaving the churchyard, he did indeed run into a man wearing the religious habit. 'Here you are,' said Osbern. 'We have been waiting for you all this time, and very boring it has been, too.'

Thus did the blessed man hasten forth in the spirit to offer reverently to his visitor the courtesy of his prayers, and not only saw him coming from afar but accompanied him on his way, and in some fashion read his footprints and counted his approaching steps.

CHAPTER 78. WULFRIC ANNOUNCES THE DEATH OF A MONK OF WINCHESTER

A regular visitor to the man of God was William fitzWalter, the lord of the village. Knocking one day at the window, he had a long and tedious wait before the holy man responded. When at last he appeared, it was to say: 'I know you have been much put out by my delay and your long wait. But please excuse me; I was occupied and could not meet your wishes – or my own – any quicker.' 'Doing what, master?' 'One of the brothers from the monastery at Winchester died a short while ago, and it came to me that I might ease his passing with my prayers. I was very anxious to do this for him, and it was this I was engaged in.' The knight took care to ascertain the name of the monk and the hour of his passing. He then sent with all haste to Winchester, wanting to know if things were really as Wulfric said. The messenger rode day and night, and arrived at his destination just as the monk was being carried out with due solemnity for burial, which facts he reported back to his lord. The holy man in the interim sent for the knight. 'Is it true,' he asked, 'that you still don't trust me and sent to Winchester to find out whether I had spoken the truth?' And the knight, convicted of prevarication, learned that absent or present was the same to Wulfric, and that even the heart's hidden depths were not hidden from him. This I had from his son, Walter of Glastonbury.

CHAPTER 81. HOW WULFRIC FORETOLD THAT THE QUEEN'S PRIDE WOULD BE BROUGHT LOW

In the days of King Stephen the queen came to Dorset – to Corfe Castle if my memory serves me right – and the noblewomen of the district converged in haste to pay their customary respects. Among them was the wife of William fitzWalter, who approached the queen with due reverence, at pains to show all possible deference and courtesy. But because her husband William had not yet given his allegiance to King Stephen, the queen with regal hauteur turned her face away. Thereupon, having been made to look foolish in the eyes of the other women, she went off to Haselbury and poured her embarrassment into the ears of the man of God, whom she loved dearly for his holiness and his benignity. Having comforted her with quiet kindliness, Wulfric bode his time until a day not far removed when the queen herself sought out the man of God. Mindful of the affair he had been called upon to judge, he showed her no special marks of respect, but, revealing himself to her in all his prophet's grandeur, he said: 'It was you, was it not, who disdained to rise and greet a faithful and holy woman, and shamed her, and would not receive her with a kiss? I tell you, the day will come when you will consent to this mouth of yours bestowing its favours on the poor and base-born, and, far from spurning, you will kiss any mouth that offers itself to yours.'

Those who remember how things fell out, how King Stephen was captured and how the queen, anxious to get him freed, courted the common people (by whose help the king's release is thought to have been hastened), will notice that Wulfric's prophecy was fulfilled to the letter.[16] This I had from the son of the woman in question, Walter of Glastonbury.

CHAPTER 89. THE WOMAN WHO CONFESSED HER
SINS AND RECEIVED MUCH IN RETURN

There came to the man of God two exceedingly rich women, the one being Bence, the mother of Alfred of Lincoln, the other Agnes, late sister to the Countess of Gloucester. When Bence commended herself urgently to his prayers, the man of God nodded his assent and promised to pray for her as long as he lived. But when Agnes made the same request with an equal urgency, he was silent for a while, until, as she pressed more insistently, he finally said: 'I shall pray if so be I may.' Beaten back, she returned to the fray yet again and more boldly, while he stood his ground unbudging. At this point he went up as usual to the altar to celebrate mass. On his return Agnes asked him whether he had prayed for her. 'Indeed not,' he said. 'When I started to do so, I was prevented.' She insisted on knowing why she was thus excluded. 'You have not kept the holy days in your grand and splendid buildings, and God's saints have gone unhonoured, and you yourself to date have led a less than holy life.' Thereupon in the presence of God, who scrutinizes the heart, and of his saint, she threw herself on the ground in lamenta- Wisd. 1:6 tion. 'It is true,' she said, 'that is the way things are, but from now on with God's help I will live a stricter life.' Then in greater privacy she renewed herself inwardly through confession and the absolution of her sins, and rose up stronger in her determination to lead a better life. As one who was already washed white, she received kind words of comfort from the holy man: 'Have no fear: from now on I will pray for you faithfully. Hold steadfastly to your purpose though, in the knowledge that you have not many days to live on earth.' The woman went home and took care to make better use of the brief span that remained to her, and to make up with penitential practices for the waste of earlier days.

CHAPTER 90. HE FORETELLS THE DEATH OF KING HENRY

King Henry I of England made plans to cross to France, and common talk brought the news to the man of God, who commented: 'He will go, but he will not come back; or if he does, it will not be safe and sound.' These words were repeated to the king, who took them hardly and sent to him to ask if he were indeed the author. 'If I said it,' said the man of God, 'I don't regret it, for I did not speak it of myself.'

The king departed as he had arranged. Some time later the man of God sent for the lord of the village and said: 'The king died yesterday: consider what you will do.' The knight was dumbfounded and enjoined him to silence. 'It is easy enough for me to be silent, but by tomorrow it will be in every mouth.' He went on to prophesy that the king would find mercy with God, because he had fought for peace and justice during his life and had built the abbey of Reading with royal munificence.

CHAPTER 91. THE REIGN AND CAPTIVITY OF KING STEPHEN PROPHETICALLY FORETOLD

Another who visited the man of God was Count Stephen, who afterward reigned over England; being a blood relation of the king, his possessions in England were many and great. He was accompanied by his brother Henry, Bishop of Winchester, a man august and grand in every way. Looking at the count, the holy man said: 'Greetings, king!' The other two stared at one another, supposing him to have fallen into some purely human error, but he insisted: 'It is to you, Stephen, that I say, Greetings, king. God has delivered the kingdom of England into your hand; as for you, strive your utmost after peace and justice, and take care to honour and defend the Church of God.' In fact, when the kingdom came to Stephen in accordance with God's design, what with others trying to wrest it from him, the peace of England was utterly destroyed, as Wulfric had earlier foretold.

The lord of the village called one day on the man of God and asked him how he fared. 'Well, except in so far as I feel sorrow for our friend.' 'Which friend is this?' 'King Stephen will be delivered tomorrow into the hands of his enemies and taken prisoner.' The knight groaned and said: 'What next, master? Will he not be freed?' 'Yes, indeed he will be freed, and he who took him prisoner will drink in turn of the same cup.'[17]

King Stephen himself came subsequently to him, and Wulfric, after many reproaches and much admonishment, promised him among other things that he was to reign as long as he lived. No less noteworthy is it that he urged the king to do penance for a particular sin which he identified to him, adding that until he repented there was no possibility of his throne being made firm or peace established. The king began to weep profusely at these words, and, confessing his sin, he presented his cheek to the prophet to be struck and spat upon.

CHAPTER 94. ADVANCE NOTICE GIVEN OF THE ARRIVAL OF WILLIAM FITZWALTER

The bailiff of Haselbury came to the man of God one day, being about to set out to see his lord, who was at the time residing somewhere else. He made a point of commending himself to Wulfric's prayers, afraid, given the general unrest, of falling among robbers. 'There is no need for you to go to him,' said the man of God, 'he will be coming here tomorrow.' The other expressed some doubt, having had no forewarning of this arrival. 'Well, I have no doubt at all,' said Wulfric. 'He is having his horses foddered this very minute. After that he will wait a while, and then he will ride through the night, arriving here at daybreak. So make sure there is food prepared for him, which you can serve him when he gets here, for it will be a very tired and famished man you will receive.' All this was said in such firm tones that the bailiff, not daring to resist the Holy Spirit, awaited in faith the promised arrival and was exactly rewarded. Thus it was given to Wulfric to prophesy not only in spiritual matters but also in day-to-day affairs, and to arrange for the physical comfort of the man who ministered to his own material needs, repaying like with like. This I had from William, the guest-master.

CHAPTER 96. WALTER OF GLASTONBURY

Because I have made frequent use of the testimony of Walter of Glastonbury, it is time that I myself bore witness to my witness and spared a few words to establish his credentials. He owed his intimacy with the holy man in the first instance to his father and mother, and, more importantly, as will be apparent, to what was to happen in his life that Wulfric, by God's grace, foresaw and foretold. In the time of King Stephen the lad was left in London by his father in the house of one of the citizens, as surety in a money matter. He had entered freely on his captivity, but it was a wretched and anxious time all the same, and, when he found himself fretting more and more at the monotony of his confinement, he sent to blessed Wulfric to ask him to pray for him, expecting his intercession to effect a sure and swift release. The reply that he got from the holy man was that he would have to wait a little while longer, for the day of his liberation had not yet come. 'When it does come,' he said, 'release will be simple and sudden.' Disheartened and depressed by this reply, he settled down to wait and wait again on the outcome of the prophecy. When a number of years had passed and he was still a prisoner, Wulfric's little while seemed to him very long. 'What does he mean by little?' he muttered to himself. Then, shortly before the promised day, Wulfric sent him someone to whisper words of comfort in his ear: 'Keep your spirits up. This is it: you have been freed!' So finally, as the man of God had promised, at a particularly opportune moment he broke from his fetters and presented his family and friends with a red-letter day at his home-coming.

His was the charm of an innate simplicity, a quality which endeared him greatly to the man of God, and the frequent and close contacts that resulted gave him an insight into Wulfric's inner life. It happened one day that there was some general talk in the saint's presence about which of the fitzWalter sons would turn out to be the most powerful. The man of God gave his voice to Walter. 'This is the one,' he said, 'who will be the best provided for of all the brothers.' Walter took this on the purely human level as designating him as his father's heir, and – since pride is forever swelling in our human nature – he placed inordinate hope in Wulfric's words, began to conceive new plans and ambitions, behaved more arrogantly, and adopted a more self-indulgent way of life. When these changes came to his mother's notice, she grieved for her son quite as much as if he were dead, and turned to the holy man for help. His response was: 'Do not weep; this life will not detain him long.' This reply came to the ears of the young man, who interpreted it to mean that his death was imminent, and, as is the way with boys when rain starts falling, put an end to his playing. It even entered his mind to renounce the world, and he began to discuss the matter with the man of God. But the idea that had surfaced sluggishly was discussed without urgency, and, with an excess of precaution hardly befitting religious vows, he dragged out the tardy undertaking over a long period. Eventually the holy man said to him: 'The plan you spoke about will be implemented earlier than you yourself intended, and all will come to pass much faster than you hoped.' And indeed, soon after, at the request of the Lord Henry, Bishop of Winchester, for reasons arising that it would take too long to enumerate, he took the habit in the abbey of Glastonbury.

He has lived there ever since, giving no occasion for complaint, held indeed in high favour, and has now attained a ripe old age. He is prepared to give an account of blessed Wulfric's life to all who ask – at a suitable time – and both his religious profession and his age preserve him from any suspicion of untruth. Any good and simple man is ashamed to lie; in a monk such a thing is totally unbecoming. Further, it is deceitful, wicked and altogether abominable for a witness to the truth, when his testimony is brought forward publicly, to side with falsehood and uphold a lie. And lastly, to see a white-haired ancient cutting japes and playing the fool is unpleasant enough; but for such a one, on the very threshold of eternity, to spend his time concocting idle tales is not merely unattractive, it must appear thoroughly repellent.

CHAPTER 99. THE SIGNS THAT HERALDED HIS DEATH

It is time now to speak of the blessed man's death. Long before the event he had foreknowledge of it, a knowledge infused by the Holy Spirit in those living words that he used to utter in Wulfric's ear. It was also clearly confirmed to him by outward signs, for, when a year or more, as is thought, remained of his life and he was sitting in his cell, his hauberk, its rings miraculously parted, slipped suddenly from his shoulders to his knees. His heart fell with it, and, snatching at the slipping mail, he called his boy and with his help hitched the hauberk back on to his shoulders, fastening it with stronger laces. Thereupon he came out in blisters all over his body, and the flesh, which the Holy Spirit had rendered so recently as hard as iron, was now found to be, of itself, no more than flesh. Thus mail and flesh together, each in its own way, foretold that his service in Christ's army was coming to its end. For the flesh, to which the Spirit had Rev. 14:13 already said that it might rest from its labours, was justly indignant at the reimposition of its burden. Moreover, that most humble of men had to be humbled still further after such victories in the field, so that the wealth of glory won might be perfected and safeguarded by humility.

Thus it was that the man of God called together his most trusted friends, namely Brother William the guest-master, Henry of Corscomb, Osbern the priest and others similarly esteemed, and, having related the happenings one by one, he took counsel as to what he should do. The others were for reporting the business to the bishop, so Osbern the priest was sent and brought back the following instruction: he was to take off the hauberk and not wear it any more, but keep it by him wrapped in a cloth. So the man of God took from his sacred shoulders this aider and abetter in his feats of arms, and conserved it in a linen cloth; and from that time on, like a veteran, he awaited in peace the hour of his releasing. When one of our monks said to him in the course of conversation that he hoped, God willing, to be found worthy to attend his deathbed, the holy man replied: 'If that is what you want, it will be exceedingly simple. I shall send to you shortly before that day and you will hurry over, and your abbot as well should he so decide.' And to a private question as to the manner of his end, he answered that he would not be thrust out of this life on the point of some violent pain, but as his natural strength failed and vitality ebbed he would pass on peacefully on a flood-tide. Speaking of his death to Robert, Bishop of Bath, he said: 'When you hear that I have departed this life, make sure that you do not delay in coming to officiate at the commending of my soul to God and the committing of my body to the earth.' This was neither an entreaty nor the anxiety of a self-important man to procure in advance the ministrations of the great at his funeral rites. Frank and free in his simplicity, he enjoined even on the bishop what he foresaw in spirit should and ought to be done.

Meanwhile, with what longing sighs he, her son and citizen, had called on the Jerusalem he was so soon to see, with what loud shouts he hailed her now that he was on the point of entering her glory and partaking in the feast, there is no man fit to think about, let cf. Ps. 41:5 alone describe. One thing is certain: hovering in happy anticipation, with wings already spread for flight and swelling heart, he will have Job 39:26 darted out to meet joy on the way. Indeed I do not doubt that he had already sped towards Christ the Bridegroom coming from the wedding feast to fetch him to it, and been blessed with foretastes of cf. Mt. 22:2ff. ineffable joy. For if from day to day his body decayed and, wearing out like a garment, hastened to yield up to death what was its own, Ps. 101:27 / Heb. 1:11 so too from day to day was his spirit as surely renewed and hastened towards its own, which, thanks to his long and holy life of poverty, was undoubtedly even then the kingdom of heaven. And so, urged daily on towards his final goal, when his days were nearly spent the blessed man sent for Osbern the priest to speak with him in private.

CHAPTER 100. THE DISPUTE OVER HIS BODY FORETOLD

'Osbern,' he said, 'the hour of my calling is at hand; on the fifth day – that is, Saturday – as it draws towards evening, I shall have to be ready.' Osbern groaned at this and his face fell. 'Do not,' said Wulfric, 'let this trouble you nor take it too much to heart. I am going to my Lord whom I have served, and the day that now approaches is the day I have long desired. If you have a care, let it be this: when I have passed on, see that you bury my body here at once. Otherwise you will find yourself in trouble, for I tell you now that, thanks to the intrigues of men who will come to demand it with force of arms, my body will be a great nuisance to you. However, I trust in my Lord that they will not prevail and that it will not be given to them to take it hence. This is the place in which God called me to labour, and here he wills that I should take my rest.' Having said this, he made a pure and humble confession of his sins – for life cannot be lived without sinning – and, having received absolution from the priest, he was fortified according to rite with the other sacraments of the Church. After this he took to his bed and consented to rest his limbs, weak with debility and age.

Sad news runs swiftly: the neighbouring faithful, learning that their father was ill and that the physician of all the world was himself abed, came flocking to weep over him and receive his dying blessing. Mindful of his words to Brother William and of the love he bore him to the end, he sent for him as he had promised, so that the monk might once more see his dear Wulfric in the light of this world and exchange a last farewell. He hastened over and received in legacy the saint's blessing; and indeed he was at pains that day to load himself with Wulfric's blessings and rejoiced in the riches he had stored up in the past, knowing that in a little while he would Jn. 14:19, 28 not see him any more because he was going to the Father.

So it was that this sun, whose brightness had illumined the world till then by word and example, both knew and made known to others the time of his setting. And, lest death should seize him unawares and disquiet him by the dreadful manner of its coming, Christ did not suffer it to come like some thief or brigand to his little lad. Seen from afar, it walked before him, and, when it came, if not sweet, it was certainly less bitter. Thus it was that Wulfric, child of Christ deservedly beloved, full of years and virtue, on the day and hour of his predicting and with his joined hands pointing heavenward, passed from our light to light eternal. Osbern the priest, who had received his instructions about hastening the burial, did not feel he could properly smuggle into the next world a man of such glory, unhonoured and without paying this world its due of funeral rites. So he deferred complying with Wulfric's wishes and yet did not counter the will of God, in that the holy man's prediction about the wrangle over his burial place came to pass, and it was seen that this was indeed the place that the Lord had provided for his saint's repose.

CHAPTER 101. THE QUARREL FOR POSSESSION OF THE BLESSED MAN'S BODY, WHICH THE MONKS OF MONTACUTE STARTED IN VAIN

Along came the monks of Montacute, with a strong contingent of soldiers and others procured for the purpose, demanding as of right the body of the holy man on account of his being their brother – as they said – and receiving his daily pittance from them, and having vouchsafed himself to them for burial. But Osbern and those who took their stand with him put a different case. They accepted that the man of God was the monks' brother as regarded participation in spiritual benefits, as in the case of other holy men; nor could they deny the daily provision of victuals. But that he had chosen to be buried at Montacute, of this, they said, they had no knowledge whatever; on the contrary, they knew for an absolute certainty that he had consecrated this place to himself and himself to this place. As the argument continued in this vein, the monks abandoned reason for force in their struggle to achieve their ends, and set hasty hands to the body, which lay exposed in the church according to custom. Osbern thereupon, hemmed in so tight a corner, discovered with heaven's help the narrowest of ways out. Slipping from the church, he locked the door, leaving all the intruders shut in and shut up, and urgently set about summoning help from every quarter. Meanwhile, those within were not idle; they made a frenzied attack on the wall where the holy man's window had been in order to open a way for themselves and the sacred treasure after which they were vainly slavering. Outside, the villagers confronted them, striving with might and main to block up the opening and nullify their efforts. When finally the wall was breached, handling the sacred body without any reverence, the men within prepared to push it out to those of their faction who had scrambled through to receive it. The villagers, who were every bit as excited, struggled manfully to push the venerable body exposed to their view back inside again. Since there is no pursuing so fierce a fight without loss of peace and innocence, blood was shed and wounds were inflicted, but – God battling for his saint – none mortal.

The strife and confusion were at their height when back came

Osbern with a strong force gathered from Crewkerne and other places to which he had sent when his forewarning of the dispute had prompted him to make provision. Unlocking the church, he made his entry, and, by parading his new-found strength, he destroyed the morale of the invading party, dissipated their belligerence and deflated their presumption. Afterwards he showed himself conciliatory to the monks and convinced them with sensible argument that it would be best for both sides to refer the matter to the bishop and wait on his decision. And so the monks, their purpose unaccomplished, returned home more than a little shamefaced and mortified. However, it is silly and ill-considered to make fun of men who have mistaken their enthusiasm for religious zeal and whose pious ambitions have been frustrated, not by the decree of any human agency, but by the judgement of almighty God.

Subsequently the bishop, hearing of Wulfric's death, came over as the latter had foretold and was taken in to him, and there in the cell that had seen the flowering of his virtues, with all the reverence worthy of such holiness, the bishop buried the sacred and precious treasure. And, lest memories of pleasurable disorder should disturb in some degree the weaker minds, he calmed everything down with a few words to the people, reminding them how, long ago in the early days, the entire city of Jerusalem had been thrown into turmoil on St Paul's account.

CHAPTER 102. HOW WULFRIC'S BODY WAS TWICE TRANSLATED

For the rest, after the funeral rites had been celebrated with due decorum, Osbern the priest, fearful that thieves might dig up his treasure and steal it, reburied it secretly on the north side of the altar, smoothing the surface of the grave to match the surrounding floor, in case a rough finish should give cause for suspicion. Time passed, and, when he discovered, from whisperings overheard, that he had been found out, he looked around for a still safer cache, and finally hid his secret in the western part of the church in a spot known only to God and himself, using, I have no doubt, the lowliness of this inferior position as a sign. It was on the tenth day of March in the year of Our Lord 1154 that Wulfric fell asleep, in the first year of the reign of King Henry II, and in the everlasting reign of Our Lord Jesus Christ, to whom with the Father and the Spirit be all honour and glory, world without end. Amen.

ADAM OF PERSEIGNE

Adam of Perseigne followed a well-worn path into the Cistercian Order. He started off as a Canon Regular, moved to the black monks and finally joined the Cistercians at Pontigny, where he became in due course novice master before ruling as abbot over the monastery of Perseigne from 1188–1221. His sermons are still largely unpublished. His surviving letters, some sixty in all, tell us something about the man and something too about the Order at the end of its first hundred years. His influence, like that of St Bernard, extended far beyond the confines of his abbey. Among his correspondents are found abbots and monks of his own and other orders, princes and nobles, a king of England and, more interestingly, a number of well-born women, notably Marie and Alix of Champagne, who regarded him as what today would be termed their spiritual director. The Cistercians had been slow to accept any contacts with women, even refusing at first to respond to the wish of nuns to find a place in the Order, but during the later part of the twelfth century attempts were made to meet the growing aspirations of the laity and of women in particular, both lay and religious.

Adam expected from his correspondents an authentic commitment to the spiritual life, and his letters, rich in teaching, were for keeping, poring over and no doubt for passing round. He must have been a good novice master, for human relationships were important to him. He left many letters of friendship, including six to a nun of Fontevrault named Agnes, who later became superior of a newly founded Cistercian community near Nogent-le-Rotrou. The letters to Agnes remain a little stilted, as though he were trying his footing on ground that had long been signposted as slippery and unsafe, and he makes it clear more than once that he was not as free to visit her as he would have wished. None the less, spiritual friendship, which

Aelred preferred to cultivate for mutual support within the community, had, by Adam's day, not only passed beyond the walls but crossed the gender boundary.

His Epistola 15, given here in part, was written in response to a plea for spiritual sustenance. The recipient, a certain Nicholas, was probably a younger man, a relation or a friend. Like Agnes, he was living in a community with which Adam had regular contacts (greetings are sent to abbot, prior and bursar), and the letter will have been shared with all.

Two Letters

LETTER 57

To his dear Agnes, wishing that she may not disregard God's
discipline but ever set her mind on the higher gifts.   1 Cor. 12:31

As ever, dearest friend, I am wholly yours, my soul clings to yours,
and the bond that unites us is the love of Christ. I heard that the
heavenly goldsmith had recently been subjecting the gold of your
devotion to more stringent testing in the fire of suffering, as he
presses on to fashion for himself from that same gold a royal
diadem. How happy you would be if you should prove serviceable   Isa. 62:3
for the making of so glorious a diadem, one which needs the heat of
the furnace and repeated hammerings to bring it to perfection. Take
heart therefore and wait patiently for the Lord. Be valiant in action,   Ps. 26:14
steadfast in endurance, in loving tender and in all things wise. The
love that merits only praise is that which combines wisdom with
sweetness, and to which a certain spiritual steel ensures perseverance.
Love of Christ is sweet indeed when he is the soul's one object of
delight; it is wise when it is ruled in all things by discernment,
which — never doubt — is the mother and guardian of all the virtues.

Certainly where discernment's brake is lacking, whatever thought,
or speech, or action seeks to put into effect is found to be lacking in
proportion. Discernment treads warily in every situation; it is never
precipitate, embarks on nothing unadvisedly; instead, wholly submissive to Providence, it subjects itself lovingly to the judgements of
God. It is not merely that it does not doubt their justice: it positively
revels in their delightfulness. Love that may have been tender and
wise but lacked the steel of fortitude must necessarily run the risk of
non-perseverance, because as long as love soldiers in the flesh it must
withstand many a trial of strength. But when discernment governs

its activities and when, in self-distrust, it commits itself to wisdom's rule and judgement, then it triumphs with ease. For discernment always proceeds with caution and is refreshed in the struggles of this present life by a certain inner relish, which lures it ever onward, and the strength it draws from its confident hope gives it a high courage that keeps it from succumbing.

Entrust yourself therefore wholly to God's governance, submit yourself without reserve to the welcome decisions of your Bridegroom, so that, in all security of conscience, you accept without hint of an objection whatever your Master may ordain for his dominion, his property, which is what you are. Indeed your God possesses and has possessed you until now, and by his grace will ever possess you wholly until the end. Yourself the possession of the one and only, and happily in turn possessing him, you whom his love once clothed with his own self he will nowise strip hereafter of so blessed an enjoyment.

Truly as I am truly yours, although I share your joy in the progress that patience and tribulation bring about in you, I also share intensely, through my compassion with you, in your afflictions, and so extraordinary is the part I take in your joy and in your pain, giving thanks with you and suffering with you, that I hardly know where I am between these twin demands on my affection. For it is no less love's duty to congratulate you on your progress than to grieve over the infirmities that our frail nature lays on you, and, just as you feel for me a true and strong affection, I feel no less for you this double-sided tenderness.

For the rest, as your affection divined, I was recently at Loroux, but because I was absolutely not my own master I was quite unable to come and see you, the Abbot of Cîteaux not granting permission. I mention this for fear you might feel yourself belittled if you heard it from another source.

Greet all the holy community on my behalf, and with especial warmth those with whom you know I have the closest ties. Don't desist from asking for prayers on my behalf, for I have not yet ceased to be in need of them. Farewell.

FROM LETTER 15

To his dear Nicholas, Brother Adam, a sinner, wishing that in the Holy Spirit he may love faithfully and find happiness in love returned.

Let us therefore make the crossing to Bethlehem and not disdain, as we leave the business of the world behind, to approach the humble lodging-place of Christ. Here a child was born to us, here a son was given, who emptied himself that we might be filled to overflowing, who shrank that babes might grow in knowledge. This blessed hut, this inn – to be preferred above the palaces of kings – has become the classroom where the Word instructs us children from the crib, exemplifying in his speechless infancy a new and wondrous precept of humility. *Isa. 9:6 / Phil. 2:7*

And so, my son, if you would witness to the truth, do not forsake the inn at Bethlehem. There the infant Word lies wailing in the crib, yet that cry is far more eloquent than Cicero's oratory or even than the angels' silver tongues, for it gave fluency to children. There he who feasts the angels is sustained with a little milk, yet our simplicity nourished at this humble source will grow into adulthood. There inaccessible light is wrapped in common swaddling clothes, which yet serve to wipe away the grime of sin. In that manger the wheat of heaven is turned to barley, yet this fodder gives packhorses the strength to bear their burdens. *Wisd. 10:21 / 1 Tim. 6:16*

Now the cloister within the monastery I call Christ's lodging-place, his inn; no, rather it is the monastery itself, into which you turned when you left evil ways for good. The cloister is the stable, the stall of discipline to which you, like a docile animal, bound yourself with the tether of your vow. And what should I call the barley in the manger but the order observed in the cloister, or again the understanding of God's word which is extracted with difficulty from the husk of the letter, or indeed the most blessed body of Christ, received in the sacrament of the altar? The awn and the straw of the barley represent both the discomfort and difficulties inherent in the religious life and the figures and outer envelope of Holy Scripture; they signify too the sacramental species under which we partake of the flesh of Christ. Again, what are these species –

colour and savour, form and mass – by which so great a mystery is bodied forth, but those swaddling clothes in which the infant Word lies wound in his narrow crib? By frequent use of these sacramental species in faith and love and humble imitation, by the bland milk of simplicity are infants nourished, until, matured in years, they can Heb. 5:12–14 take stronger meat.

Loving one's neighbours is this stronger meat, rejoicing in one's own abasement, following Christ even to the ignominy of the Cross, being nailed to that Cross, embracing patiently an undeserved punishment, being lost in yearning and contemplation to the reality of all things earthly. That is the food of the mature and of those Heb. 5:14 who, like the Apostle, have their faculties trained by practice. Would that you might be one of them, one who is able to take advantage of such solid fare. Best for me if the infant occupant of that crib, who chose a stable for his birthplace, should dispense to my weakness a few sups of his milk. Would that it were given to me to be beside him at his mother's breast and thus learn from his infant cries what I might safely know and joyfully retain.

A DESCRIPTION OF CLAIRVAUX

This delightful piece is unattributed. The author could have been a frequent visitor to Clairvaux or a member of the community. From the way he writes and from the fact that he feels no need to establish a bona fides, the latter seems the more likely.

The Clairvaux he loves and describes is not the 'little huddle of huts' seen by William of St Thierry on his first visit to the community four years after its implanting.[1] Those were replaced as soon as possible by a stone-built church, cloister and monastic complex. But the spate of recruits rendered these in turn inadequate – and not the buildings only. Bernard and his companions had settled in the upper reaches of a cleft in the hills that opened into a wider and more fertile valley running down to the Aube. A growing community required larger gardens, orchards, meadows, perhaps even a better water supply. When Bernard returned in 1135, the prior and other 'provident men' who 'periodically compelled God's servant to come down from heaven where he habitually dwelled and made him aware of the needs of the house',[2] pressed for a move down valley to wider acres closer to the river. Bernard resisted: such a step would be costly, wasteful of what had been achieved and create a wrong impression in the region. The elders, who had to deal with the practical problem of forcing several quarts into a pint pot, prevailed. 'Support for God's work came flooding in', workmen were hired and the brothers fell to with a will. Arnald of Bonneval describes the digging of the network of channels, ducts and sluices designed to feed and power the workshops – the same system on which our author dwells with loving admiration. For the first time (the close-pressing forest having preserved their privacy before) the monks built a wall, 'throwing a great girdle round the monastery and its broad expanse. The house rose, and, as for the church, it shot upward and outward as though it had a living and moving soul within it.'

It was this latter Clairvaux that William referred to – almost with regret – as enjoying sufficiency and peace; this Clairvaux that appeared to many as a prefiguration of the heavenly Jerusalem that the twelfth century, from Abelard on, hymned with an almost desperate yearning. But there is nothing desperate in this piece. Its writer is blessedly serene, his mood elegiac: the birds are always singing in the orchard, the fruit is ever swelling on the bough, no sharp and sided hail flies in these fields. Everything is fixed at the moment of perfection as in an illuminated manuscript. This is a landscape with figures, each one rich with meaning and allusions, a medieval canvas stretched on a classical frame, with Ovid peeping like a faun round a tree-trunk. The soaring buildings, so central even in decay to our picture of the monastic life, hardly figure here. It is the co-operation between man and nature that has captured the author's imagination. Instead of the struggle to wrest a living from a grudging soil, he depicts a nature open-handed and rich in courtesies, a creation that mirrors the bounty of its maker and invites the monk to gaze at the reflection.

A Description of Clairvaux

Should you wish to picture Clairvaux, the following has been written to serve you as a mirror. Imagine two hills and between them a narrow valley, which widens out as it approaches the monastery. The abbey covers the half of one hillside and the whole of the other. With one rich in vineyards, the other in crops, they do double duty, gladdening the heart and serving our necessities, one shelving flank providing food, the other drink. On the ridges themselves it is often the monks' work (pleasant indeed and the more so for being peaceful) to collect dead brushwood and tie it in bundles for burning, sorting out the prickly brambles and cutting and tying only what is fit for the fires. Their job too to grub out the briars, to uproot and destroy what Solomon calls the bastard slips, which throttle the growing branches or loosen the roots, lest the stout oak be hindered from saluting the height of heaven, the lime from deploying its supple branches, the pliant ash that splits so readily from growing freely upwards, the fan-shaped beech from attaining its full spread. Wisd. 4:3

Farther on, the rear of the abbey extends to the wide valley bottom, much of which lies inside the great sweep of the abbey wall. Within this cincture many fruit-bearing trees of various species make a veritable grove of orchards, which by their nearness to the infirmary afford no small solace to the brothers in their sickness: a spacious promenade for those able to walk, an easeful resting-place for the feverish. The sick man sits on the green turf, and, when the merciless heat of the dog days bakes the fields and dries up the streams, he in his sanctuary, shaded from the day's heat, filters the heavenly fire through a screen of leaves, his discomfort further eased by the drifting scent of the grasses. While he feeds his gaze on the pleasing green of grass and trees, fruits, to further his delight, hang swelling before his eyes, so that he can not inaptly say: 'I sat in the shadow of his tree, which I had desired, and its fruit was sweet to my taste.' A chorus of brightly feathered birds caresses his ears with sweetest melody. Thus for a single illness God in his goodness provides many a soothing balm: the sky smiles serene and clear, the earth quivers with life, and the sick man drinks in, with eyes, ears and nostrils, the delights of colour, song and scent.

S. of S. 2:3

Where the orchard ends the garden begins, marked out into rectangles, or, more accurately, divided up by a network of streamlets; for, although the water appears asleep, it is in fact slipping slowly away. Here too a pretty spectacle is afforded to the sick, who can sit on the grassy banks of the clear runnels watching the fish at play in the translucent water, their manoeuvres recalling troops in battle. This water, which serves the dual purpose of feeding the fish and irrigating the vegetables, is supplied by the tireless course of the river Aube, of famous name, which flows through the many workshops of the abbey. Wherever it passes it evokes a blessing in its wake, proportionate to its good offices; for it does not slip through unscathed or at its leisure, but at the cost of much exertion. By means of a winding channel cut through the middle of the valley, not by nature but by the hard work of the brethren, the Aube sends half its waters into the monastery, as though to greet the monks and apologize for not having come in its entirety, for want of a bed wide enough to carry its full flow. And should this stream in spate surge forward in a tumultuous sally, repulsed by the fronting wall under which it has to flow, it falls back into itself, and the current once again embraces the reflux. As much of the stream as this wall, acting as gatekeeper, allows in by the sluice-gates hurls itself initially with swirling force against the mill, where its ever-increasing turbulence, harnessed first to the weight of the millstones and next to the fine-meshed sieve, grinds the grain and then separates the flour from the bran.

The stream now fills the cauldron in a nearby building and suffers itself to be boiled to prepare the brothers' drink (should husbandry have been ill-rewarded by a poor vintage, and malt, in default of grape juice, have to supply the want).[3] Nor does it hold itself acquitted yet. The fullers, next door to the mill, invite it in, claiming with reason on their side that, if it swirls and eddies in the mill, which provides the brothers with food, it should do no less by those who clothe them. The stream does not demur, nor indeed refuse any request made of it, Instead, raising and lowering by turns the heavy pestles (unless you prefer the term mallets or, better still, wooden feet – the expression which seems most suited to the gymnastic occupation of the fullers), it frees these brothers from their drudgery. And should their gravity be broken by some jest, it frees them too from punishment for their sin.[4] O Lord, how great are the consolations that you in your goodness provide for your poor servants, lest a greater wretchedness engulf them! How generously you palliate the hardships of your penitents, lest perchance they be crushed at times by the harshness of their toil! From how much back-breaking travail for horses and arm-aching labour for men does this obliging torrent free us, to the extent that without it we should be neither clothed nor fed. It is most truly shared with us, and expects no other reward wheresoever it toils under the sun than Ecc. 1:3 that, its work done, it be allowed to run freely away. So it is that, after driving so many noisy and swiftly spinning wheels, it flows out foaming, as though it too had been ground and softened in the process.

The tannery is next to capture the stream, and here it displays its zeal in the fashioning of all that goes to make the brothers' footwear. Thereafter, its water decanted into a succession of channels, it carries out a dutiful inspection of each workshop, diligently inquiring where it can be of service and offering its ungrudging help in the work of cooking, sifting, turning, whetting, watering, washing, grinding and softening. Lastly, to ensure that no cause for gratitude be wanting, that its tasks be left in no respect unfinished, it carries the waste products away and leaves everything clean in its wake, and, while Clairvaux renders it thanks for all its blessings, it courteously returns the abbey's greetings as it hastens away to pour back into the river the waters siphoned off into the monastery. The two currents are indistinguishably mingled and the river, shrunken and sluggish since the diversion, surges forward under the onrush of water.

Now that we have returned the stream to its bed, let us go back to those rills we left behind. They too are diverted fr)m the river and meander placidly through the meadows, saturating the soil that it may germinate. And when, with the coming of the mild spring weather, the pregnant earth gives birth, they keep it watered too lest the springing grasses should wither for lack of moisture. As it is, these have no need to depend on drops begged from the clouds, fostered as they are by the care of the kindred river. These rills, or more properly trenches, their job done, are swallowed once more by the river that spewed them forth, and the Aube, now fully replenished, rushes off on its steep downhill course. And we, who have kept it company all this way, until it, in Solomon's words, has

Ecc. 1:5 returned to its place, let us too return to our point of departure and, wasting no words, leap lightly over the wide expanse of the meadow.

Here is a spot that has much to delight the eye, to revive the weak spirit, to soothe the aching heart and to arouse to devotion all who seek the Lord. It brings to mind the heavenly bliss to which we all aspire, for the smiling face of the earth with its many hues feasts the eyes and breathes sweet scents into the nostrils. Both the sight and the scent of the meadow put me in mind of tales of long ago. Their scent recalls to me that the smell of Jacob's garments was compared

Gen. 27:27 to the fragrance of a fertile field; their colour, how the splendour of Solomon's purple was displayed. And yet he, who lacked neither the skill derived from wisdom nor the means that power affords, could

Mt. 6:28-9 not in all his glory rival the lilies of the field. And so it is that, while
Lk. 12:27 agreeably employed in the open, I get no little pleasure from the mystery beneath the surface.

This meadow is refreshed by the floodwaters of the Aube, which runs through it, so that the grass, thanks to the moisture at its roots, can stand the summer heat. Its extent is great enough to tire the community for the space of twenty days when the sun has baked to hay its shorn grassy fleece. Nor is the haymaking left to the monks alone: alongside them a countless multitude of lay-brothers and voluntary and hired helpers gather the mown grass and comb the shorn ground with wide-toothed rakes.[5]

Two granges divide this meadow between them, the Aube serving as an equitable judge and surveyor in the settling of disputes.

Ps. 77:54 Assigning to each its share, like a marking-rope it sets the bounds that neither dares cross to invade the other's portion. You would take these granges not for the living quarters of lay-brothers but for monastic cloisters were it not that ox-yokes, ploughs and other farm implements betray the inhabitants' status, and that no books are opened there. As regards the monastic buildings themselves, you will admit that they are well-fitted in size, siting and appearance to a large community of monks.

In the part of the meadow nearest the wall, a watery lake has been created from the solid field. Where in former times the sweating labourer mowed the hay with a sharp scythe, today the brother in charge of the fish-ponds, seated on a wooden horse, is borne over the smooth surface of this liquid field. Wherever he goes, a light pole serves him for spurs to speed his progress, for a curb when turning. The net destined to entangle the fish is spread under the water, and its favourite baits are set, but primed with a hidden hook to catch the unwary – an example which teaches us to spurn delights, for pleasure harms and suffering is its price. Only the man who has never sinned or never done true penance for sin can possibly ignore that the outcome of pleasure is pain. May God keep pleasure far removed from us – that pleasure at whose doorway death stands posted, and which a wise man likens to bees on the wing, which, as soon as they have shed their sweet burden of honey, turn and strike the addicted heart with a deep-seated sting.[6] The high bank surrounding the mere is faced with wattle made from withy roots to prevent the soil from slipping into the water that washes it. A brook some thirty feet distant keeps the water-level constant by means of feeder ditches, which carry and regulate both inflow and outflow.

But while I am winging my way across the plain, breathless with the exertion, whether it be describing the vivid surface of the meadow painted by Wisdom's own hand or the ridges of the hills with their shaggy pelt of trees, I am taxed with ingratitude by that sweet spring from which I have drunk times without number and whose deserts I have ill requited. It has often quenched my thirst, humbled itself to wash not only my hands but my feet, and done me many a kindness and service – good offices which merited a better reward. For now it reproaches me bitterly with having assigned it the last place, and that only just, in my topographical list, when the first, by right of reverence, was its due. And indeed I cannot deny that my memory was laggard when it gave others precedence. This spring, like the waters of Siloam which move silently, glides to and fro unheard down subterranean channels. Its Isa. 8:6 course cannot be detected by the faintest murmur, and, as though it feared discovery, it hangs its head and turns its face aside. Why should I not think it wanted to be passed over in silence when it secretes itself under cover? Like all good springs it sallies out over against the rising sun, so that midsummer finds it greeting the roseate splendour of dawn full in the face. A small but pretty hut, or tabernacle to use a more reverential word, encloses it and protects it from any dirt. It wells out of the hillside only to be swallowed by the valley, and in the very place of its birth it seems to die, nay, even

Lk. 11:29
Jon. 1:17 to be buried. But do not look for the sign of Jonah the prophet, expecting it to lie hidden away for three days and three nights: at once, a thousand feet away, it rises again in the abbey cloister, as it might be from the bowels of the earth, and, as it were restored to life, offers itself to the sight and use of the brethren, lest its future lot should be with any but the holy.

THROUGH MEMORY'S DOOR

The *Vita Prima* is proof that already in St Bernard's lifetime the garnering of reminiscences had begun. Once death had tipped him backwards into history – or onward into eternity – the process accelerated. It was not only Bernard who must be commemorated, it was the whole Clairvaux phenomenon that had to be captured and fixed on the page for future generations, since every miracle, every word of wisdom and spiritual experience provided not only a goal but food for the long journey. The first of several collections of edifying stories was compiled at Clairvaux in the 1170s. Entitled the *Liber visionum et miraculorum*, it was recently discovered among the Clairvaux manuscripts at Troyes. It was rapidly followed by the *Liber de miraculis* written by Herbert of Clairvaux, a Spaniard who had entered Clairvaux in St Bernard's day and spent most of a long life there. Both collections were plundered by Conrad von Eberbach when he came in 1220 to write the *Exordium Magnum*, a more ambitious and altogether better-organized work, but one which falls outside the time span of this anthology. There is much repetition and a degree of tedium in these compilations, but the stories offer a slant on St Bernard not afforded by the *Vita Prima*. They show him in his domestic role, the father of his monks, all-knowing, infinitely caring, the guarantor of their salvation. While he lived, he was their champion against the devil; dead, his example and his prayers were still potent. Many of the stories concern simple monks, named and nameless. None the less, ubiquitous in death as in life, Bernard's presence permeates the material. Indeed he looms so great as virtually to obscure his predecessors. For the Cistercians of the late twelfth century, he had become the Order.

Eight Stories from Exemplum Collections

ABBOT AND NOVICE

II, 23 While blessed Bernard was still a novice, he used to recite in silence every day the seven penitential psalms for the repose of his mother's soul. One day, having begun his recitation as usual after compline, he broke off before completing it – whether from negligence or absent-mindedness I could not say – went to his bed and fell asleep. Abbot Stephen, aware in spirit of this oversight, sent for him the following day and said: 'I wondered, Brother Bernard, why you abandoned those psalms of yours yesterday after compline, or if you entrusted their saying to someone else?' At these words the young man, bashful and devout as he was, reddened and threw himself at the abbot's feet.

A DEATH DEFERRED

I, 13 Blessed Bernard went one day to visit a dying brother after compline. Perceiving that the man was close to death and would soon pass over, he said to him: 'Dearest brother, you know that our community is tired now from work and will shortly have to get up for vigils. Should you in your turn fall asleep, they, to their great disturbance, will have to cut short their rest and will celebrate the great night office with less solemnity. So, that you may prosper and live long in the land which you are about to enter and make your own, I bid you in Christ's name to wait for us till the hour of the divine office.' To this the dying man replied: 'I shall do your bidding, my lord, provided you support my intention with your prayers.' What more? The abbot went off to the dorter and the

<small>Dt. 5:16, 23:20 etc.</small>

brother did not die before the term appointed. But as soon as the sign was given for the tablet to be banged for vigils and the din rang out, he breathed his last. Nor did it happen only with this brother, but at other times and with other monks whose deaths were deferred for one or more days at the abbot's behest.

THE DROVER'S HELPMEET

I, 15 There was another brother in the monastery who worked as a drover, a simple man and pure of heart. He once in his sleep had the quite delightful vision of Our Lord Jesus Christ beside him on the other side of the pole, holding the goad in his own sweet hand and driving the oxen with him. Straight after this he fell ill, took to his bed and ended his life after six days of pain and travail. Brother Bernard, reflecting on the vision that the monk had related, and knowing him to be pure and simple of heart, rejoiced exceedingly and declared confidently that the brother walked with God. Since God had worked at his side, he had translated him, for infinite Compassion could not desert in his last agony the servant he had so courteously toiled alongside in the field.

THE GALLOWS-BIRD

II, 15 There was a day when God's servant, Bernard, went to see Count Theobald on business. As he approached the town where the count was then to be found, he met a large crowd conducting a notorious brigand to the gallows. The tender-hearted abbot, taking hold of the thong that bound him, said to his executioners: 'Hand this murderer over to me: I want to string him up with my own hands.' The count, meanwhile, hearing that the man of God had come, hurried to meet him, for he always showed him the greatest honour and affection. He was horrified to find him, rope in hand, with the prisoner in tow. 'Ah, reverend father, what is it you want to do? Why have you called back from the gates of hell this gallows-bird who deserves a thousand deaths? Can you save a man who has turned himself into a devil? His reform is a lost cause, and dying is the only good thing he'll ever do. Let a lost soul go to his ruin, for his pernicious life has imperilled many another.' 'I know, best of men,' replied the abbot, 'that this is a villain of the deepest dye, deserving of the harshest torment. Don't imagine I want to free a sinner of this kind unpunished; my intention is rather to hand him over to the torturers that he may get his just deserts – and the longer the process lasts, the juster it will be. You sentenced him to a short agony and a sudden death; I shall see that he is crucified slowly and dies a very protracted death. You would let the body hang on the gibbet for a day or two; I shall ensure that he lives and hangs, nailed to the cross, for many years in continual expiation.'

Silence greeted these words: the very Christian prince did not dare make further objections to the saint. So at once that kindest of fathers stripped off his tunic and clothed his prisoner in it, and, after shaving the latter's head, took him into the Lord's fold, making a sheep from a wolf, a lay-brother out of a robber. From that day on Phil. 2:8 the brigand made himself obedient to the abbot, even unto death, living at Clairvaux, if I am not mistaken, thirty years or more in the Order. Constant was his name, and I myself saw the man and knew him.

A WORD OF COMFORT

There was an occasion when blessed Bernard, sitting in chapter, said something wondrously comforting. And although his words cheered every heart, as will an utterance full of joy and consolation, I will admit that there was one present among us that day whom the burden of conscience terrified perhaps overmuch. This is what, among other things, the abbot said: 'Why are you so forlorn? If Judas who betrayed and sold the Lord were here where you are now, he would obtain mercy.' The man who heard these words bore witness and wrote this down.

COUNTERWEIGHTS

A man of Flemish birth, named Arnulf of Majorca, exceedingly rich and addicted to pleasure, surrendered himself in secret to St Bernard.

His circumstances were so involved that the two men agreed to keep the business under cover until the day he was due to leave his land and kindred; for he was the head of a great lineage, blessed with sons and brothers and so entangled in riches and possessions that, unless he took wise dispositions in advance, he would be unable to tear himself free without causing injury and offence. So no one but these two knew of the decision.

Meanwhile the word of God came to a certain herdsman taking his oxen out to plough: 'Go and tell Arnulf of Majorca to take you with him to Clairvaux, where he is going to become a monk, and you are to enter with him.' The drover, hearing the voice but seeing not a soul, began to pray intently that, if the word was of God, the Almighty might open his ear again and reinforce the message by repeating it. When he had heard the oracle a second time, he went to the appointed man: 'I have a message for you, my lord,' he said. And having been taken aside, he fell at the other's knees. 'I beg you for Christ's sake,' he said, 'to take me with you to Clairvaux and save my soul along with yours.' The account of the revelation, which he gave, filled Arnulf of Majorca with wonder and delight, and he took the herdsman with him, to be the inseparable companion of his journey and conversion and to share, as we believe, in the heavenly reward.

When this grand personage arrived at Clairvaux, he gave generously of his substance to that and other houses, which induced blessed Bernard to state publicly that Christ's power and glory were not less manifest in the conversion of Brother Arnulf than in the raising of Lazarus after four days, for it was plain, since he lay Jn. 11:39 walled and entombed in pleasures like one in the grave, that, living, he was dead. When he received that brother's confession, made with many groans and tears, of all the sins he had accumulated in the world, blessed Bernard, seeing the bitter remorse that filled his heart and his spontaneous pursuit of all that was good, bade him say three times the Our Father and persevere in his purpose. At this Brother Arnulf, much put out, exclaimed: 'Please, Father, do not mock your servant.' 'In what way am I mocking you?' 'Seven or ten years' fasting would not be enough for me, even in sackcloth and ashes, and you tell me to say three Our Fathers and persevere in the Order!' But the saint replied: 'Do you then know better than I what you should do and how to ensure your salvation?' 'God preserve me from such wicked presumption! But for his sake I beg you not to spare me in the present, that it may go easier with me in the future. Give me the kind of penance now that will win me, after my death, eternal rest without further expiation.' 'Do as I have said,' replied the blessed Father, 'and I promise you that, when you have laid down the burden of the flesh, you will fly straight to God without any hindrance.'

PEASE PORRIDGE

On the Monday of Easter week one Andrew, Archdeacon of Verdun and a man of the highest birth, was converted to the religious life. He had come to Clairvaux on a visit and had at the time no intention of remaining. But when he went into chapter to ask for the prayers of the community and saw the orderliness of that holy throng and their almost angelic demeanour, he was deeply moved, and the spirit of the Lord seized on him and he was
1 Sam. 10:6 changed on the spot into another man. So wholeheartedly did he quit the world that he did not return home for as much as an hour to take leave of his friends or dispose of his house and chattels. He abandoned everything, breaking off rather than loosing his ties, that he might cleave the sooner to Christ.

It has to be said, however, that this Andrew endured many temptations in the course of his noviciate. He was like some ultra-tender woodworm, soft and delicate in the extreme, having been cocooned and cosseted from his mother's womb. Having reluctantly unlearned the dainty habits of his early life and found the newly undertaken labour to be very arduous, like Lot fleeing Sodom he
Gen. 19:18–19 decided that he could not save his soul by making for the heights and resolved in consequence to turn aside to a less demanding order. Having mentioned the matter several times to Dom Robert, the abbot, his courage finally failing him he succumbed to temptation and declared to him one day that he could not endure the life a moment longer. The abbot pleaded and coaxed and at last extorted the promise that he would force himself to stick it out for three more days. Hardly had the abbot obtained this assurance than he had the community praying to God for the man.

Later that day, when this novice sat down at table, he found a bowl of split peas in front of him – the kind of pulse he detested above all others and which sometimes even made him retch. But at the first spoonful he found it amazingly tasty, richer in flavour even than meat. At once he seized the spoon and, moving the bowl closer, frugality forgotten, he devoured his portion to the last mouthful. As he was eating, he kept sticking his finger in his mouth, expecting to come across some of the crisp morsels of fat bacon in which he fancied the concoction had been fried. When the meal was over, he hurried off to inquire of the abbot whether he had ordered the dish to be seasoned with lard or some other fat for his especial benefit. This the abbot denied, and so the cooks were sent for. They too protested that in truth they had put in nothing bar salt and water. At this the novice realized that he had been favoured with a divine visitation and rendered thanks to God; nor from that day on could he be deflected from the Order of his choosing.

When on the next day and the next and for a long time after he still found the same delicious flavour in victuals of that sort, he finally learned from experience that the Lord is able, when he wishes   Lk. 3:8 to console his servants, to imbue greens and pulses with the same rich savour that he has imparted to meat and fish. So it came about that he often confessed to deriving more pleasure now from eating pease-pudding and greenstuff than he used to get from feasting on fatstock and game.

A BURDEN SHARED

From the beginning the devil has thwarted the virtuous and does so still today, but God in his kindness sees to it that he does them no lasting hurt. That this is so is universally known, yet it is rare that anyone makes an adequate response to God. Out of many examples let me relate a recent one, which, being close in time, will hold more interest and act as a sharper spur to all lovers of God to praise him.

It happened at Grandselve, a daughter house of Clairvaux. Thither came a young knight to fight in God's cause. He knocked, and the door was opened to him; he was received, tried and made a monk.   Mt. 7:7 Day by day he grew towards perfection, progressing in the monastic ideal beyond many of his contemporaries in the Order. The whole community rejoiced, but the abbot above all, inasmuch as he had given birth to one who bore the likeness of Christ within him. This good soldier was wounded, hit by an arrow shot in the dark. He began to flag and weary of the life, to swing between listlessness and agitation. A venom snaked its way into his breast, pain took hold of his heart and a sword pierced his very soul. His expression grew sombre, his look less kindly, his words became sharp and his movements slack; he was readier to break silence and give way to levity. In fact the whole man was changed for the worse and totally altered.

This radical change was noticed and caused concern. The whole community was upset, especially the abbot, who was stirred to the very depths. He turned himself from a father into a mother, preparing to give birth anew, remoulding in his son the deformed likeness of Christ. He soothed, cherished, caressed. He bored through the wall and made a breach. The brother made his confession and admitted that he was a sinner indeed, overwhelmed by a mountain of offences, a torrent of wickedness and a sea of wrong doing, and that God had no part in him, since he was just and repaid everyone according to his deeds. 'How,' he asked, 'if God judges rightly, will he not destroy me, who have gone against him to this very day, shrinking from no act which sexual desire suggested. How could he put himself in opposition to what is just and moral?

'There has been nothing that my lust stopped short of, nothing so vile that my brutish and bestial mind shuddered at the thought. Thus have I run headlong throughout life, bereft of sense, acting against reason, and, because I have ignored God, he now will have nothing to do with me. There is only one thing left for me: to return to the world and make the most of the time remaining, lest my reward be hardship in this life and nothing in the next, for my wickedness is too great for any claim to mercy.'

The abbot trembled as he listened. He reproached himself with keeping a bad watch. He lamented bitterly not having held the wolf at bay. With protracted sighs he deplored the fact that the sheep had been dragged off and was now following of its own accord. 'What are you saying, dearest son? Why has this calamity overtaken you so suddenly? Who has tripped you up? You were running well. You were already nearing the goal, and we were rejoicing at your progress; now we must weep over your fall. Tell me,

1 Kgs. 3:26

cf. Phil. 3:21

Ez. 8:8

Rom. 2:6,
Rev. 22:12

Gal. 5:7

why do your sins fill you with terror? Have you not confessed them all to me?'

'I have kept nothing from you.'

'If I were to take your sins on me and ensure that you were absolved from them, would you take comfort, serve God and not leave the monastery?'

'Oh! what are you saying?' replied the other. 'What you propose is nothing! I would happily put up with a hideous dungeon in perpetuity, frog-infested lakes, sword, fire, scorpions and every punishment imaginable. The harshest treatment would be as a soothing balm, pain would seem like pleasure and every sort of torment and suffering light and transient if only I were sure of God's forgiveness.'

'Come here,' said the abbot, 'and give me your hand. See, I absolve you this very day. I take all your sins on me and will account for them all to God on the Day of Judgement. I absolve you, I set you free. O God,' he prayed, 'who are with us and see us, confirm my judgement. Require this man's sins of me. Hold him blameless and innocent, and, laying nothing to his account, exact the whole of his debt from me.'

The monk was satisfied. With heartfelt thanks he threw himself on the abbot's face and began at once to behave cheerfully and confidently, holding to his purpose and making progress in the monastic life by fighting the good fight, finishing the race and keeping the faith. Three years remained to him, and, being come to perfection in that brief space, it was as though he had lived long. His soul was pleasing to God, so God hastened to withdraw him from the wickedness around him. In short, he was carried off so that evil might not warp his understanding nor deceitfulness seduce his soul. For two days he lay at the point of death, neither speaking, eating nor feeling. Then, coming to himself, he asked for the abbot. His eyes were all that moved as he turned them reverently on the approaching man. Gen. 50:1

2 Tim. 4:7
Wisd. 4:13

Wisd. 4:14
Wisd. 4:11

'Father,' he said, 'and truly a father to me. I ought to adore your footsteps. I should have licked the ground you stood on and offered myself to you as a very footstool. It is through you that I am saved. It is you who have furnished me with life and crown. You are for me the means of salvation and grace, of all, in brief, that heaven holds of honour and glory.'

'How do you know this?' asked the abbot.

'By revelation. These two days past I have been in heaven. I saw what awaits me, but your merit and your reward were shown to me too. Two beds there were, spread with silks and purple cloth. On one lay a gold and jewelled crown, and on the other, two. Nothing like these was ever seen and nothing heard of that could equal them. And I was told: "The couch with one crown is yours, the other with two is your abbot's. He has deserved one crown for his own way of life and the other for your conversion. For Scripture tells us that, as Christ laid down his life for us, so ought we to lay down our lives for the brethren. He has discharged this duty, laying down his soul[1] for you, and in the doing saved both you and him."'

1 Jn. 3:16

It happened just as he had said. As the brothers rose from the midday meal, he paid his final dues and joined the angels in joy, to benefit those to come by his example and sharing his glory with the man who imperilled his own soul for his sake. This fellow worker and witness was then Abbot of Grandselve; he went thence as abbot to Clairvaux and is now Archbishop of Clermont. He is reported to be still alive today, holy by all accounts, bright in his deserts and blest in his reward, a man for whom a couch has long been spread in heaven.

Notes

Also included in the Notes are bibliographical details and sources for both Latin texts and other English translations.

INTRODUCTION

1.   The degree of distortion depends on whether one accepts the date of 1112, given in the *Vita Prima*, for Bernard's entry, or that of 1113, favoured by many modern scholars. If the first is the true one, then the founding of La Ferté was indeed consequent on Bernard's arrival; if the latter, it followed within a few weeks and was therefore independent of the new contingent, since there must have been forward planning.

2.   John Morson O.C.S.O., *Via Veritas et Vita: Christ in the Sermons of Guerric of Igny* (Achel, 1972).

Bibliographical Details: For a general history of the Order one may consult Louis Lekai, *The Cistercians: Ideals and Reality* (Kent, Ohio, 1977). For an understanding of monastic spirituality, see Jean Leclercq, *The Love of Learning and the Desire for God: A Study of Monastic Culture*, 2nd edn. (SPCK, 1978) and Louis Bouyer, *The Cistercian Heritage* (1958). Cistercian Publications have both published and reprinted in English translation a number of individual studies and composite works on Cistercian spirituality and the historical background.

CÎTEAUX: THE EARLY YEARS

Bibliographical Details: The latest evaluation of the early development of the Order can be found in Jean-Baptiste Auberger, *L'unanimité cistercienne primitive: mythe ou réalité?* Studia et Documenta, III (Achel, 1986).

The Little Exord

Source: For the Latin text of the *Exordium Parvum*, see: Jean de la Croix Bouton et Jean-Baptiste Van Damme (eds.), *Les plus anciens textes de Cîteaux*, Cîteaux-Commentarii Cistercienses, Studia et Documenta, II (Achel, 1974).

1. *Rule*, ch. 55.
2. *Rule*, ch. 39.
3. *Rule*, ch. 53.

The Admonition of Stephen Harding

Source: Auberger, *L'unanimité cistercienne*, p. 327.

1. Gesta Regum Anglorum IV, 334, in *PL* 179, 1287; see also 1289–90.
2. Stephen Harding's Bible and other manuscripts from Cîteaux are in the municipal library at Dijon.

BERNARD OF CLAIRVAUX

Source: All translations are based on the text of *SBO*.

1. Letter 228.
2. Zoë Oldenbourg, *Saint Bernard* ['Le mémorial des siècles'] (Paris, 1970), p. 51.
3. Letters 187 and 189.

Bibliographical Details: The best Life of St Bernard at present available in English is Watkin Williams, *St Bernard of Clairvaux* (Manchester, 1935). Two others are in preparation. Although dated, E. Vacandard's *Vie de saint Bernard* (Paris, 1895) is comprehensive and still useful.

For the vast output of works, articles, etc. on St Bernard the following bibliographies may be consulted: Jean de la Croix Bouton, *Bibliographie Bernardine: 1891–1957* (Paris, 1958); Eugène Manning,

Bibliographie Bernardine: 1957–1970 (Documentation Cistercienne, Rochefort, 1972).

From the *Vita Prima* by William of St Thierry, Arnald of Bonneval and Geoffrey of Auxerre

Source: PL, 180. The *Fragmenta* have been more recently edited by Robert Lechat in *Analecta Bollandiana*, 50 (1932).

1. William's illness and his convalescence at Clairvaux took place at the latest in 1124.
2. The three Sundays preceding Lent are known respectively as Septuagesima, Sexagesima and Quinquagesima.
3. Cf. Sermons on the Song of Songs, 27, 9, *SBO* I, p. 188.

Bibliographical Details: For two views of the reliability of the *Vita Prima*, see A. H. Bredero, 'Études sur la *Vita Prima S. Bernardi*' in *AC*, XVII (1961), pp. 1–72 and 215–60, and XVIII (1962), pp. 3–59; and W. E. Goodrich, 'The reliability of the *Vita Prima S. Bernardi*. The image of Bernard in Book I of the *Vita Prima* and his own letters: a comparison' in *AC*, XLIII (1987), pp. 153–80.

From *An Apologia for Abbot William*

Source: SBO, 3. This translation comprises the last two thirds of the treatise. There is an excellent translation of the whole by Michael Casey (CFS 1, 1970) to which Jean Leclercq has written a substantial introduction.

1. Cf. St Bernard's Letter 88 (James 91). This is the Oger who is represented in the *Apologia* as staying at Clairvaux and waiting impatiently for the work to be finished. For another of Bernard's letters to him, see p. 97.
2. Cf. Letter 84 *bis* as quoted by Leclercq in his introduction to the CFS translation of the *Apologia*, p. 6.
3. Here Bernard is being less than accurate: there had been an open quarrel with Cluny over the defection of his cousin Robert of Châtillon, and the wound continued to fester until Peter the Venerable returned the young monk in 1128. Bernard, meanwhile, had written Robert a famous, emotional and bitterly satirical letter couched in terms at times identical to those he was later to use in the *Apologia*.

4. See Leclercq's introduction to CFS translation, pp. 15–23.

5. Many of the abuses pinpointed by St Bernard were singled out for correction in the Statutes enacted under Peter the Venerable. See *PL* 189, 1025–48.

6. *Rule*, ch. 55, 36, 39. Some of these points, like the use of fat, were a matter of fine interpretation.

7. *Rule*, ch. 48.

8. Literally 'the very one who instituted the wearing of tunics', i.e. St Benedict, author of the Rule.

9. St Gregory the Great, in Ezech. I, vii, 5, *PL* 76, 842.

10. *Rule*, ch. 36.

11. The four great abbots who governed Cluny, with the briefest of interregnums, from its early years until the death of the last in 1109, a span of nearly two centuries. Their reforming zeal extended itself further and further afield at the behest of princes and popes. Very many monasteries placed themselves under the authority of Cluny and more were founded. The total of large and small houses reached 1,184 under St Hugh, of which over two thirds were in France. This compares with the 694 Cistercian houses achieved by the end of the thirteenth century, scattered over a wider geographical area.

12. *Rule*, ch. 55.

13. Monks commonly saw themselves as the heirs and continuators of the apostolic community. Cf. William of St Thierry's *Life of St Bernard*, p. 31.

14. Lit. 'galabrunum aut isembrunum'. I am indebted to Michael Casey for the rendering. The Latin words refer to fabrics with no exact modern equivalent, the essential being that they were luxury articles. For further elucidation see *Apologia*, trans. M. Casey, p. 60, n. 149.

15. Lit. 'discolor barricanus'. Cf. as above. Catskins (ibid. p. 60, n. 149) were also in the luxury class. The Cluniacs defended their use of sheepskins on the reasonable grounds that the climate in Burgundy was much colder than in Italy, where the Rule was drawn up.

16. *Rule*, ch. 36.

17. Persius, *Satires*, II, 69.

18. The issues treated in this chapter are more complex than those of food and drink and clothing, and St Bernard's own attitude is at times ambivalent. As with the treatise as a whole there is both an immediate historical context and a wider moral one. The French

abbeys had been since Carolingian times centres of exchange, where laymen could hope for spiritual benefits in return for material donations; centres of culture, where artistic skills were practised and preserved; centres of learning, offering (until the advent of the cathedral schools) the only access to knowledge. In each of these roles they served as magnets, drawing in people whose privilege it was to enrich and embellish them. Poverty eluding them, they claimed to be poor in spirit; the splendour of the liturgy, the grandeur of the architecture, the elaborate ornamentation of church and cloister were all for the glory of God.

The new orders, in their flight into the wilderness, cut themselves off from the sources of wealth and from the reciprocal obligation to impress. Simplicity and austerity were central to their understanding of the religious life; poverty was a fact. Bernard pushed back the frontiers of renunciation still further. The figurative illuminations of the Cîteaux scriptorium were left behind. The visual arts had no place in religion save as a stimulus for spiritual dullards; for monks, light and line should suffice. This narrowly focused view became for a generation at least that of the whole Order (Aelred certainly shared Bernard's passion for all that was 'denuded, unpolished and unadorned': cf. in *The Mirror of Charity*, II, 24 a passage clearly inspired by the *Apologia*). Yet for all the verbal ferocity of his attack on what he terms the 'greater' abuses, Bernard's aim is strangely wavering. More than once he goes to the assault only to back away. His fine fury at money wasted on buildings while human beings starve peters out in a quotation from the Psalms: 'Lord, I have loved the beauty of your house.' It is only the grotesques that receive no quarter, but they are in the cloister, where there is no excuse. In an age of tourists he has been castigated as a puritan; in fact, for a man so temperamentally extreme, he seems surprisingly fair-minded.

From *The Life of Malachy the Irishman*

Source: SBO, 3.

1.   2 November, the Feast of All Souls, when the Church on earth prays for the departed.

Three Sermons on the Song of Songs

Source: SBO, 1 and 2.

1.   'Propter gratiam'. There is certainly a play here on the word *gratia*, which carries the meanings both of 'gratitude' and 'grace'. Whereas the first is undoubtedly due to teachers, St Bernard was as surely balancing 'nature' and 'grace', 'carnal' and 'spiritual'.

Bibliographical Details: *St Bernard's Sermons on the Canticle of Canticles*, trans. by a Priest of Mount Melleray (Dublin, 1920). Not the most recent but probably the most accessible.

From *On Consideration*

Source: SBO, 3.

1.   *Rectus* and *pravus* have a dual meaning of which St Bernard will have been keenly aware.

2.   An echo of the Augustinian view of the soul as reflecting the Trinity in its tripartite division into memory, understanding and will.

Nine Letters

Source: SBO, 7 and 8.

1.   See Letter 500 to Burchard, Bishop of Worms.

2.   Bernard has slipped here into the allegorical mode.

3.   *Heroides*, 1:11.

4.   Later to become abbot of Igny. See p. 127.

5.   The antipope Anacletus.

6.   Although it is uncomfortable to the modern ear, I have kept as close as possible to Bernard's Latin, particularly his *humilitas* and *sublimitas*, in order not to lose what I believe to be an intentional double meaning, i.e. the gulf in moral worth that he perceived between himself and Peter the Venerable and the distance between their respective positions in the monastic hierarchy of their day, greater than hindsight would suggest.

Bibliographical Details: The standard translation of St Bernard's letters is that by Bruno Scott James (1953).

WILLIAM OF ST THIERRY

Source: PL, 180, 205ff.

1. 'On the Nature of Body and Soul', *PL*, 180, 695.
2. From a Latin rendering of the Hebrew. The cherubim, being the highest order of angels, were nearest to the divine knowledge and therefore fuller of it.
3. It is unsure whether William wrote *canis*, the dog, or *carnis*, the flesh. An element of wordplay was probably present.

Bibliographical Details: There is a full study of William of St Thierry by J.-M. Déchanet *O.S.B.*, *Guillaume de Saint-Thierry: l'homme et son œuvre* (Bruges, 1942); translated in the Cist. Studies Series (Cist. Pub., 1972).

GUERRIC OF IGNY

Source: *PL*, 185; *Sources Chrétiennes*, 2 vols. (Paris, 1970, 1973).

1. See p. 98.
2. 'Ecce venit rex: occurramus obviam salvatori nostro.' The antiphon of the invitatory psalm from the office of vigils for the First Sunday of Advent; see J. Morson and H. Costello (eds.), *Guerric of Igny: Liturgical Sermons I* (Cist. Pub., 1971), p. 7, n. 1.
3. A reference to the conventual mass celebrated daily.
4. The theme of the three comings, with emphasis placed on the Middle Advent, is found in other Cistercian writers and notably in St Bernard's Advent sermons nos, 3 and 5 (ibid., p. 10, n. 29).
5. Cf. Luke 2:22–38. The feast of the Purification is traditionally known as Candlemas.

AMEDEUS OF LAUSANNE

Source: Text of the Homilies in *PL*, 188.

AELRED OF RIEVAULX

Source: Text of Aelred's writings in *PL*, 195 and *CC, Cont. Med.*, 1, ed. A. Hoste and C.H. Talbot, 1971. The *Oratio pastoralis* is only in the latter volume, ed. A. Wilmart.

1. Jocelyn of Furness, *Vita s. Waldeni*, Acta Sanctorum, iii Aug., c. 257.

Bibliographical Details: For a good introduction to Aelred, see A. Squire, *Aelred of Rievaulx: A Study* (1969).

From *The Life of Aelred* by Walter Daniel

1. First in the Bulletin of the John Rylands Library, VI (1921–2); then in book form with an excellent introduction and facing translation in 1950, reprinted 1978.
2. Archbishop Thurstan.
3. Probably Waltheof, King David's stepson and boyhood companion of Aelred, who was at this time prior of the Augustinian canons at Kirkham. He later entered Rievaulx and ended his life as abbot of Melrose.
4. I have followed Powicke here, although Walter uses the term *coturnix*, a quail, a word with which he would have been familiar from the Vulgate (cf. Ex.16:33).
5. For the details of food and drink, cf. *Rule*, ch. 39 and 40.
6. Ibid., ch. 22.
7. Ibid., ch. 33.
8. Ibid., ch. 6 and 42.
9. Ibid., ch. 5.
10. Ibid., ch. 63.
11. It was hunting-dogs that were banned by the Order, whether for the use of the monks (God forbid!) or the convenience of the local lord.
12. Walter Espec, Lord of Helmsley and Wark, was indeed a man of power and influence in the north of England, though his relevance here lies chiefly in his three religious foundations: he installed the Canons Regular at Kirkham in 1122, before inviting the Cistercians to Rievaulx ten years later. It was St Bernard who sent the initial contingent from Clairvaux. In 1135 Walter Espec made a further grant of land at Wardon in Bedfordshire, on which Abbot William of Rievaulx established the first daughter house, known as Sartis, 'the clearing'. Aelred left a striking portrait of his patron in his account of the Battle of the Standard, in which Walter Espec played an important part both as tactician and negotiator. According to Aelred he was 'a giant of a man with limbs in proportion to his

great height. Black of hair and heavily bearded, he had a wide brow, large, keen eyes, a full countenance and a voice like a trumpet.' 'De bello Standardii', *PL*, 195, 703.

13. Swineshead, a Savigniac foundation, opted in 1148 to join the Cistercian Order.

14. Walter refers to three classes of men living at Rievaulx: *monachi*, *conversi* and *laici*. The first comprised the choir monks; the second the lay-brothers, the backbone of the workforce and responsible for the outlying granges; the third, also known as *mercenarii*, was made up of laymen associated with the spiritual and material life of the monastery, who formed, as communities grew, an essential addition to the labour force. Powicke estimates that the 140 choir monks of Aelred's day would have been complemented by some 240 *conversi* and 260 laymen or *mercenarii*. Cf. Powicke, p. 38, n. 2.

15. Cf. Christ on the road to Emmaus. Likewise Aelred, when considering an applicant, would pretend to be 'going further', or passing him over, and thus give an appearance of surrendering to the wishes of the community.

16. Walter had to counter criticism of his work. Voices were raised to question the miracles attributed to Aelred and to ask for the names of witnesses. These, in an apologia addressed to a certain Maurice, who may have been the prior of the Augustinian canons at Kirkham, Walter supplies. He insists further that he stands by all he wrote, yet, although saints work miracles, miracles do not make the saint – virtue does. He goes on to illustrate his point with a new and dramatic anecdote, which I have slotted into its chronological place in Aelred's life.

17. Henry Murdac.

18. Cf. Powicke, p. 62, n. 1: 'Monks, in the winter months, retired for the night at 6.30, so the fourth watch when Ailred died was about 10.30 p.m. on the day before the Ides of January, i.e. 12 January 1167 (n.s.).'

From *On Spiritual Friendship*

1. Brian Patrick McGuire, *Friendship and Community: The Monastic Experience 350–1250* (Cist. Pub., 1988), p. 298.

2. Cf. St Augustine, *Confessions*, II, 3. Aelred was steeped in St Augustine, and the *Confessions* was one of three works in his private oratory at the time of his death.

3.　Ibid., III, 4.

4.　A monk who was at Rievaulx with Aelred when the latter was novice master and whom he continued to hold in friendship.

5.　Cf. Cicero, *De amicitia*, XV, 55. Aelred's debt to Cicero is vast and more than once acknowledged. It would in any case have been obvious to his contemporaries. The dialogue form and tripartite division were used by Cicero, and it has been estimated that a third of the latter's treatise passed into Aelred's. The full gamut of references is given by C. H. Talbot in the notes to *Christian Friendship by St Ailred of Rievaulx* (Catholic Book Club, 1942). What is lacking in Cicero, Aelred looks for and finds in Scripture, in the sapiential and historical books of the Old Testament as well as in the New. In the process of abridging, the lists of examples that Aelred draws from Scripture have had to be sacrificed, leaving Cicero deceptively in the ascendant.

6.　No identification has been suggested for Gratian.

7.　Sallust, *Catilina*, 20, 4.

8.　*De amicitia*, XIII, 47.

9.　Ibid., XXI, 76; the expression is Cato's.

10.　*De officiis*, III, ch. 22, 135.

11.　*Confessions*, IV, 8.

12.　L. Annaei Seneca, *Monita*, 97.

13.　Aelred's first friend is usually identified with the Simon whom he laments most movingly in the *Mirror of Charity*, I, 34.

14.　Powicke identifies this second friend with a certain Geoffrey of Dinant whom Aelred brought back with him to Rievaulx in 1142; cf. Powicke, p. 50.

From *The Mirror of Charity*

1.　The altar, seen symbolically as both crib and cross, Christ being incarnated in the host and sacrificed at its breaking.

2.　*Confessions*, X, 33.

The Consolations of Scripture

1.　From Sermon 27 of a series of 32 on the 'proclamations' of Isaiah, known as *De oneribus*.

Pastoral Prayer

1.　Cf. *Rule of St Benedict*, ch. 64.

ISAAC OF STELLA

Source: Isaac of Stella's sermons have been edited, with facing French translation, in *Sources chrétiennes*, 3 vols. (Paris, 1967–87). Text also in *PL*, 194.

1.　An etymological derivation found in St Jerome, *Liber de nominibus hebraicis*.
2.　'animalis', cf. 1 Cor. 2: 14. The Pauline opposition of animal/carnal and spiritual is frequently echoed in Cistercian writings.
3.　'omnino nesciam, tu scis' (lit. 'I do not know at all, you know'). Cf. 2 Cor. 12: 2: 'nescio . . . Deus scit.'

GILBERT OF HOYLAND

Source: Sermons and letters in *PL*, 184.

1.　From Sermon 41 on the Song of Songs.

Two Letters

1.　Seneca, *Epistulae Morales*, 3.
2.　Ovid, *Heroides*, 5: 15.
3.　Rendering 'desides' in place of 'inutiles' (*PL*, 184, 289C). This is one of several alternative readings given in two Bodleian MSS and indicated by Lawrence Braceland; see *Works of Gilbert of Hoyland*, (CFS 4, 1981) p. 91, n. 2.
4.　Seneca, ibid., 81.
5.　'ut de domestica aliquid philosophia ingeram', i.e. Christian as opposed to pagan wisdom.
6.　'in cujus duplicitatis suggillationem geminum mihi forsitan calicem transmiseris.' This is a very obscure passage and I am not sure that I fully understand Gilbert's subtleties. Richard had the advantage of knowing the context. Lawrence Braceland believes that Gilbert

received from Richard a crosier, two chalices and a woollen chasuble. Apart from the unlikelihood of anyone sending a present of two chalices, I do not think the Latin supports the inference. As for the chasuble, there is no mention of it, and I believe that Gilbert was allowing his mind to be led from one verse of Scripture to the next, from the broken reed to the smouldering flax and thence to the flax-weavers of Isaiah. Wool comes in as a contrast. In the Bible the whiteness of wool symbolizes innocence and there is a specific warning against the interweaving of wool and flax: cf. Deut. 22:10: 'You shall not wear a mingled stuff, wool and linen together.'

7.   There are many letters of encouragement to conversion; indeed they became something of a genre. This is a fine example and clearly written from the heart.

8.   'pigrior aliquantulum fueram et tardante scripsi dextera', supplied only by MSS B and R: see Braceland, ibid., p. 98. n. 3.

9.   The trivium (grammar, rhetoric, logic) leading on to the quadri-vium (arithmetic, geometry, astronomy, music) as taught in the Schools. The thought here is closely based on Seneca (*Ep. Mor.*, 88), who claimed that the arts were only of value if they tended towards the acquiring of virtue. Seneca was for Gilbert what Cicero was for Aelred: a mentor and companion to be left finally behind in a leap to the spiritual.

10.   Adopting the reading of MSS B and R, 'quo nitendum sit' (Braceland, ibid. p. 98, n. 4) in place of 'utendum' (*PL*, 184, 291D).

11.   'Quam artium omnium artem dixerim'. It seems to me that 'ars' is used here in its sense of 'knowledge', but cf. William of St Thierry's affirmation in his treatise *On the Nature and Dignity of Love*: 'ars est artium ars amoris' ('the art of arts is the art of love'), a theological response to Ovid's *Ars amatoria*. Medieval scholars were both, as one of them said, 'dwarfs on the shoulders of giants' and latter-day Davids taking up the challenge of the Classical Goliath.

12.   Reading *pignore* not *pingere* (see *PL*, 184, 294B).

JOHN OF FORD: THE LIFE OF WULFRIC OF HASELBURY

Source: Text, edited with an excellent introduction and notes by Dom Maurice Bell, in *Wulfric of Haselbury, by John, Abbot of Ford* (Somerset Record Society, XLVII, 1933).

1. Ford, or Forde, was founded from Waverley in 1136 and established on its present site (formerly in Devon, now in Dorset) in 1141.

2. According to Gerald of Wales, who counted himself among his friends, he was a better monk than abbot, a better abbot than bishop, and a better bishop than archbishop. Giraldus Cambrensis, *Itinerarium Kambriae*, II, XIV, Rolls Series, 21/6, p. 149.

3. It is noteworthy that the completing of the Abbot of Clairvaux's great unfinished work of mystical theology was entrusted successively to two Englishmen. Rievaulx and Ford in particular were important centres of learning in the twelfth century, and the English in general (for one must not forget the expatriates Stephen Harding and Isaac of Stella) played a disproportionate part in the intellectual life of the Order.

4. All the details of how the Life came to be written derive from the two prefatory letters to Bartholomew and Baldwin. See *Wulfric*, ed. Bell, pp. 7–12.

5. It is logical to assume that John finished the Life before composing the dedicatory letters. In the last chapter (105) he describes a miracle as taking place 'fifteen years ago and fifteen years after the holy man's death', which he tells us elsewhere occurred in 1154. This corresponds perfectly with the dating of the letters: the first, to Bartholomew, was written before the latter's death in December 1184; learning of this event, John penned a second epistle to Baldwin, addressing him as Archbishop of Canterbury, an office in which he was consecrated in May 1185.

6. Today the foundations lie under the east end of the Early English north aisle, which is open to the chancel and serves as vestry.

7. *Wulfric*, ch. 105, p. 132.

8. Literally 'the new man'. See Eph. 4: 24.

9. *Wulfric*, Notes, p. 143.

10. John may well be referring to a version given by both Henry of Huntington and Gervase of Canterbury. For details see *Wulfric*, Notes, p. 46.

11. This kind of criticism of the Order was frequent at the time John of Ford was writing. In the mouth of Wulfric it would be surprisingly early.

12. Henry, abbot of Tintern and Waverley, would be only a name on a charter and in the Annals of Waverley had not John of Ford so vividly preserved his *ipsissima dicta*. Since he was, on his own admission, a successful freebooter during the anarchy, we may suppose him born no later than 1115. On entering the Order his elevation was very rapid, and he was abbot of Tintern before Wulfric's death in 1154 (he visited him in that capacity [ch. 51]) and still held the office in 1157. He died as abbot of Waverley in 1182 (*Wulfric*, p. xxxvii).

13. Almost certainly Baldwin, since Henry of Waverley died the year after the former moved to Worcester. The journey probably took place between 1175 and 1180.

14. Tintern, founded in 1131 from l'Aumône, the house that had founded Waverley two years earlier.

15. 1130–38.

16. After Stephen's capture at the Battle of Lincoln in Feb. 1141, the queen, Matilda of Boulogne, threw herself on the mercy of the citizens of London, appealing to them to intervene on her husband's behalf.

17. Robert, Earl of Gloucester, in whose castle the king was held and whose capture in Sept. 1141 led to Stephen's liberation two months later.

ADAM OF PERSEIGNE

Source: Letter 57 in *Archives historiques du Maine*, vol. XIII, *Correspondence d'Adam, abbé de Perseigne* (Le Mans, 1951). Letter 15 in *PL*, 211, 630.

A DESCRIPTION OF CLAIRVAUX

Source: PL, 185, 570–74.

1. See p. 31.
2. This and the next quotations are from Arnald of Bonneval's account in the *Vita Prima*, II, II, 29–31.
3. i.e. ale was brewed when wine was short.
4. 'absolvit ... absolvit'. Work was done in silence and to break it would be a sin. Perhaps the noise of the water covered any pleasantries that slipped out.
5. Ovid, *De Remedio Amoris*, v. 192.
6. Boethius, *The Consolation of Philosophy*, III, VII.

THROUGH MEMORY'S DOOR

Source: The passages with two exceptions are from Herbert's *Liber de miraculis*, PL, 185, 1274ff. The text of the story entitled 'A Word of Comfort' is taken from Brian Patrick McGuire, 'A Lost Clairvaux Exemplum Collection Found: The *Liber visionum et miraculorum* compiled under Prior John of Clairvaux 1171–9', in *AC*, 39 (1983), pp. 26–62. It also figures prominently in the *Exordium Magnum*, but I have used the earlier version. The last story, which concerns, not St Bernard, but Pons, Abbot of Grandselve, a former monk of Clairvaux, is from a collection compiled at the monastery of Langheim in Bavaria. It has been edited by Brian Patrick McGuire in 'Rebirth and Responsibility: Cistercian Stories from the Late Twelfth Century', *Cahiers de l'Institut du moyen-âge grec et latin*, 57 (Copenhagen, 1988), pp. 148–58.

1. *Anima* has the dual meaning of 'life', as in the Gospel, and 'soul'.

READ MORE IN PENGUIN

In every corner of the world, on every subject under the sun, Penguin represents quality and variety – the very best in publishing today.

For complete information about books available from Penguin – including Puffins, Penguin Classics and Arkana – and how to order them, write to us at the appropriate address below. Please note that for copyright reasons the selection of books varies from country to country.

In the United Kingdom: Please write to *Dept. EP, Penguin Books Ltd, Bath Road, Harmondsworth, West Drayton, Middlesex UB7 ODA*

In the United States: Please write to *Consumer Sales, Penguin Putnam Inc., P.O. Box 12289 Dept. B, Newark, New Jersey 07101-5289.* VISA and MasterCard holders call 1-800-788-6262 to order Penguin titles

In Canada: Please write to *Penguin Books Canada Ltd, 10 Alcorn Avenue, Suite 300, Toronto, Ontario M4V 3B2*

In Australia: Please write to *Penguin Books Australia Ltd, P.O. Box 257, Ringwood, Victoria 3134*

In New Zealand: Please write to *Penguin Books (NZ) Ltd, Private Bag 102902, North Shore Mail Centre, Auckland 10*

In India: Please write to *Penguin Books India Pvt Ltd, 11 Community Centre, Panchsheel Park, New Delhi 110017*

In the Netherlands: Please write to *Penguin Books Netherlands bv, Postbus 3507, NL-1001 AH Amsterdam*

In Germany: Please write to *Penguin Books Deutschland GmbH, Metzlerstrasse 26, 60594 Frankfurt am Main*

In Spain: Please write to *Penguin Books S. A., Bravo Murillo 19, 1° B, 28015 Madrid*

In Italy: Please write to *Penguin Italia s.r.l., Via Benedetto Croce 2, 20094 Corsico, Milano*

In France: Please write to *Penguin France, Le Carré Wilson, 62 rue Benjamin Baillaud, 31500 Toulouse*

In Japan: Please write to *Penguin Books Japan Ltd, Kaneko Building, 2-3-25 Koraku, Bunkyo-Ku, Tokyo 112*

In South Africa: Please write to *Penguin Books South Africa (Pty) Ltd, Private Bag X14, Parkview, 2122 Johannesburg*

READ MORE IN PENGUIN

A CHOICE OF CLASSICS

Aeschylus	**The Oresteian Trilogy**
	Prometheus Bound/The Suppliants/Seven against Thebes/The Persians
Aesop	**The Complete Fables**
Ammianus Marcellinus	**The Later Roman Empire (AD 354–378)**
Apollonius of Rhodes	**The Voyage of Argo**
Apuleius	**The Golden Ass**
Aristophanes	**The Knights/Peace/The Birds/The Assemblywomen/Wealth**
	Lysistrata/The Acharnians/The Clouds
	The Wasps/The Poet and the Women/ The Frogs
Aristotle	**The Art of Rhetoric**
	The Athenian Constitution
	Classic Literary Criticism
	De Anima
	The Metaphysics
	Ethics
	Poetics
	The Politics
Arrian	**The Campaigns of Alexander**
Marcus Aurelius	**Meditations**
Boethius	**The Consolation of Philosophy**
Caesar	**The Civil War**
	The Conquest of Gaul
Cicero	**Murder Trials**
	The Nature of the Gods
	On the Good Life
	On Government
	Selected Letters
	Selected Political Speeches
	Selected Works
Euripides	**Alcestis/Iphigenia in Tauris/Hippolytus**
	The Bacchae/Ion/The Women of Troy/ Helen
	Medea/Hecabe/Electra/Heracles
	Orestes and Other Plays

READ MORE IN PENGUIN

A CHOICE OF CLASSICS

Hesiod/Theognis	**Theogony/Works and Days/Elegies**
Hippocrates	**Hippocratic Writings**
Homer	**The Iliad**
	The Odyssey
Horace	**Complete Odes and Epodes**
Horace/Persius	**Satires and Epistles**
Juvenal	**The Sixteen Satires**
Livy	**The Early History of Rome**
	Rome and Italy
	Rome and the Mediterranean
	The War with Hannibal
Lucretius	**On the Nature of the Universe**
Martial	**Epigrams**
	Martial in English
Ovid	**The Erotic Poems**
	Heroides
	Metamorphoses
	The Poems of Exile
Pausanias	**Guide to Greece (in two volumes)**
Petronius/Seneca	**The Satyricon/The Apocolocyntosis**
Pindar	**The Odes**
Plato	**Early Socratic Dialogues**
	Gorgias
	The Last Days of Socrates (Euthyphro/ The Apology/Crito/Phaedo)
	The Laws
	Phaedrus and Letters VII and VIII
	Philebus
	Protagoras/Meno
	The Republic
	The Symposium
	Theaetetus
	Timaeus/Critias
Plautus	**The Pot of Gold and Other Plays**
	The Rope and Other Plays

READ MORE IN PENGUIN

A CHOICE OF CLASSICS

Pliny	**The Letters of the Younger Pliny**
Pliny the Elder	**Natural History**
Plotinus	**The Enneads**
Plutarch	**The Age of Alexander (Nine Greek Lives)**
	Essays
	The Fall of the Roman Republic (Six Lives)
	The Makers of Rome (Nine Lives)
	Plutarch on Sparta
	The Rise and Fall of Athens (Nine Greek Lives)
Polybius	**The Rise of the Roman Empire**
Procopius	**The Secret History**
Propertius	**The Poems**
Quintus Curtius Rufus	**The History of Alexander**
Sallust	**The Jugurthine War/The Conspiracy of Cataline**
Seneca	**Dialogues and Letters**
	Four Tragedies/Octavia
	Letters from a Stoic
	Seneca in English
Sophocles	**Electra/Women of Trachis/Philoctetes/Ajax**
	The Theban Plays
Suetonius	**The Twelve Caesars**
Tacitus	**The Agricola/The Germania**
	The Annals of Imperial Rome
	The Histories
Terence	**The Comedies (The Girl from Andros/The Self-Tormentor/The Eunuch/Phormio/The Mother-in-Law/The Brothers)**
Thucydides	**History of the Peloponnesian War**
Virgil	**The Aeneid**
	The Eclogues
	The Georgics
Xenophon	**Conversations of Socrates**
	Hiero the Tyrant
	A History of My Times
	The Persian Expedition

READ MORE IN PENGUIN

A CHOICE OF CLASSICS

Leopoldo Alas	**La Regenta**
Leon B. Alberti	**On Painting**
Ludovico Ariosto	**Orlando Furioso** (in two volumes)
Giovanni Boccaccio	**The Decameron**
Baldassar Castiglione	**The Book of the Courtier**
Benvenuto Cellini	**Autobiography**
Miguel de Cervantes	**Don Quixote**
	Exemplary Stories
Dante	**The Divine Comedy** (in three volumes)
	La Vita Nuova
Machado de Assis	**Dom Casmurro**
Bernal Díaz	**The Conquest of New Spain**
Niccolò Machiavelli	**The Discourses**
	The Prince
Alessandro Manzoni	**The Betrothed**
Emilia Pardo Bazán	**The House of Ulloa**
Benito Pérez Galdós	**Fortunata and Jacinta**
Eça de Quierós	**The Maias**
Sor Juana Inés de la Cruz	**Poems, Protest and a Dream**
Giorgio Vasari	**Lives of the Artists** (in two volumes)

and

Five Italian Renaissance Comedies
   (Machiavelli/**The Mandragola**; Ariosto/**Lena**; Aretino/**The Stablemaster**; Gl'Intronati/**The Deceived**; Guarini/**The Faithful Shepherd**)
The Poem of the Cid
Two Spanish Picaresque Novels
   (Anon/**Lazarillo de Tormes**; de Quevedo/**The Swindler**)

READ MORE IN PENGUIN

A CHOICE OF CLASSICS

READ MORE IN PENGUIN

A CHOICE OF CLASSICS

La Fontaine	**Selected Fables**
Madame de Lafayette	**The Princesse de Clèves**
Lautréamont	**Maldoror and Poems**
Molière	**The Misanthrope/The Sicilian/Tartuffe/A Doctor in Spite of Himself/The Imaginary Invalid**
	The Miser/The Would-be Gentleman/That Scoundrel Scapin/Love's the Best Doctor/Don Juan
Michel de Montaigne	**An Apology for Raymond Sebond**
	Complete Essays
Blaise Pascal	**Pensées**
Abbé Prevost	**Manon Lescaut**
Rabelais	**The Histories of Gargantua and Pantagruel**
Racine	**Andromache/Britannicus/Berenice**
	Iphigenia/Phaedra/Athaliah
Arthur Rimbaud	**Collected Poems**
Jean-Jacques Rousseau	**The Confessions**
	A Discourse on Inequality
	Emile
	The Social Contract
Madame de Sevigné	**Selected Letters**
Stendhal	**The Life of Henry Brulard**
	Love
	Scarlet and Black
	The Charterhouse of Parma
Voltaire	**Candide**
	Letters on England
	Philosophical Dictionary
Emile Zola	**Zadig/L'Ingénu**
	L'Assomoir
	La Bête humaine
	The Debacle
	The Earth
	Germinal
	Nana
	Thérèse Raquin

READ MORE IN PENGUIN

A CHOICE OF CLASSICS

Adomnan of Iona	Life of St Columba
St Anselm	The Prayers and Meditations
Thomas Aquinas	Selected Writings
St Augustine	Confessions
	The City of God
Bede	Ecclesiastical History of the English People
Geoffrey Chaucer	The Canterbury Tales
	Love Visions
	Troilus and Criseyde
Marie de France	The Lais of Marie de France
Jean Froissart	The Chronicles
Geoffrey of Monmouth	The History of the Kings of Britain
Gerald of Wales	History and Topography of Ireland
	The Journey through Wales and The Description of Wales
Gregory of Tours	The History of the Franks
Robert Henryson	The Testament of Cresseid and Other Poems
Robert Henryson/ William Dunbar	Selected Poems
Walter Hilton	The Ladder of Perfection
St Ignatius	Personal Writings
Julian of Norwich	Revelations of Divine Love
Thomas à Kempis	The Imitation of Christ
William Langland	Piers the Ploughman
Sir Thomas Malory	Le Morte d'Arthur (in two volumes)
Sir John Mandeville	The Travels of Sir John Mandeville
Marguerite de Navarre	The Heptameron
Christine de Pisan	The Treasure of the City of Ladies
Chrétien de Troyes	Arthurian Romances
Marco Polo	The Travels
Richard Rolle	The Fire of Love
François Villon	Selected Poems
Jacobus de Voragine	The Golden Legend